D1557180

The Episcopal Church's History:
1945-1985

The Episcopal Church's History: 1945-1985

David E. Sumner

MOREHOUSE-BARLOW
Wilton, Connecticut

Morehouse-Barlow Co., Inc.
78 Danbury Road
Wilton, Connecticut 06897

Library of Congress Cataloging-in-Publication Data

Sumner, David E., 1946-
The Episcopal Church's History, 1945-1985.

Bibliography: p. 211
Includes index.
1. Episcopal Church—History—20th century.
2. Anglican Communion—United States—History—20th century. I. Title.
BX5882.S85   1987   283'.73   87-7677

ISBN 0-8192-1402-7

Printed in the United States of America

To the honor and glory of God

*with special appreciation to my wife, Lisa,
and all the friends whose assistance made this
book possible*

Acknowledgments

The author would like to thank the editors of the following publications for permission to quote from copyrighted materials:

The Witness, P.O. Box 359, Ambler, PA 19002

The Living Church, 816 E. Juneau Ave., Milwaukee, WI 53202

The Historical Magazine of the Protestant Episcopal Church, P.O. Box 2247, Austin, TX 78768

The Christian Century, 407 S. Dearborn St., Suite 1405, Chicago, IL 60605 for permission to reprint from these articles:

"Still No Women" © 1955 The Christian Century Foundation (10/2 issue)
"Going Public; Seminaries in Search of Support" by Christopher W. Bugbee, © 1981 The Christian Century Foundation (7/13 issue)
"Common Prayer and an Uncommon Convention" by Jean Caffrey Lyles, © 1976 The Christian Century Foundation (10/6 issue)

Excerpts from pp. 83 and 84 in *Take A Bishop Like Me* by Paul Moore, Jr. © 1979 by Paul Moore, Jr. Reprinted by permission of Harper & Row, Publishers, Inc.

Excerpts reprinted from *Among Friends* by Henry Knox Sherrill, © 1962 by Henry Knox Sherrill, by permission of the Atlantic Monthly Press.

Quote from p. 317 in *The Death and Life of Bishop Pike* by William Stringfellow and Anthony Towne, © 1976, reprinted by permission of Doubleday & Company, Inc.

Excerpt from p. 903 in *American History: A Survey,* Sixth Edition, by Richard N. Current, T. Harry Williams, Frank Freidel, and Alan Brinkley, © 1983, by permission of Alfred A. Knopf, Inc.

Information from *They Took Their Stand: The Integration of Southern Private Schools* by Zebulon Vance Wilson, © 1983, reprinted by permission of the author.

The author gratefully acknowledges the Rt. Rev. Arthur E. Walmsley's and the Rt. Rev. Roger Blanchard's kind permission to quote from their remarks about Henry Knox Sherrill recorded in the Columbia University Oral History Project.

Frederick H. Borsch, Dean of the Chapel at Princeton University, has also kindly granted his permission to use his quotation from *New Perspectives on Episcopal Seminaries.*

Contents

Foreword

The last forty years have been among the most exciting in the Episcopal Church's history, and I am happy to introduce a book which reports on this era. I am acquainted with David Sumner, having met him at the 1984 Anglican Consultative Council meeting in Lagos, Nigeria.

During these forty years, the Episcopal Church adopted a new *Book of Common Prayer,* a new hymnal, voted to welcome women into the fullness of ministry as deacons, priests, and bishops. We've accepted the challenges and opportunities of the civil rights era, worked for peace with justice, and sought to further open our doors to all seeking to find a new life in America. The progress in ecumenical relations during the latter part of the twentieth century is greater than at any other time since the Reformation. Not only have we witnessed the development of the World Council and National Council of Churches, the Episcopal Church has reached a number of milestones in its relationship with other denominations, resulting in bilateral covenants. Modern developments in communications and transportation have enabled us to establish closer ties with our Anglican brothers and sisters throughout the world. These "bonds of affection" have developed largely through the work of the Anglican Consultative Council which was established by the 1968 Lambeth Conference.

My four predecessors as presiding bishop during this time each made unique contributions to the church's life. The beloved Henry Knox Sherrill, who held the office from 1947-1958, was a giant in the field of ecumenical relations. He served as one of the first presidents of both the National Council and World Council of Churches. Arthur Lichtenburger (1958-1963) brought courageous leadership in civil rights during a time of great turmoil. An unfortunate illness shortened his term of office. With his tremendous leadership abilities and energy, John E. Hines (1964-1973) carried us further into the civil rights movement and helped pave the way for greater leadership roles by women and minorities.

John M. Allin took over the reins of office at a time of division and distrust within the church and the nation. He brought a remarkable spirit of reconciliation into the office, and brought unity when many social and ecclesial issues threatened to divide us. But most of all, he expanded our vision outside the parochial walls with *Venture in Mission,* one of the most successful mission projects in the history of the Episcopal Church.

When I said "There shall be no outcasts" in my acceptance speech at the 1985 General Convention, I affirmed my hope and conviction that this church should be open to everyone. As David Sumner points out, this statement also summarizes much that has happened during the last forty years. He reminds us that at the end of the Second World War, women could not be deputies to many diocesan conventions, much less our General Convention. Many parishes prohibited women from serving on vestries. Blacks were systematically excluded from leadership roles in many dioceses and parishes. The talents and ministry of the laity were yet to be widely recognized. It is shameful to admit, but the church's leadership at that time was almost all white, male, and ordained.

We may say that "We've come a long way," but yet there is still a long way to go. As we move toward and into the twenty-first century, I hope we all—clergy and laity—will reach out to all of humanity with the reconciling and redeeming love of our Lord Jesus Christ. We celebrate the unity in our diversity but we know that our true unity comes through commitment to Jesus.

Edmond Lee Browning
Presiding Bishop
I Advent, 1986

Preface

Writing recent history is risky business! Throughout this book's research, other historians have given me that warning. As the work progressed, I realized why. First, some events and people that seem insignificant now may prove more significant in years ahead. Likewise, some that seem historical at this point may prove less important as time passes.

Second, it is risky because many of the people I have written about are still living. Some of these people will undoubtedly feel that more emphasis should have been given to certain areas, while less should have been given to others. There are people who will feel that they, or others they know, should have been included. But some topics are simply "judgment calls," and that is part of the risk of writing recent history. As time passes, a consensus will develop as to the events and personages that are truly historical in this particular era of Episcopal Church history.

I am convinced, however, that the need for this book far outweighs its risks. There is currently no book on Episcopal Church history containing anything which occurred after 1955. I soon realized that my main task was simply to uncover the facts of modern history and write about them. I have deliberately avoided interpretation except where it seemed necessary. While the "compiler" task is in some ways unglamorous, it is at this point necessary. Future historians will have the luxury of giving more interpretation to this era than I have been able to do.

The sources used for this book include magazine and journal articles, pamphlets and booklets, theses and dissertations, the Diocesan Press Service, Forward Movement tracts, correspondence and, in some classes, interviews. While the sources of information have been numerous and quite scattered, almost all are published and accessible to other scholars in some form.

I have tried to write this book for two audiences. First, I have tried to write for new Episcopalians and adult converts who may not know much about the church's recent history. Therefore, I have tried to write in a style that is interesting and entertaining to lay audiences. It is also my hope that "cradle Episcopalians" find it interesting and informative as well. Second, I have tried to write for scholars, seminary students and historians. I have been careful to document the facts, verify the information, and cite all sources. With the extensive index and appendices, the book is intended to serve as an easy and accessible reference work.

Almost everything that has happened since 1945 falls into the major areas given by the chapter outlines. For these reasons, I chose a topical, rather than a chronological approach to writing history. Had I chosen the chronological approach, for example, it would have been confusing to switch back and forth between Prayer Book revision, women's ordination, or the civil rights movement as these developments unfolded. Therefore, I chose to take each topic and "tell its story" as it happened. While this approach may fail to grasp the unity and interconnectedness of all historical events, it allows the telling of these stories with greater coherence and historical detail within each topic.

The reader should not look for an account of every person, every event, or every organization he or she has heard about in recent years. The purpose of this book isn't to explain "everything you've always wanted to know about the Episcopal Church." Its purpose is to tell the story of the Episcopal Church within the context of certain major themes that have developed over the last forty years.

Like so many books, the credits and thanks due are numerous. My friend, the Very Reverend W. Robert Insko, suggested the idea for the book in 1980 when he pointed out there was currently no book on modern Episcopal Church history. The genesis for the research and development of the topics began while working on an STM in the summer graduate school at the School of Theology of the University of the South. The late Urban T. Holmes, former dean, provided me with a list of suggested chapter topics. Most of the research has been conducted in libraries at Sewanee, the General Theological Seminary, the Yale Divinity School, the Henry Knox Sherrill Center at the Episcopal Church Center, and the Archives of the Episcopal Church in Austin, Texas. While the library staffs at all of these places have been courteous and helpful, I want to especially thank Dr. Nelle Bellamy and Elinor S. Hearn at the Archives; Grace Harvey at the University of the South, and Miss Avis Harvey at the Henry Knox Sherrill Center.

Chapters four and five on civil rights are a condensation of my STM thesis, titled "The Episcopal Church's Involvement in Civil Rights: 1943-1973," for the University of the South. This work occurred between 1979-1983 and my adviser, the Reverend Dr. Donald S. Armentrout, deserves thanks for his encouragement and inspiration as a teacher and writer.

A number of people have read various chapters and provided suggestions or corrections. They include: The Very Reverend James Fenhagen, dean of General Theological Seminary; John Goodbody, retired communications executive from the Episcopal Church Center, New York; the Reverend Dr. J. Carleton Hayden of Morgan State University; the Reverend Dr. Samuel Garrett, retired from the Church Divinity School of the Pacific; the Reverend Dr. Marion Hatchett of the University of the South; Dr. David Holmes of the College of William and Mary; the Reverend Preston Kelsey, II, director of the Board for Theological Education; the Reverend William Norgren, ecumenical officer for the Episcopal Church; Mary Eunice Oliver of San Diego, California; Dr. Thomas Reeves of the University of Wisconsin, Parkside; the Reverend Harrison Simons, parish priest of Oxford, North

Carolina; the Reverend Dr. Frank Sugeno of the Episcopal Theological Seminary of the Southwest; Dr. Fredrica Thompsett and the Reverend Suzanne Hiatt of the Episcopal Divinity School; and the Reverend Almus Thorp, Sr., retired dean of Bexley Hall Seminary and director of the Board for Theological Education. Personnel from numerous seminaries, church offices, and periodicals have provided requested information by correspondence or sending copies of other materials; to try to name all of them would surely omit some of them.

I am also indebted to Presiding Bishop Edmond Lee Browning who has written a foreword for this book. I first met Bishop Browning in 1984 when he was a delegate and I was on the communications staff at the Anglican Consultative Council meeting in Lagos, Nigeria. The humility, sincerity, and informal style of the former Bishop of Hawaii impressed me and the other assembled delegates and staff from forty-six countries. Little did any of us know that thirteen months later he would be selected presiding bishop of the Episcopal Church.

Perhaps most credit should go to the Diocese of Southern Ohio, and its bishop, the Right Reverend William G. Black. Between 1981 and 1986, I was employed there as director of communications and editor of the diocesan newspaper, *Interchange*. Without the opportunities that that job provided, this book would have never been written. In this position, I discovered that the role of journalist and the role of historian, especially a modern historian, go side by side. Research on this book sometimes provided material for the diocesan newspaper, while material in the diocesan newspaper (and several other diocesan newspapers) often provided valuable historical data for the book. I am thankful for continuing education budget support which provided for research trips to the Episcopal Church Archives and other libraries.

Few authors give a list of thanks without expressing deep gratitude to their spouse. My wife, Lisa, came into my life in 1983 after this book was begun, but before it was finished. Her love has brightened my life and my writing. Her encouragement and enthusiasm has helped make it possible. Numerous friends in my local parish, diocese, and throughout the church have also provided encouragement and ideas. This book is dedicated to Lisa, and to all of these friends. More importantly, it is my gift to the Episcopal Church. Having come to it as an adult, I found a faith and a ministry which gave my life new purpose and meaning. This book is a result of that.

David E. Sumner
Cincinnati, Ohio
August 1986

1

The Episcopal Church Enters the Global Era

"IN THE BEGINNING GOD created the heavens and the earth." The familiar words of the first chapter of Genesis took on new meaning when they were broadcast by three Apollo 8 astronauts as they orbited the moon approximately 210,000 miles in space on December 24, 1967. The Christmas Eve message had been the choice of Colonel Frank Borman, a lay reader of the Episcopal Church. He was joined in the reading by Captain James Lovell, also an Episcopalian, and Lieutenant Colonel Bill Anders, a Roman Catholic. Since the astronauts obviously were unable to attend services, the Christmas Eve Eucharist at St. James' Cathedral in Chicago was broadcast to them via Mission Control in Houston.[1]

Like the astronauts in 1967, the Episcopal Church was thrust into the twentieth century following the second world war. One advantage the astronauts had was that their journey's destination was planned in advance. The church was not always so fortunate. Sometimes it marched forward with courage and determination: at other times history seemed to drag the church kicking and screaming.

> With the controlled splitting of the atom, humanity, already profoundly perplexed and disunified, was brought inescapably into a new age in which all thoughts and things were split—and far from controlled . . .[2]

This passage from *Time* magazine, written two weeks after the atomic bomb was dropped on Hiroshima in 1945, might also describe the modern age in which the Episcopal Church found itself.

New Directions in a New Age

There were many bold changes in sight for the Episcopal Church, beginning with the 1946 General Convention and the election of Henry Knox Sherrill, Bishop of Massachusetts, as the presiding bishop. At the convention, a debate began over the acceptance of women deputies that would not be settled for another twenty-one years. The House of Deputies took the unprecedented step of electing as its president a layman—Owen J. Roberts, Justice of the Supreme Court.

The Right Reverend Henry Knox Sherrill preached these words in his installation sermon as presiding bishop on January 14, 1947 at the Washington Cathedral:

> So, as this month, by the act of General Convention, I assume a position of leadership within the church, I ask of every bishop, clergyman, layman, and lay woman: "Where do we stand? What do you believe? What do you plan to give of your means, above all of your life, in this cause?"

Presiding Bishop Sherrill addressed a church that had faced several years of party strife and division, and had nursed wounds that were just beginning to heal. During the previous nine years, the proposed merger with Presbyterians had divided the church. While his words were especially pertinent in 1947, the same questions could be asked of each new generation of Episcopalians. In 1947, however, World War II was over and the Episcopal Church, like the rest of the nation, was about to enter a new period of prosperity.

Episcopal Church history between 1945-1985 is characterized by three major themes: ecumenical relations, developments leading to the ordination of women, and civil rights for black Americans. While not every major issue was related to these themes (for instance, Prayer Book revision), each theme encompassed several events over many years.

On the ecumenical scene, it was an era that witnessed the establishment of the World Council of Churches in 1948 and the National Council of Churches in 1951. Presiding Bishop Henry Knox Sherrill was elected as the National Council's first president in 1951 and he later became president of the World Council of Churches.

At the 1946 General Convention in Philadelphia, the bishops and deputies defeated a merger proposal with Presbyterians—an issue that had preoccupied the Episcopal Church for nine years. George E. Demille wrote in *The Episcopal Church since 1900,* "Not since 1874 had a General Convention met in such a storm-laden atmosphere as that which assembled in Philadelphia in September, 1946. The strong advocates of unity were not ready to press for action—action swift and definite. The Anglo-Catholics had girded their loins to defend what they felt to be the essential Catholic position of the church."[3]

The Presbyterian General Assembly had previously passed the merger proposal. The Episcopal Church's Commission on Approaches to Unity presented its "Proposed Basis of Union" to the convention—and it was defeated. However, a compromise resolution was passed. What the convention said was that it did not endorse the particular plan of union, but wanted the commission to continue its deliberations. Further conversations with Presbyterians were—for all practical purposes—dead, but the resolution did open the door for future ecumenical dialogues by requesting that deliberations "continue." And so by entering through the back door, a new era in ecumenical relations with other denominations had begun.

The Joint Commission on Ecumenical Relations was established by the 1949 General Convention. In succeeding years, the Episcopal Church began dialogues with Lutherans, Roman Catholics, and the Orthodox churches. When the Consultation on Church Union formed in 1961, the Episcopal Church immediately joined.

Women's issues first surfaced at the 1943 General Convention when the Episcopal Church Women asked the convention to place two women on the Joint Commission on Holy Matrimony. The Diocese of Missouri sent a woman deputy to General Convention in 1946, who was seated, and four dioceses sent women in 1949, who were refused seating. Each General Convention for the next eighteen years debated whether or not to permit women deputies. They were finally approved in 1967 and first seated in 1970.

Women's rights issues later emerged in debate over admission to the seminaries, the role and meaning of deaconesses, ordination to the diaconate and, finally, ordination to the priesthood. Bishop James Pike ordained a woman deacon in 1965—five years before the church gave its formal approval. And in an unprecedented action, eleven women were ordained in Philadelphia in 1974—two years before the church made its historic decision to allow the ordination of women. While the House of Bishops soon declared these ordinations "invalid," most of the women found some place to exercise their ministry.

In the 1940s, both local congregations and the national church were beginning to confront the racial issue that was to preoccupy the nation for the next thirty years. Resolutions on civil rights for black Americans were discussed at every General Convention between 1943-1973. The 1943 General Convention passed a resolution on race relations as "embodying a Christian approach to a new world order."

Civil rights disputes forced the resignation of faculty members at Sewanee's School of Theology in 1952 and a change in the site of General Convention from Houston to Honolulu in 1955. The Episcopal Society for Culture and Racial Unity (ESCRU), founded in 1959, became the church's leading voice for racial justice and equality until it disbanded in 1970. While the General Convention Special Program (1967-1973) brought with it more conflict and controversy, it resulted in progress in terms of its commitment to helping minorities. After 1973, the church retreated from the public arena and turned its focus to the debate over who could be ordained and what kind of Prayer Book the congregations should be using.

Along with certain public issues, the church dealt with internal matters as well. From 1894 to 1962, the headquarters for the Episcopal Church was located at 281 Park Avenue South in New York City. Due to crowded conditions there, some departments had been relocated in Greenwich, Connecticut and Evanston, Illinois. As plans developed for a new church center, there was debate over its location. An article in *The Living Church* read, "A midwest site was urged . . . Washington, D.C. extended its invitation as a 'strategic location.' A cathedral-based center was discussed; Westchester County, New York, was toured; many diocesan dinners were attended; but after a careful and detailed survey, the answer always was: New York City."[4]

In 1960, the church's executive council acquired title to property located at the northeast corner of 43rd Street and Second Avenue. Construction began a year later, and on February 21, 1963, Bishop Frederick Warnecke of Bethlehem, Pennsylvania, chairman of the Site Committee, presented the master keys of the new twelve-story Episcopal Church Center to Presiding Bishop Arthur Lichtenberger.

The Episcopal Church settled one of its oldest debates—its official name—in a remarkably amicable way at the 1979 General Convention. Since 1789, the church's legal title was "The Protestant Episcopal Church in the United States of America." Throughout the church's history, Anglo-Catholics had objected to the word "Protestant" in the church's name. In voting to drop the word "Protestant," the convention made both "The Episcopal Church" and "The Episcopal Church in the U.S.A." legal names. In doing so, it settled an issue that had been raised at almost every General Convention since 1877.

Other important changes took place in the church at the close of World War II, particularly in the unprecedented increases in the number of men enrolled at seminaries. George E. Demille writes in *The Episcopal Church since 1900,* "Not only had the numbers increased; there was a notable increase in quality. For these men had back of them years of grappling with reality, years of facing death; they had a seriousness and a maturity far above the normal."[5]

While the quality of the clergy was increasing, most church leaders recognized a deteriorating quality of Christian education in Episcopal churches across the land. Between 1933 and 1943, church school attendance dropped from 510,000 to 388,000, a decrease of over 20 percent. This was the lowest figure for church school attendance since before the turn of the century, and became one of the major issues that the Episcopal Church would address in the late 1940s.

More than the particular events themselves, the post-war era marked another singularly important transition for the Episcopal Church: When Henry Knox Sherrill was elected presiding bishop at the 1946 General Convention, he became the first full-time presiding bishop elected specifically to hold that office. Henry St. George Tucker, who was presiding bishop from 1937-1946, had continued to hold his diocesan post as Bishop of Virginia. But the 1943 General Convention enacted the canonical change that made the office a full-time one and required the presiding bishop-elect resign his diocesan position.

The demands of history often produce the men and women to meet the particular needs of the times, and Henry Knox Sherrill was no exception. Sherrill's leadership, particularly his ecumenical leadership, brought the Episcopal Church into the national and international arena in a new way. Arthur Walmsley, Bishop of Connecticut, said in a 1982 interview:

"Up until the time of Henry Sherrill, we did not have a national identity. We were still very much a collection of dioceses; we had a low profile . . ."[6]

The full-time office enabled Sherrill to give the time needed to make the church visible among its ecumenical and Anglican partners. Roger Blanchard, the former Bishop of Southern Ohio, made an observation similar to Walmsley's:

Henry St. George Tucker was a transition person from the old to the new. But when Henry Sherrill was elected, he gave up his diocese, knowing when he was elected that he would give up his diocese. He enabled the church to become a national church in a way it was never before. It took its place in the Anglican Communion in a way that it never had before because he brought a sense of unity, of wholeness, of a national church rather than a collection of ninety-plus dioceses . . .[7]

With the election of Henry Sherrill, the Episcopal Church entered its own "new age." And today, as much so as forty years ago, Charles Dicken's famous words, "the best of times and the worst of times," could also aptly describe the Episcopal Church's modern history. Indeed, it could be said of any period in its history, for there were always opportunities for the church—and there were concomitant problems as well. Writing in the *Anglican Theological Review* in 1948, Norman Pittenger pointed to some of the dangers facing the Episcopal Church at that time:

The first is the danger of becoming, or remaining, a "high brow" church. We appeal to the more highly educated and wealthier members of society; we have little to do with the working people, the great mass of American citizens. The second danger is that we remain predominantly an Anglo-Saxon communion, despite the growing number of other people who now belong to us.

. . . A third danger is that we have hardly yet touched Negroes of America. If once we attempted to key our message to the colored people of this land and provided adequately for work amongst them, we could offer a religious home for huge numbers of men and women who would bring to us a warmth of religious feeling, a depth of conviction, and a broad sympathy and understanding . . .

In the fourth place, we have a strange fear of cooperation with non-Episcopalians. If we are sure of our position, we need not be afraid to work with all men of good will, and especially with our Protestant brethren in many fields of Christian interest and service.[8]

The words of Pittenger were prophetic ones. We smile at some of them, perhaps smugly, as the progress the church has made in the past thirty-five years is reviewed. But there is a ring of uncomfortable familiarity to some of his words. Pittenger's message has been heard before and probably not very long ago. Some problems take more than a generation to solve.

2

Women Become General Convention Deputies

AT THE 1949 CONVENTION of the Episcopal Diocese of Olympia, (Washington), Ruth Jenkins was asked by a group of delegates if she would consent to nomination as a deputy to General Convention. She asked them to consult with Bishop Stephen Bayne on the matter. When asked, the illustrious bishop replied with a smile, "I don't know anyone I'd rather see thrown out of General Convention than Ruth Jenkins."[1]

When Ruth Jenkins took over the administration of the Annie Wright Seminary in Tacoma, Washington in 1942, the girls' school had a quarter of a million dollar debt. Ten years later, the debt had been cleared, the enrollment jumped from 130 to 300, and the faculty increased from 25 to 47. In honor of her achievements, the College of Puget Sound awarded her an honorary Doctor of Humane Letters degree.[2] Ruth Jenkins was eminently qualified to be a deputy to General Convention by every standard—except her sex.

The Diocese of Olympia elected her as a deputy to the 1949 General Convention, and she received the highest number of votes of any of the four it elected. But along with three other elected women deputies, the San Francisco convention refused seating, saying in effect that the time for women deputies had not yet come.

And the time would not come for over twenty years. The 1967 General Convention was the first to approve a change in the Episcopal Church's constitution permitting women deputies.

The General Convention of the Episcopal Church meets every three years, and has since 1789. It is divided into the House of Bishops and the House of Deputies, similar in some ways to the House and Senate in the United States Congress. The House of Deputies consists of four lay and four clerical deputies from each of the dioceses. As the supreme governing body of the Episcopal Church, any change in the church's constitution or canons (ecclesiastical procedures) must be approved by both bodies.

7

The 1946 General Convention was taken by surprise when the Diocese of Missouri sent Mrs. Randolph Dyer as a deputy. Mrs. Dyer was a member of St. Peter's Church in St. Louis, and the granddaughter of Bishop Huntington of Central New York. At the first meeting of the House of Deputies on September 10, Mrs. Dyer's seat was challenged. After considerable debate, she was seated, with voice and vote, and with the understanding that the question would be settled for future cases by "proper canonical procedure" and authorization.

At the next General Convention in 1949, the Diocese of Olympia sent Dr. Jenkins; the Diocese of Nebraska sent Mrs. Elizabeth D. Pittman; and the Diocese of Missouri sent Mrs. E.V. Cowdry. The Diocese of Puerto Rico elected Mrs. Domingo Villafane as a deputy, but she was not present at the General Convention.

This time the matter was brought up in a resolution to change the word *laymen* in Article I, Section 4 of the constitution to *laypersons*. It was defeated in the House of Deputies and never reached the House of Bishops. On the following day, the House adopted a resolution providing for the seating of the women by courtesy, but without voice or vote. The three women deputies declined the invitation, pointing out it was "irrelevant."

A statement read on their behalf by Dean Sidney E. Sweet of Missouri declared:

We, the three women who were elected members of the House of Deputies, and who were refused seats at the opening session, thank the House for its permission to be seated without voice or vote, which was accorded us yesterday. But we regretfully wish to inform the House that such action is irrelevant to the main issue. We were elected by our diocese, not as women, but as lay deputies. We feel the real issue has not been met by this convention. The question is not one of courtesy to women, but whether or not women may represent in its councils the church they are proud to serve.[3]

Many years later, Dr. Jenkins commented, "Then a sop was offered the women deputies in the form of a 'courtesy' resolution to allow them seats without voice or vote. I walked out, and into the arms of my bishop who was as disgusted as I was."[4] After describing the defeat, *The Christian Century* observed, "No such reluctance appeared, however, when the women sought permission to present the convention with an offering of $2 million which they had raised for the work of the church . . . The money was welcomed in while the women were being locked out."[5] "Next time I hope we don't rebuff the women the same day they present their United Thank Offering," was a comment said making its way around convention halls.

In one resolution, the 1949 San Francisco convention reaffirmed the church's recognition of the office and work of deaconesses as "the one and only order of the ministry for women which we can recommend our branch of the Catholic church to recognize and use." Despite its recalcitrance against women, the convention recognized that an issue was at hand. It appointed a Commission on Women to study "the place of women in the church" and to report to the 1952 General Convention on its findings.

Dr. Jenkins was appointed as a member of the commission, along with two other women: Miss Leila Anderson and Mrs. Edward G. Lasar. Bishop Malcolm Peabody of the Diocese of Central New York was chairman. The commission presented a favorable report to the 1952 General Convention and recommended that the constitution be changed to allow women to become deputies. "Because of the theological and historic principles stated above . . . this commission believes there is no basis of distinction in principle between men and women in the church."[6] The report also pointed out that there were eight other provinces of the Anglican Communion (countries) where women served in similar church legislative bodies.

The commission presented its resolution to the convention:

"Resolved, the House of _____ concurring, the Article I, Section 4 of the constitution be changed to read in the place of the word "Laymen," "Lay Deputies, men or women," and in place of the word "Layman," "Lay Deputy, man or woman."

It failed.

The *Boston Globe* stated, "It was the laymen and not the clergy that defeated them." The clerical deputies in the House of Deputies passed the resolution, but the lay orders defeated it. Why? It could be because the seats of lay deputies were most threatened. In 1952, the clerical deputies had nothing to lose by supporting the resolution. In floor debate, a deputy from Providence, Rhode Island, offered the most candid remarks: "Women have their power, God bless them, but we men must assume ours also. I think there are other ways in which the position and force of women can be integrated without taking a place away from a man," he said.

According to the *Boston Globe* account, others gave reasons for their opposition to the resolution—some that seem quite similar to later arguments advanced against the ordination of women: Jesus chose only male apostles, the Bible taught different roles for men and women, and only the "feminist" women wanted leadership positions.

Dr. Ronald Jardine from Harrisburg, Pennsylvania, spearheaded the opposition, saying that Jesus Christ was a male and all the apostles were men. "Men and women have divergent roles to play in life," he argued. According to the physician, the "rank and file" of the churchwomen didn't want this. Those who did, he asserted, were "career women" who wanted to "inject themselves into high positions."

A bishop from Texas asserted there was a "practical angle." He said that giving the vote to women would tend to make busy laymen lax in their church interests, and subsequently more inclined to turn the reins of the church over to the "distaff side."

The Reverend Theodore P. Ferris, the renowned rector of Trinity Church, Boston, led the losing forces who sought to seat women. "We want the best brains and the deepest spiritual understanding," he said. "If these are present in a woman, I don't want the House to be deprived of them."

And two delegates chided their peers for lagging behind secular society in women's rights. Governor Elbert N. Carvel of Delaware said, "This is not the nineteenth century; it is the twentieth century. Women have proven themselves in government and have made a contribution to the efficient and effective operation of our states before we are allowing them to prove themselves in our church." The Rev. Leland W.F. Stark of Washington, D.C., said, "Every argument against this resolution was urged long ago against suffrage. It bothers me that secular bodies move so much faster than the church."

Arguments for the seating of women were to no avail, however. Nor did they carry the day in 1955 at the convention in Honolulu. *The Christian Century* reported of this effort:

It was conducted at a humorous, almost ribald level, with hearty laughter at every occasion of discovering a double meaning in some innocent remark of a speaker. The possibility that the convention might be a body that made serious decisions affecting people's lives, that people ought to have a chance to speak and vote on serious discussions affecting their lives—all these never seemed to enter anybody's head. It was just rather whether we liked this group in our club, whether they might take over and squeeze us out. It was not the importance, intelligence, or competence of women that was on trial in this debate.[7]

The lack of leadership roles for women in the church was not limited to the national level of the General Convention. *The Episcopalian* reported in 1964 that women could not serve on vestries or be delegates to diocesan conventions in thirty-four of the church's seventy-seven dioceses. Five dioceses restricted women from serving on parish vestries and being elected diocesan convention delegates. Only thirty-nine dioceses gave women the canonical right to serve "in any and all lay positions within the diocese and parish" in 1964.[8]

The proposal to allow women to be seated as deputies at General Convention was again defeated at the 1958, 1961, and 1964 Conventions. Dr. Clifford P. Morehouse, president of the House of Deputies, wrote in 1964:

The old argument, that if women were allowed to sit in the House of Deputies they would soon outnumber the men and the men would not take their fair share in the work of the church, is not only untrue, but is an unwarranted slander upon the loyalty of the men of the church. . . . The truth of the matter is that men and women are equally loyal communicants of the church and the practice of segregation by sex is no more admirable than that of segregation by race or color.[9]

The culmination of the twenty-one year old battle came in 1967 in Seattle. The resolution passed in both houses to change the wording in Article I, Section 4, to read *laypersons* rather than *laymen*.

The *Convention Daily* stated, "At every convention since 1949 which decided that the word *laymen* was not generic, attempts have been made to change the constitution to read *laypersons*. These attempts were defeated by increasingly narrow margins, and were crowned with success by yesterday's vote."

The action was ratified at the 1970 General Convention in Houston, and twenty-eight elected women deputies were seated October 12. In all, forty-three women deputies (including fifteen alternates) served at various times during this convention in Houston.

One of those women, Mary Eunice Oliver, writes, "As the women deputies went forward to be welcomed for the first time, Dr. Coburn (president of the House of Deputies) called the church to repent. I began to cry. It was as though all the rejection, agony and frustration of women poured out from me . . . I was at peace . . ."[10]

3

The Path to Women's Ordination

THE REVEREND JEAN DEMENTI tells this story about her arrival in Alaska in January, 1951 to become a missionary nurse. "My plane trip was ten hours long, and I had had practically no sleep for three days and nights before that. When I arrived in Fairbanks at 6 a.m., Bishop William Gordon met me, took me to the Gordon home, and sat me down in the kitchen. . . . I couldn't imagine having a bishop cook my breakfast."

She became a missionary nurse at a boarding school in the town of Nenana. Two years later she was acting superintendent at the Hudson Stuck Hospital in Fort Yukon, and in 1955, she became nurse-evangelist to Shageluk and St. Luke's Mission. Ordained to the diaconate in February, 1972, she continued her work: "It isn't everybody who can deliver a baby, baptize her, prepare her for confirmation, marry her, and even—God forbid—bury her, which I have done." In January, 1977, Jean Dementi was one of the first women regularly ordained to the priesthood in the Episcopal Church, but her ministry had already begun some twenty-six years earlier.[1] In the 1980 election for bishop coadjutor of Alaska, she became the first woman in the Anglican Communion nominated for the office of bishop. At the time, she was serving as rector of St. Jude's Church, North Pole.

The story of the Episcopal Church's decision to ordain women was a recognition of what certain women already had accomplished in their ministries, but such recognition was not granted without a pitched battle. Just as the early Christians learned that the faith excluded neither "Jew nor gentile," many churches came to believe that their ordained ministries should exclude neither "male nor female." Archbishop of Canterbury Donald Coggan told the 1976 General Convention in Minneapolis, "Saint Peter ratted on the old conservatives and admitted those dirty gentiles. The ordination of women is nothing compared to that." It was the September 16, 1976, session of the House of Deputies that took the final vote which would allow women to canonically enter the priesthood of the Episcopal Church.

12

"My friends, fellow deputies, and members of the gallery," began the Reverend John Coburn, president of the House of Deputies. "We now come to a solemn moment in the life of our church which will affect its course in the years to come. The matter has been debated fairly and well. Before asking for the vote, may I request that we keep five minutes of silence during which we will ask for the guidance of God's Holy Spirit."[2]

As president of the House of Deputies, John Coburn delayed his consecration as Bishop of Massachusetts so he could preside over this historic session of General Convention. Held in Minneapolis, this convention approved changes in the Episcopal Church's canons that allowed the ordination of women as deacons, priests, and bishops.

The precedent-shattering change in the status of women in the Episcopal Church was accomplished in the simple language of a new Section 1, of Title III, Canon 9:

Section 1. The provisions of these canons for the admission of Candidates, and for the ordination to the three orders: bishops, priests and deacons; shall be equally applicable to men and women.

The mood was excited and tense. A majority of votes was required in both the House of Bishops and the House of Deputies. The House of Bishops had passed the measure a day earlier. The outcome was less certain in the House of Deputies. The vote, announced at 6:36 p.m. on September 16, 1976, came when the chair called the House to order and asked the secretary to read the result.

"Clerical votes: 114 votes cast, 58 needed for affirmative action. Sixty votes yes; 39 votes no; 15 votes divided.

"Lay votes 113, 57 votes needed for affirmative action. Sixty-four votes yes; 36 votes no; 13 votes divided. The resolution carried in both orders."[3]

The Episcopal Women's Caucus had worked towards this moment for five years. The Reverend Pat Park, a leader in the Women's Caucus, was quoted saying shortly before the vote, "We know that we have approximately enough votes to win. There are enough swing votes to have us very worried. But we have a fairly good idea that it will pass."[3]

Controversy over the issue simmered for several years, and was far from over after the convention made its decision. Bishop Stanley Atkins of the Diocese of Eau Claire (Wisconsin), said a few days later, "I'm sad, I'm pensive, and I'm filled with foreboding for the future. There is a deep rift in the soul of the Episcopal Church."[4] His sentiments reflected those of members of several groups in the church which had worked equally hard to defeat the measure. Another opponent, Bishop Paul Reeves of Georgia, called it "the most grievous blunder that has been made in the 200-year history of the Episcopal Church."[5]

Historical Precedents

The decision in Minneapolis was not an isolated historic one, even within the Episcopal Church. Most Protestant denominations in the United States had already ordained women. Both the United Methodist Church and the United Presbyterian Church began admitting women to full clergy rights in 1956. The Presbyterian Church in the United States (Southern branch) began in 1964. The American Lutheran Church and Lutheran Church in America began ordaining women in 1970. The African Methodist Episcopal Church began admitting women in 1948. Churches with a predominantly congregational policy had begun long before. The Congregational churches (later to become the United Church of Christ) ordained women in 1853, and the Disciples of Christ began to do so in 1888.

Within the United States, the women's movement had been gaining momentum since the early 1960s. Betty Friedan's book, *The Feminine Mystique* (1963), is often cited as the first major document of the current women's movement in the United States. It attacked traditional views of women's "proper role," arguing that for many women, being a housewife and mother was not sufficiently rewarding and fulfilling. In 1966, Friedan joined with other feminists to create the National Organization for Women (NOW), which was to become the largest and most influential feminist organization in the country. "The time has come," asserted the NOW founders, "to confront with concrete action the conditions which now prevent women from enjoying the equality of opportunity and freedom of choice which is their right as individual Americans and human beings."

In the 1972, Congress approved the Equal Rights Amendment (ERA). By the end of the first year, thirty states had ratified it. One church historian writes, "Of all the feminist crusades of the 1960s and 1970s, none united more women from more different backgrounds than the campaign for passage of the Equal Rights Amendment."[6] However, by 1979, ERA was still three states short of ratification. Congress extended the seven-year limit another three years, but it failed to gain the thirty-four needed states by 1982.

The influence of the feminist movement upon women's ordination in the Episcopal Church is debatable. Supporters are more likely to describe the church's decision to ordain women in spiritual and theological terms; opponents of women's ordination accuse the church of succumbing to the pressures of the secular feminist movement.

The Episcopal Church became the second province within the Anglican Communion to adopt canonical change formally allowing the ordination of women. The Anglican Church of Canada ordained its first woman on November 1, 1976. There were, however, three prior incidents of the ordination of women as priests in the Anglican Communion.

In 1944, Bishop R.O. Hall of Hong Kong ordained Florence Li Tim-Oi as priest. On June 4, 1944, he wrote to William Temple, Archbishop of Canterbury:

"... I am not an advocate for the ordination of women. I am, however, determined that no prejudices should prevent the congregations committed to my care [from] having the sacraments of the church . . ."[7]

Subsequently, the 1948 Lambeth Conference asked for either the resignation of Bishop Hall, or a renunciation of the title of priest by Florence Li. To spare her bishop further embarrassment, she consented to the latter course of action. She said, "I wrote to Bishop Hall: I would like to keep quiet to help the church . . ." Although she did not continue to exercise the ministry, she privately insisted that she remained a priest of the Anglican Communion.[8]

Some years later, in 1971, the Synod of Hong Kong and Macao became the first Anglican province to officially permit the ordination of women to the priesthood. Bishop Gilbert Baker, acting with the approval of the synod, subsequently ordained to the priesthood Jane Hwang and Joyce Bennett. Both had already served several years as deacons.

The Diaconate

The debate over the ordination of women to the priesthood began in the 1960s with debate over the entry of women into the diaconate. This debate was more theologically complex in one sense because women at that time were allowed to become "deaconesses," but not deacons. The church never really resolved whether or not "deaconess" was an order of the ministry, but finally abolished the office when it voted to allow women into the diaconate in 1970.

The orders of ministry in the Episcopal Church are different from that of many other Protestant denominations. A deacon in the Episcopal Church is a member of its ordained ministry, though not a priest. Like priests, a deacon is given the title of "The Reverend." A person who aspires to the ordained ministry must first be ordained a deacon. If the person is later approved by the appropriate committees and boards, then he or she may be ordained to the priesthood.

"Deaconess" was the historic ministry for unmarried lay women in the Episcopal Church, beginning in the late nineteenth century. However, the church was never clear about whether deaconesses were "ordained" or simply "set apart." If they were ordained, then they were in Holy Orders—an Anglican term normally including the three orders of bishop, priest, and deacon. If they were "set apart," then the office was little more than a specialized lay role for women.

According to the church's canons, the duty of a deaconess was "to assist in the work of the parish, mission, or institution to which she may be appointed, under the direction of the rector or priest in charge." Furthermore, deaconesses were charged to assist in the administration of baptism; read Morning and Evening Prayer and in some cases give sermons at these services; organize and carry out the church's work among women and children; give instruction in the Christian faith; and "care for the sick, the afflicted, and the poor."

In 1964, the General Convention changed the canons to read that deaconesses were "ordered" rather than "appointed" and adopted a special liturgy for use in the ordination of women as deaconesses. The convention also dropped the celibacy requirement for deaconesses. Furthermore, it declared deaconesses to be "an order of the ministry"—adding a fourth order to the three Anglican orders of ministry. The changes, nevertheless, added more theological confusion than clarity to the issue, a point later made by James Pike, Bishop of California. Pike became involved in the debate because of his desire for women—and particularly a deaconess in his diocese—to be allowed to become deacons.

William Stringfellow and Anthony Towne explained the theologically confusing issue in a fairly succinct manner in their book, *The Death and Life of Bishop Pike:*

> The underlying issue, which the St. Louis vote had apparently only succeeded in confusing, was whether deaconesses are merely specialized laywomen or in holy orders; and, if in holy orders, whether in the diaconate, the so-called third order of ministry with the same status as male deacons . . . or in a fourth order reserved for deaconesses. In effect—although the debate on these matters was by no means coherent—the bishops opted for the view that deaconesses constituted a fourth order.[9]

A deaconess in Bishop Pike's diocese was the first woman to become a focus in this debate. Mrs. Phyllis Edwards of San Francisco, a former schoolteacher and widowed mother of four children, attended theological school and was ordered a deaconess in the Diocese of Olympia (Washington) in 1964. After moving to San Francisco, Mrs. Edwards distinguished herself with her ministry to the poor in the inner city.

As a result of the 1964 General Convention's action, Bishop Pike announced his intention of admitting Mrs. Edwards to the diaconate. He believed the term "ordered" could refer to nothing other than ordination to the full ministry, just as it did for male ordinands. Therefore she did not need "re-ordination" in order to be admitted to the diaconate. After objections from national and local church leaders, however, Pike deferred a decision until he could bring the issue before the September 1965 House of Bishops meeting in Glacier Park, Montana.

In a resolution of the 1965 meeting, the bishops stated that "when a deaconess is 'ordered' with prayer by the bishop and the laying on of hands, together with a formula giving authority to execute the office of deaconess in the church of God, she receives an indelible character for this ministry in the church of God."[10] Bishop Pike observed, however, that the resolution did not answer the question he had raised: whether the present deaconesses stood in need of another ordination.

A week later, on September 13, 1965, Bishop Pike held a service of "investiture" at Grace Cathedral to give recognition to Mrs. Edward's status as a deacon. At the 1965 service, Mrs. Edwards took the oath of conformity to the doctrine and discipline of the Episcopal Church, which is required of all who are ordained to the diaconate. Bishop Pike conferred upon her the New Testament and stole, historic marks of the diaconate. Like all male deacons, she was thereafter listed among the "clergy" of the Diocese of California and known as "the Reverend Mrs. Edwards."

Pike's successor, the Right Reverend C. Kilmer Myers, became bishop in 1966, and allowed Mrs. Edwards to continue to function as a deacon. In fact, in 1969 she was performing one of the functions of a priest canonically denied to deaconesses, but not to deacons. She was helping to distribute the elements at St. Aidan's Church where she had been appointed acting vicar. The bishop also allowed her to perform burials, officiate at baptisms in case of an emergency, and officiate at (but not bless) marriages. In effect, as California's Suffragan Bishop Richard Millard put it, "Mrs. Edwards is functioning in this diocese as a deacon."[11]

The entire Anglican Communion was grappling with defining the status of deaconesses, so the question was not limited to the church in the United States. After considerable debate, the 1968 Lambeth Conference recommended ". . . that those made deaconesses by laying on of hands with appropriate prayers be declared to be within the diaconate."[12]

Two years later, the United States church settled its dilemma by following the Lambeth Conference recommendation. The 1970 General Convention in Houston concurred with the 1968 Lambeth Conference statement that "those made deaconesses by the laying on of hands . . . be declared to be within the diaconate." Canon 50, "Of Deaconesses," was repealed and replaced with a new Canon 26, "On Women in the Diaconate." However, four Anglican provinces—Canada, New Zealand, Hong Kong, and Kenya— had already allowed women into the diaconate before the United States church made its decision.

Theological Education

Women began to enter seminaries much earlier than anyone ever thought of ordination for women. Theological education and ordination were separate matters, and not all students—male or female—planned ordination. The first seminary to adopt a formal policy for admitting women to the bachelor of divinity program was the Episcopal Theological School in Cambridge, Massachusetts, in 1958. When this school merged with the Philadelphia Divinity School in 1974, it was renamed the Episcopal Divinity School. A special committee at the seminary had studied the advisability of the course of action and took special note of a resolution adopted by the House of Bishops in September, 1957. Although the resolution did not recommend admitting women to seminaries, it stated that, "The theological education of women and their professional life and service in the church are matters of special concern to us."[13]

The committee also noted that thirty-eight Episcopal women were studying for advanced theological degrees at three leading inter-denominational seminaries in the 1957-58 academic year. So in the fall of 1958, the Episcopal Theological School admitted three women to its bachelor of divinity program: Judith Adelman, Catherine Boyd, and Roberta Evans. All three graduated in 1961. That same year, the seminary also began admitting men who were not postulants for ordination (i.e., officially sponsored) to the bachelor of divinity program.

Although the Cambridge, Massachusetts, seminary was the first to adopt a policy of admitting women, it was not the first to graduate a woman. Two other seminaries awarded the bachelor of divinity degree to a woman prior to that time. The first Episcopal seminary to graduate a woman was the Berkeley Divinity School in New Haven, Connecticut, in 1939. Clara Olds Loveland transferred from Yale Divinity School of Berkeley in 1937. She received the bachelor of divinity degree, cum laude, on June 8, 1939. In 1954, Jane Buchanan transferred to the Church Divinity School of the Pacific in Berkeley, California, from St. Margaret's House, a school for training deaconesses and women church workers, also in Berkeley. She graduated in 1955.

In 1963, Virginia Theological Seminary was the second seminary to adopt a policy of admitting women to the bachelor of divinity program. After the first two seminaries began to admit women, all of the remaining Episcopal seminaries admitted women in due course. The Church Divinity School of the Pacific began admitting women regularly in 1967, as did the Episcopal Theological Seminary of the Southwest in Austin, Texas. Seabury Western, General Theological Seminary and the School of Theology at the University of the South all began admitting women in 1971—after the 1970 General Convention decision that permitted women to become deacons.

Under these circumstances, it was inevitable that two training schools for women lay workers faced declining enrollments and eventual closure. Windham House in New York City closed in 1967 and St. Margaret House closed in 1966. But until these two schools closed, they were responsible for training many of the "DRE's" (directors of religious education) and missionary workers among the Episcopal Church's notable women.

Heather Huyck, an Episcopal Church historian, says that most of these first women who entered seminaries did so without hopes or plans for ordination:

Seminary training not only gave women professional credentials. As important, it exposed women to men who were themselves preparing for the priesthood . . . most of the women who first enrolled in seminary did not initially intend to become priests. They wanted to study further, to be able to grapple with theological issues. For many women, only in hindsight did they perceive seminary as one logical step in fulfilling their calling to the priesthood. At the time, their goal was much more limited.

However, Huyck states that seminary served an additionally important function for women who were eventually ordained: It gave them a chance to meet each other.

Seminary provided women with another major advantage—a place to meet other women facing similar issues . . . During seminary, women discovered they were not alone. Seminary was crucial for "finding" each other and forming the network eventually instrumental in bringing women's ordination to the Church.[14]

Women's Ordination: Organized Efforts Begin

While the 1970 General Convention approved the ordination of women to the diaconate, it was also the first convention to vote on the ordination of women to the priesthood. The House of Deputies—with lay and clerical deputies—failed to approve it because its clerical deputies turned it down. Huyck comments that the vote "orchestrated by a very small group of people at the 1970 Houston General Convention did much better than any of its supporters had expected. Part of the explanation comes from the unprepared, even non-existent opposition."[15]

Others pointed out that this was the first time in several conventions that the clerical deputies in the House of Deputies voted on the conservative side of an issue, while the lay deputies took the progressive stand. As pointed out in the previous chapter on admittance of female deputies, it could have been a matter of which deputies felt their convention seats to be the most threatened.

The years 1970 and 1971 marked a turning point for women's ordination. The vote on ordination of women to the priesthood at the 1970 General Convention resulted in the formation of women's networks and organizations working for ordination. Secular discussions about women were affecting the church. By 1971, there were large numbers of women who had graduated from seminary and had developed expectations and hopes for ordination to the priesthood. Few women were any longer content to become directors of religious education or other lay workers.

The 1968 Lambeth Conference had previously paved the way for further discussion on the ordination of women to the priesthood. After heated debate, the bishops defeated a resolution which stated that "there are, in principle, no conclusive theological reasons for withholding priesthood from women." However, a softened version, which passed, stated that "The Conference affirms its opinion that the theological arguments as at present presented for and against the ordination of women to the priesthood are inconclusive." (Resolution No. 34)

Furthermore, another resolution let down the gates by recommending that member churches make canonical provision "for duly qualified women to share in the conduct of liturgical worship, to preach, to baptize, to read the

Epistle and Gospel at the Holy Communion, and to help in the distribution of the elements." One observer reported, "If Lambeth X did not open the door for women to be admitted to the priesthood, it surely unfastened the latch."[16]

Another seminal event occurred when the Anglican Consultative Council (ACC) declared in 1971 that it was acceptable for a bishop to ordain a woman to the priesthood with the consent of his national church or province. The ACC, created by the 1968 Lambeth Conference, served as an international "general convention" of Anglicans. Although its resolutions were not binding on member churches, this decision paved the way for the provinces to at least consider the matter without fear of reprisal from other members of the Anglican Communion. It was shortly after this that the Synod of Hong Kong and Macao gave Bishop Baker its consent to ordain two women to the priesthood.

Organized efforts toward the ordination of women to the priesthood probably began with the formation of the Episcopal Women's Caucus in October, 1971. The caucus grew out of a conference in Alexandria, Virginia, on the ministry of women and sponsored by the Episcopal Church's Board for Theological Education.

One of the caucus' first actions was to issue a statement protesting the action taken by the House of Bishops at a meeting which was held almost concurrently. The bishops requested the establishment of a committee to "study the status of women in ministry." The Women's Caucus got word of the bishop's resolution through a television news report. The Women's Caucus responded with a letter to the bishops, stating:

We deplore the action of the House of Bishops in forming yet another committee for an 'in depth study of the ordination of women as priests and bishops' . . .

Citing previous reports by the Episcopal Church and the Anglican Communion, the letter further stated:

We . . . are convinced that further study constitutes negative action on this question. Therefore, we, the Episcopal Women's Caucus, declare that we cannot collaborate in negative action by serving on this committee. We will refuse to serve, if asked, and we call upon all women . . . to join us.[17]

The signers of the statement represented nineteen dioceses, as well as several seminaries. In the end, the bishops couldn't get any women to serve on their study committee, so they made it an "in-house" study.

In May of 1972, the Women's Caucus adopted a statement of purpose: "The Episcopal Women's Caucus is an ad hoc group of lay women, seminarians and ordained women whose purpose is to actualize the full participation of women in all levels of ministry in the Episcopal Church."

The organizers and members of the Episcopal Women's Caucus hoped that the 1973 General Convention would endorse their cause. The logic that

1970 had gone so unexpectedly well would bring certain victory in 1973 overlooked the development of organized opposition. If the 1970 vote had roused its supporters, it had roused its opposition as well. The American Church Union (ACU) and other like-minded groups developed systematic opposition to women's ordination. Shortly after the 1973 General Convention, the ACU and other groups banded together to form the Fellowship of Concerned Churchmen—an umbrella organization whose sole purpose was to oppose the ordination of women to the priesthood.

At the November 1972 meeting of the House of Bishops in New Orleans, the bishops endorsed women as priests and deacons "in principle." It was a close vote, however. Seventy-four voted in favor of the proposition, while sixty-one voted against it. As of August, 1973, twenty-seven dioceses had voted in support of ordination of women to the priesthood. Thirteen dioceses had either rejected such a plan or asked for further study before action was taken by General Convention. There were ninety-seven women deacons at the time, with forty-two who had been ordained since the 1970 General Convention.

The 1973 General Convention's failure to approve the ordination of women was a great disappointment to women and their supporters. It was defeated in the House of Deputies, without the motion ever reaching the House of Bishops. Although a majority of both clerical and lay deputies approved the motion, it was defeated because of parliamentary rules that counted divided votes from diocesan delegations as negative votes. The actual vote was clerical deputies: yes-50, no-43, divided-20; lay deputies: yes-49, no-37, divided-26. The rules required a majority of all votes in both orders for a motion to pass.

"We were devastated, as a group and as individuals," the Reverend Barbara Schlachter later recalled ". . . Sisterhood and morale were at an all-time low. But out of the ashes, out of the darkness, we rose again."[18]

On December 15, 1974, five women deacons presented themselves to Bishop Paul Moore of the Diocese of New York at a service of ordination for five men. The women took the unexpected action hoping (but not expecting) that the liberal bishop would go ahead and ordain them. During the service at the Cathedral of St. John the Divine, Bishop Moore permitted the women to go through the service but did not ordain them. Moore wrote in his book, *Take a Bishop Like Me:*

> There they stopped, knelt down, and looked up to me with what seemed the pain of a thousand years. They looked up and offered to their bishop their vocation to the office of priest . . . My hands involuntarily began to move forward to lay upon their heads, upon their lives, the burden and glory of priesthood. I knew I could not; yet in that moment, as the congregation gasped and leaned forward in their seats . . .[19]

The five women were Carter Heyward, Barbara Schlachter, Emily Hewitt, Carol Anderson, and Julia Sibley, all of whom had been ordained to the diaconate by Moore. Since Bishop Moore had been a strong advocate for women priests, and sometimes a gadfly among the House of Bishops, it seemed to be a good occasion to make their point. But he had made it clear in an earlier meeting with the women that he would not ordain them. The Reverend Suzanne Hiatt, currently a faculty member at the Episcopal Divinity School, wrote: "When the bishop finally refused to lay hands on them, they walked out, taking with them about a third of the congregation, including the bishop's chaplain."[20]

"The Philadelphia 11"

It was a hot summer in 1974, two years before the Episcopal Church was to vote on the ordination of women to the priesthood for the third time. Amongst the heat and debate of the issue it was not surprising, perhaps, that irregular ordinations would eventually occur.

In February of 1974, the Episcopal Women's Caucus met and divided into three groups, each galvanized to take a different approach. One group decided to concentrate on educating the church on the issue of women and sexism. A second group was to concentrate on political organization for the 1976 General Convention; the third group decided that neither education nor political organization were sufficient in forcing the Episcopal Church to ordain women to the priesthood. They eventually decided to seek irregular ordinations.

On July 10, 1974, a self-constituted planning group (five bishops, seven priests, six deacons, and four laypersons) met in Ambler, Pennsylvania. They agreed to participate in an ordination to be held on the Feast of Saints Mary and Martha (July 29) at the Church of the Advocate in North Philadelphia. As the home parish of one of the ordinands, the rector and vestry had already extended an invitation for the proposed ordination ceremony.

In an open letter to the church, dated July 19, 1974, Bishops Daniel Corrigan, Robert DeWitt, and Edward R. Welles, II, announced their intention to ordain several women to the priesthood on July 29 at the Church of the Advocate. The letter stated, in part:

> On Monday, July 29, 1974, the Feasts of St. Mary and Martha, God willing, we intend to ordain to the sacred priesthood some several women deacons . . . We are painfully conscious of the diversity of thinking in our church on this issue and have been deeply sobered by that fact . . . We note that the House of Bishops is on record as being in favor of the ordination of women . . . There is a ruling factor which does require action on our part. It is our obedience to the Lordship of Christ, our response to the sovereignty of His Spirit for the Church.[21]

Bishop DeWitt was the former Bishop of Pennsylvania, the diocese in which the ordinations were to take place. Edward Welles was the retired bishop of West Missouri. Daniel Corrigan was the retired suffragan bishop of

Colorado. Ordination by retired bishops is equally valid (in principle), but they faced far fewer political and ecclesiastical risks than active bishops would have faced by participating.

A fourth bishop, Antonio Ramos of Costa Rico, was present but did not participate in the ordination. He was the only currently active diocesan bishop. Bishop DeWitt later wrote, "We decided collegially that Tony Ramos, although present at the altar, should not ordain, considering that his youth (37) and status made him vulnerable to the heaviest reprisals."[22]

A letter was also released from the eleven deacons who were to be ordained. It stated in part:

We rejoice in their (the bishops) courage and feel privileged to join them in this action of Christian obedience. We are certain God needs women in the priesthood to be true to the Gospel understanding of human unity in Christ. Our primary motivation is to begin to free priesthood from the bondage it suffers as long as it is characterized by the categorical exclusion of persons on the basis of sex.[23]

The letter was signed by the eleven women deacons. They were: Merrill Bittner, Alla Bozarth-Campbell, Allison Cheek, Emily Hewitt, Carter Heyward, Suzanne Hiatt, Marie Moorefield, Jeanette Piccard, Betty Schiess, Katrina Swanson, and Nancy Wittig.

". . . I beg you to reconsider your intention to present yourself for ordination before the necessary canonical changes are made," said Presiding Bishop John Allin in a telegram to the eleven women. Bishop Lyman Ogilby, successor to DeWitt as Bishop of Pennsylvania, said that though he favored the ordination of women, he had "not given consent or approval for having this ordination in the Diocese of Pennsylvania."

Their pleas were ignored. The ordinations took place on July 29 before a congregation of 2,000 worshippers at the Church of the Advocate. The Reverend Paul Washington was rector of the inner city parish and agreed to host the ordinations.

"I participate in this service today not because I wanted to speak out, but because I could not remain silent," said Dr. Charles V. Willie in the ordination sermon.[24] The Harvard education professor was later to resign as vice president of the House of Deputies when the House of Bishops refused to recognize the Philadelphia ordinations.

The service was interrupted when Bishop Corrigan, the officiating bishop, said, "If there be any of you who knoweth any impediment or notable crime (in these women), let him come forth in the name of God . . ."

Several priests proceeded to the chancel steps and were permitted to read statements. They included representatives of the American Church Union and the Coalition for the Apostolic Ministry, two of several organizations working against the ordination of women. Following their statements, the officiating bishops responded that they were acting in obedience to God, adding, "Hearing his command, we can heed no other. The time for our obedience is now."

Two weeks later, the House of Bishops held an emergency meeting at O'Hare Airport in Chicago, called by Presiding Bishop Allin. The House declared the ordinations invalid. The vote was 129-9, and 8 abstentions. The bishops said:

We express our conviction that the necessary conditions for ordination to the priesthood in the Episcopal Church were not fulfilled on the occasion in question, since we are convinced that a bishop's authority to ordain can be effectively exercised only in and for a community which has authorized him to act for them . . .[25]

The normal process for ordination in the Episcopal Church requires two to three years of examinations by Commissions on Ministries, Standing Committees, and Boards of Examining Chaplains of each local diocese, as well as the local parish vestry. These eleven women did not have the approval of their bishops and standing committees for the ordination. Some of their bishops, while not objecting to the womens' qualifications, did object to their participation in the Philadelphia service.

The repercussions following this event were numerous. Two dioceses held ecclesiastical trials for priests who permitted women to celebrate the eucharist in their parishes: Peter Beebe in the Diocese of Ohio and William Wendt in the Diocese of Washington, D.C. Both men were convicted of disobeying a "Godly admonition" from their bishops against allowing the women to celebrate the eucharist in their dioceses.

Despite their August vote which declared that the Philadelphia ordinations were invalid, the House of Bishops endorsed "in principle" the ordination of women at their next regularly-scheduled meeting. By a roll call vote of 95 to 75, with 6 abstentions, the bishops endorsed the principle of women's ordination at their October meeting in Oaxtepec, Mexico. This was the second time, since the House also gave its approval to the "principle" of women's ordination by a narrow margin in 1972. Still, the 1974 vote did not change the action the House took in August declaring the ordination of the eleven women invalid. The House also urged its bishops to refrain from further attempts to ordain women "unless and until such activities have been approved by the General Convention" in 1976.

In January of 1975, the trustees of the Episcopal Divinity School in Cambridge, Massachusetts, offered faculty appointments with full priestly duties to the Reverend Suzanne Hiatt and the Reverend Carter Heyward, two of the Philadelphia 11. Ordained faculty members at the seminary celebrated services of Holy Communion in the chapel, and a school official said the two women would serve in the same way. They did so, beginning in March, 1975.

Meanwhile, the second of the three groups formed from the Episcopal Women's Caucus in 1974 planned the political strategy for the 1976 General Convention. This group later formed the *National Coalition for Women's Ordination to the Priesthood and Episcopate.*

The policy board of the coalition held its first meeting January 17-18, 1975, in Chicago to map strategy, develop plans and enlist support for the canonical changes that would allow the ordination of women to the priesthood. The Reverend Patricia Park of Alexandria, Virginia, and the Reverend George Regas of Pasadena, California, were chosen co-chairpersons of the coalition. The policy board adopted a statement, which read in part:

... The board intends to coordinate a massive campaign over the next eighteen months to secure a positive action for women priests at the Minnesota convention, for the board sees the church perilously close to schism if the issue of women's ordination is not dealt with justly, promptly, and forthrightly.[26]

While the women were planning for General Convention in succeeding months, the church was again caught by surprise with another irregular ordination when the Right Reverend George Barrett, the retired Bishop of Rochester, ordained four women deacons to the priesthood in a service in Washington, D.C. They were Lee McGhee, Alison Palmer, Betty Rosenberg and Diane Tickell. The service was held September 7, 1975 at the Church of St. Stephen and the Incarnation.

The Bishop of Washington, William F. Creighton, said he had "informed Bishop Barrett that he does not have my permission to ordain deacons to the priesthood in this diocese," a position supported by the Diocesan Council and Standing Committee. The ordinations were "seriously impelling the prospect of the acceptance of women in the priesthood," Creighton said in a statement.

Later he wrote to the three women canonically resident in the diocese, "directing and admonishing" them "not to perform any priestly function in any parish of this diocese." The fourth woman, Diane Tickell, was canonically resident in the Diocese of Alaska.

While Bishop Creighton opposed these irregular ordinations, he had announced a few months earlier that he was not going to ordain any more men to the priesthood until the 1976 General Convention acted on the question of women priests. "To continue to ordain men who are deacons while being compelled to refuse ordination to women who are deacons has become conscientiously impossible and a form of injustice of which I can no longer be a part," said Creighton in a statement to the press.[27] Bishop Creighton said at the April 1, 1975, press conference that the three men seminarians who had planned for ordination in June, expressed approval for his decision, even though it meant their ordination would be delayed.

The House of Bishops considered the irregular ordinations at their next meeting, September 19-26, in Portland, Maine. "We cannot get involved in judicial processes, not because anybody is frightened, but because we don't have that sort of energy," said Presiding Bishop Allin. He asked that there be "no trials" for the bishops who participated in the irregular ordinations, and the House ended up merely censuring the bishops who violated normal rules of church order. The bishops also voted to "decry the action" of Bishop Barrett for his part in the Washington, D.C. service.[28]

The beginning of 1976 found the Episcopal Church anxiously awaiting the September General Convention. Few were willing, at that point, to predict the outcome of the vote on the ordination of women.

In April, Presiding Bishop Allin reaffirmed his "position" of not taking a position on one side or the other with regard to women's ordination. In an interview following his return from the Anglican Consultative Council meeting in Trinidad, he said his own position had been misunderstood by some based on an address he had given at the Mississippi diocesan convention in January. At that meeting, Allin had said that "I think we're going to vote to ordain women" at the Minneapolis General Convention, and "I hope we will celebrate the fact."

The presiding bishop said the statement had caused confusion and misunderstanding, and "I certainly did not intend to announce a change in my own position," that he was neither for nor against the ordination of women.[29] This was his "public position" prior to the September 1976 vote, but a year later he was to make the public announcement that he could not approve of women as priests.

Approval of women's ordination in the House of Bishops was virtually assured when sixty-seven bishops announced in June that they were co-sponsoring legislation to approve the canonical change necessary for women's ordination. "These sixty-seven, when joined by other non-sponsoring bishops who have also indicated they will vote for women's ordination, appear to represent the majority of bishops who will attend the conclave," commented the Right Reverend John Burt, Bishop of Ohio.

Part of the official statement issued by the sixty-seven bishops said that "We acknowledge that the House of Bishops in which we shall introduce this proposal is but one half of the General Convention. . . . At the same time, we believe that people throughout the church and the public at large may wish to know that even now there is a sufficient majority of bishops in the Episcopal Church to assure passage in our House . . ."[30]

The 1976 General Convention

The struggles and efforts of the women and their supporters came to fruition with the history-making sixty-fifth General Convention in Minneapolis on September 15-23. On September 15, the House of Bishops voted ninety-five to sixty-one to endorse the ordination of women to the priesthood. However, the announcement of the result did not conclude the matter for the bishops who were opposed. Bishop Stanley Atkins of the Diocese of Eau Claire immediately took the floor and read a prepared statement which thirty-eight bishops subsequently signed. It read:

We stand committed to the Episcopal Church, and we are determined to work within it. We cannot accept with a good conscience the action of this House. We believe that to do so would violate our ordination vows to be faithful and to defend the word of God in Holy Scripture.

Furthermore, we cannot acknowledge the authority of this General Convention to decide unilaterally and in the face of the expressed disapproval of our Roman, Old Catholic and Orthodox brethren a question which ought to be decided by an ecumenical consensus.

The ordination and consecration of women priests and bishops will raise for us the gravest question; that is, how far this Church can accept such ministrations without fatally compromising its position as a catholic and apostolic body?

The favorable vote by the House of Bishops was expected, but more suspense surrounded the House of Deputies vote a day later. On September 16th, the House of Deputies heard fifty-eight two-minute speeches before its vote. Bishop Paul Moore describes the afternoon this way in his book *Take a Bishop Like Me:*

"Those who were against stated their side: Jesus had not chosen women apostles. Since he was a social radical for his time, he would have chosen woman apostles if he had thought that women should be successors to the apostles . . .

The opposition countered that Jesus needed the most effective leaders for his mission and that a woman in those days simply could not carry out the kind of assignment the apostles were given. Furthermore, Jesus had said that the Holy Spirit would reveal truths later which the church was not then ready to hear. Ordaining women was a case in point . . .

Another classic argument was that since a priest takes the role of Jesus at the altar, and Jesus was a man, therefore the priest must be a man. The opposing argument was that St. John said that the Word became flesh and dwelt among us. Jesus took on all humanity in his incarnation, not just men. Therefore, any human being can be the celebrant of the eucharist.

One of the bishops who had been most active in ecumenical conversations with the Roman Catholic Church stated that the ordination of women would not only be a setback in these conversations, but would perhaps end them. 'We should wait until the whole church, all the churches, can settle this together.' The rejoinder: 'But this may not happen for centuries. If it is the right thing to do, we should lead the way . . .'[31]

Following four hours of debate and procedural action, a somber House of Deputies rose for five minutes of silent prayer and then voted by orders: The clerical order voted 60 in favor, 39 opposed, and 15 divided. The laity voted 64 in favor, 36 opposed, and 13 divided.

After the vote, a stunned silence filled the giant Convention Hall in Minneapolis. "I plea that there be no winners and no losers," said the Very

Reverend David Collins of Atlanta, chairman of the Committee on Ministry which presented the resolution. At the request of House leadership, the vote was accepted in prayer, with pleas for reconciliation on both sides.

By choosing to accomplish the change through canonical change, rather than a constitutional amendment, the convention made it possible for women deacons to be ordained as early as January 1, 1977. If the convention had chosen the constitutional route, a second approval would have been required at the 1979 Convention. The first woman to be ordained following this decision was Jacqueline Means in Indianapolis, Indiana, on January 1, 1977. Bishop Donald Davis of the Diocese of Erie presided at the service held in All Saints' Church, Indianapolis.

What happened to the fifteen women who were irregularly ordained? When the House of Bishops met on September 21, 1976, at the General Convention, they voted to require a "conditional ordination" for these women. Described as "punitive" by some bishops and "reconciling" by others, conditional ordination apparently would resemble conditional baptism. In effect, a second ordination service would occur. Supporters of the irregularly ordained women were aghast. "Agreeing to conditional ordination raised questions of the July 29, 1974 and September 7, 1975 services, the women's subsequent priestly actions and their sense of being priests," wrote Heather Huyck.[32] In a surprise move, the bishops voted to reverse their action the next day. They voted to allow the women to be "regularized" with the option of a "public event." Such services were held, beginning just after the first regular ordinations in January, 1977. The bishops' 1974 "invalidity" vote was quietly put aside.

When the final meeting of the National Coalition for Women's Ordination to the Priesthood and Episcopacy met on January 2, 1977, the decision to dissolve the coalition was unanimous. The group gathered in Alexandria, Virginia, to witness the ordination to the priesthood of the Reverend Patricia Park, who was co-chairperson of the coalition and an assistant at Immanual on the Hill Church for several years.

"We can disband with joy, giving thanks and praise to God," said the Reverend George F. Regas, in addressing this final meeting. "Our stated purpose was to achieve canonical action in 1976," said the Reverend Mrs. Park. "Our work together is finished."

After the 1976 Convention

About forty women were ordained by the end of January 1977 and an additional sixty by the end of the year. According to a survey by the Diocesan Press Service, about two-thirds of these women were already in some sort of stipendiary position. But opposition to women priests and women's ordination was far from over. Some bishops remained fervent in their opposition to the ordination of women, and refused to consider candidates in their dioceses. However, their numbers diminished as they retired and were replaced—in many dioceses—by new bishops who were not opposed to the ordination of women. Some parishes voted to leave the Episcopal Church and form separate denominations.

While ecumenical ripples continued to develop in succeeding years, the only alliance to actually break came when Prime Bishop Thaddeus Zielinski of the Polish National Catholic church (a United States church) suspended the church's intercommunion agreement with the Episcopal Church. Regardless, Roman Catholic Bishop Carroll Dozier of Memphis said he doubted the vote on women would jeopardize ecumenical conversations. "There are few things in the Catholic church which are decided through hurried decisions," he remarked.

Shortly before the United States decision, the Anglican Church in Canada made its own decision to ordain women. Archbishop Edward Scott said in an interview that the ordination decisions by the United States and Canadian churches may have some "creative impact upon relationships" with the Roman Catholic and Orthodox churches. "I wonder . . . if waiting for a universal consensus does not in fact rule out any action. If we are prepared to act, but also to recognize that our action must be tested by experience . . . then we may be helping the whole church reflect at a deeper level," said the Canadian primate.

The controversy in the Episcopal Church developed into the question of whether women priests was "the law of the land" or whether individuals could oppose the action and remain loyal and faithful Episcopalians. A subsequent meeting of the House of Bishops, held in Port St. Lucie, Florida in October, 1977, considered the question.

At the opening session of the House, Presiding Bishop Allin made the announcement that he was a "presiding bishop who is unable to accept women in the role of priest." He offered to resign the office "if it is determined by prayerful authority that this limitation prevents one from serving as the presiding bishop of this church." Later in the meeting, the bishops considered and approved a resolution in response to Allin's offer to resign. Adopted by a unanimous vote, the resolution affirmed "the continuing leadership of Bishop Allin" and stated that the House of Bishops "respects the right of the presiding bishop to hold a personal conviction on this issue . . ."[33]

The conclave later adopted, by an overwhelming majority, a statement of conscience which affirmed that "no bishop, priest, or lay person should be coerced or penalized in any manner" for opposing the ordination of women—or for supporting and implementing it. The statement commended respect for people holding opinions contrary to the convention's action and the avoidance of any kind of pressure "which might lead a fellow Christian to contravene his or her conscience, and they need not regard themselves as 'disloyal Episcopalians.' "[34]

A year later, the Lambeth Conference expressed the same consensus by commending respect for those holding differing views on the ordination of women to the priesthood. In a lengthy resolution, the worldwide conference of bishops recognized that four of its member churches had already given approval to the ordination of women to the priesthood. It recognized the autonomy of each of its member churches "to make its own decision about the appropriateness of admitting women to Holy Orders." At the same time, the conference declared "its acceptance of those member churches" which both do and do not ordain women, and urged all its member churches to "respect the convictions of those provinces and dioceses" with differing practices. The resolution passed 316-37, with 17 abstentions.

By 1979, almost 300 women had been ordained to the priesthood, and seventy-two of the ninety-three domestic dioceses had canonically resident women who were ordained (priest or deacon). By 1985, more than 600 women had been ordained to the priesthood, with the majority serving in stipendiary positions. More than 140 were rectors of parishes, and almost 200 were assistants.

While debate still continues over the ordination of women to the priesthood, the mid-1980s brought the larger question over ordination of women to the episcopacy. The House of Bishops at the 1985 General Convention declared that it did not intend "to withhold consent to the election of a bishop of this Church on the grounds of gender." By 1986, at least three women had become final nominees for bishop in various diocesan elections, and one lost only narrowly.

At the end of World War II, women could not serve as General Convention deputies, as diocesan convention delegates or even on parish vestries in many dioceses. By 1970, women were allowed into the diaconate. By 1977, women were allowed into the priesthood. Heather Huyck, quoted earlier, sums up the story very simply: "The church could now celebrate a whole priesthood."[36]

4

Civil Rights
for Black Americans

"DOES SEGREGATION OF CHILDREN in public schools solely on the basis of race . . . deprive the children of the minority group of equal education opportunities? We believe it does . . . We conclude that in the field of public education the doctrine of 'separate but equal' has no place . . .''

Chief Justice Earl Warren uttered these historic words on May 17, 1954. This Supreme Court decision on school integration, viewed generally as the benchmark of the United States Civil Rights movement, was followed by fifteen turbulent years during which its judicial and social implications began to unravel.

In 1954, the Diocese of South Carolina became the last Episcopal diocese to remove the racial barrier for representation at diocesan conventions. That same year, John T. Walker was the first black to graduate from Virginia Theological Seminary, one of the two Episcopal seminaries in the South. A year earlier, the School of Theology at the University of the South—the other southern seminary—was integrated. In 1955, the church moved its General Convention from Houston to Honolulu to ensure that all facilities would be fully integrated.

These facts suggest that the Episcopal Church was ahead of American society in moving towards full racial equality. However, for a church which professed to be one body, "neither Jew nor Greek" (Galatians 3:28), the record was not as spotless as one might hope.

Towards the end of the nineteenth century, conditions for blacks in the Episcopal Church worsened. By canonical action or tacit agreement, conventions excluded black delegates and established separate convocations for blacks. The seating of a black deacon in 1881 at one diocesan convention led to the amendment of the diocesan canons to specifically exclude black delegates. Similar prohibitions occurred in several other dioceses.

Black Episcopalians were disheartened by the growing canonical segregation which, by 1900, was the rule in virtually every southern diocese. Bishop James

31

T. Holly, Bishop of Haiti and the first black Episcopal bishop, counselled blacks not to desert "the church of our love" since it was "the sovereign will and power of the Almighty God that preserved grace in the church, in spite of unworthy administrators."[1]

Faced with the de facto segregation, black Episcopalians began to agitate for a separate jurisdiction that would be made up of the southern black churches and governed by a black bishop. General Convention repeatedly rejected the plan on the grounds that it was contrary to Catholic usage, and because "Anglo-Saxon churchmen have earned by centuries of toil and suffering the right to leadership."

The 1907 General Convention in Richmond reached a compromise by permitting the election of suffragans or assistant bishops for black congregations. However, they were not granted the right of succession, nor were they able to vote in the House of Bishops. Black leadership was not enthusiastic about the idea, saying that a black suffragan would be little more than a "suffering bishop" and a "puppet" to the white diocesan bishop.

Nevertheless, two black suffragan bishops were elected in 1918: Thomas Demby in Arkansas and Henry B. Delaney in North Carolina. Both served black missions in their own and surrounding dioceses. The Reverend J. Carleton Hayden, a noted black historian, points out in his booklet, *Struggle, Strife, and Freedom: The Role of Blacks in the Episcopal Church:* "Since they had no real authority their functioning was largely ceremonial. Bishop Demby urged that the experiment never be repeated. It never was."[2]

The twentieth century brought tremendous shifts of the black population in the United States. In 1900, 90 percent of the black population lived in the South, but by 1930, only 75 percent remained. By 1980, this figure was further reduced to 40 percent. The number of black Episcopalians in the North swelled as a result of immigration of West Indians to the northeastern cities, especially New York and Boston.

A number of northern cities developed strong black congregations led by well-educated, effective priests. St. Philip's in Harlem, New York, was a chief example. Led by the Reverend Hutchens C. Bishop, the congregation grew from 300 to 3,300 during his forty-seven-year rectorship. During the rectorship of his son, the Reverend Shelton H. Bishop, it had become by 1952 the largest parish in the country, with 7,851 communicants, four priests, a sizeable lay staff, and an extensive community program.

One of the most outstanding leaders during the early part of the twentieth century was George Freeman Bragg, Jr. He became rector at St. James Church in Baltimore in 1891 when its sixty-nine communicants were worshipping in rented quarters. During his tenure, the communicants increased in number to over 500. He sent some twenty men into the priesthood, and founded an orphanage. He was also responsible for the publication of the *Church Advocate,* which he used until his death in 1940 to protest racism and encourage his fellow Episcopalians to recall their heritage, and develop strong, effective parishes.

The American Church Institute for Negroes was incorporated at Petersburg, Virginia in 1906 to coordinate the work and fund raising for the Episcopal Church's black colleges. Between 1906 and 1940, the institute raised and distributed nearly seven million dollars for its affiliated schools. When the institute was dissolved in 1968 as a gesture to integration, there were only three black colleges left: St. Augustine's College in Raleigh, North Carolina; St. Paul's College in Lawrenceville, Virginia; and Voorhees College in Denmark, South Carolina.

Civil rights resolutions came to the attention of General Convention for the first time in 1943, and with successive General Conventions for the next twenty years. But private attitudes lagged far behind public statements, and segregationist statements and incidents continued to occur in the church. For instance, a Savannah, Georgia, parish voted in 1965 to sever its ties with the Diocese of Georgia and the Episcopal Church, rather then obey the church's canon which prohibited the exclusion of membership from anyone on the basis of race. With the passage of time, however, the frequency of such incidents decreased.

In 1943, the National Council of the Episcopal Church adopted four "guiding principles designed to govern the church's Negro work." The first of these was:

Fellowship is essential to Christian worship. Since there are no racial distinctions in the mind of the Father, and 'all are one in Christ Jesus,' we dare not break our Christian fellowship by any attitude or act in the House of God which marks our brethren of other races as unequal or inferior.[3]

Subsequently, the 1943 General Convention incorporated these guiding principles into a resolution:

WHEREAS, the following principles must be kept before us as the Christian goal, to wit:
1) Fellowship is essential to Christian worship;
2) Fellowship is essential to church administration;
3) High standards must be maintained in every department of our work with the Negro, and . . . to set the spiritual and moral goals for society, and to bear witness to their validity by achieving them in her own life;
RESOLVED . . . that this convention commends the foregoing principles of Christian social relations to the clergy and laity of this church as embodying a Christian approach to a new world order.

Throughout the next twenty-five years, there were many examples of parishes acting in ways which held to the ideals of this resolution. One outstanding example could be found at Calvary Episcopal Church in Philadelphia, Pennsylvania. In September of 1945, the century-old, predominantly white parish invited a black priest, the Reverend Thomas Logan, to become its rector and bring with him the black congregation from the church where he was currently vicar.

In a letter to members, parish leaders urged everyone to join together to make Calvary truly "a house of prayer for all people . . . We rightfully scorn the Nazi ideas of race hatred and contempt. All belonging to Calvary can fight such notions by continuing to worship here."[4]

In December, 1946, President Harry Truman appointed Presiding Bishop Henry Knox Sherrill to the Presidential Committee on Civil Rights. By executive order, the commission was instructed to "inquire into and to determine in what respect current law enforcement measures and the authority and means possessed by . . . governments may be strengthened and improved to safeguard civil rights of our people." Sherrill later noted that the situation was not a happy one:

> While some progress was noted, the evidence of lynchings, of police brutality, of inequality, of the administration of justice, of voting procedures and of discrimination in regard to educational and other opportunities revealed a sad situation.[5]

Bishop Payne Divinity School Closes: A Controversy Begins

In 1949, the church's only seminary for blacks, Bishop Payne Divinity School in Petersburg, Virginia, closed its doors due to severe financial problems and increased public pressure against maintaining a segregated seminary. "The seminary has always faced problems, but the two biggest ones were the raising of funds and the recruiting of good students," wrote the Reverend Odell Harris, an alumni of the seminary, in his book *A History of the Seminary to Prepare Black Men for the Ministry of the Protestant Episcopal Church.*[6] During the last few years of its operation, the seminary had less than a dozen students each year.

The assets of the seminary were merged with Virginia Theological Seminary in 1953. As a tribute to the black seminary, Virginia's library was re-named the Bishop Payne Library. In 1951, John T. Walker became the first black student to enter Virginia Theological Seminary. After graduating in 1954, he became rector at St. Mary's Church in Detroit, a mixed congregation that was approximately 88 percent white.

Sewanee Faculty Members Resign

"We should open the existing seminaries in the South to students of all races," stated the Synod of the Fourth Province in 1951. The Episcopal Church is divided into nine provinces; the fourth includes the southeastern region of the United States. Meeting in Birmingham, Alabama, synod representatives discussed whether or not to open another seminary for blacks after the Bishop Payne School had closed. They agreed it was neither feasible nor desirable and thus aimed their resolution at integrating Virginia Theological Seminary and the University of the South's School of Theology in Sewanee, Tennessee.

Virginia Theological Seminary began to admit black students, as noted, but the trustees of the University of the South were not receptive to the resolution's intent. On June 6, 1952, the synod's "Report and Resolution regarding Negro Theological Education" was brought to the attention of the university trustees at their meeting. They voted 45-12 that, ". . . the furtherance of the church's work and happiness and mutual goodwill of both races will not now be served by the action requested by the synod."[7]

The University of the South is located in Sewanee, Tennessee, and consists of both an undergraduate college and a seminary. "Sewanee" is the more common name for both. The same trustees govern the college and the seminary, both of which are owned and supported by twenty-four southern dioceses of the Episcopal Church.

When the trustees failed to allow the admission of black students to the seminary, reaction was swift. On June 9, Dean Frances Craighill Brown and seven faculty members of the School of Theology met to draft a letter that was sent to the trustees asking them to reconsider their decision. They further stated that if their request was ignored, "We are without exception prepared to resign our positions."

Their request was denied, and they did.

Following four months of controversy without concrete results, the dean and seven faculty members submitted resignations on October 6, effective at the end of the academic year. In addition to Brown, faculty members who offered their resignations were: Robert M. Grant, R. Lansing Hicks, Robert M. McNair, J. Allen Reddick, Claude E. Guthrie, and Richard H. Wilmer, Jr. In the spring of 1953, with the situation still unresolved, thirty-five of fifty-six rising second and third year students were making plans to transfer.

Pressure from throughout the Episcopal Church eventually forced the trustees to change their decision. The most embarrassing moment of the controversy came in February, 1953, when the Very Reverend James Pike, then dean of the Cathedral of St. John the Divine in New York, refused an invitation to preach at the university's baccalaureate and receive an honorary degree. "It is clear that the present faculty stand is 'on the side of the angels' and I feel I must stand with them," he said in a letter to the trustees.[8]

Meeting again on June 4, 1953, the trustees passed a resolution instructing those charged with seminary admissions "to give all applications for admission thereto sincere and thorough consideration without regard to race." A black student enrolled in the summer graduate program that summer, and one other black student entered the freshman class in the fall.

The incident put a blemish on the university's public relations record which proved difficult to remove. In later years, the college's record in recruiting black students became one of the best in the nation. *The Black Student's Guide to Colleges,* published in 1985, recognized Sewanee as one of ten predominantly white colleges in the United States offering the "best climate for black students."

The Reverend J. Carleton Hayden notes in *Struggle, Strife, and Salvation* (cited earlier) that blacks valued the Episcopal Church "partly because it never adopted racially discriminatory legislation at the national level." However, such was not the case with the individual dioceses, which are largely autonomous. In 1954, the convention of the Diocese of South Carolina voted to extend representation to a black parish and two black missions. This was the last of a number of dioceses to eliminate the color bar for representation at diocesan conventions. Previously, the diocesan constitution had stipulated that the convention be composed of clergy and laypersons "of the white race." That phrase was removed at this convention.

In the same year, debate began over the convention's choice of Houston as the site for the 1955 General Convention. The 1952 Boston convention decided to hold it in Houston, but only after long debate as to whether black delegates would receive equal housing arrangements. Presiding Bishop Henry Knox Sherrill describes the decision this way:

> There was much discussion because of the racial problem. Bishop Clinton Quin [of Texas] was eager to have the convention in his diocese as the time approached for his retirement after a notable episcopate. He gave moving and sincere assurances that this problem could and would be solved. The convention then voted, out of the great affection and esteem in which Bishop Quin was held by all, to accept the Texas invitation despite the expressed reluctance of a considerable minority.[9]

However, in the spring of 1954, several dioceses and church leaders began voicing concern over the Houston choice. The Diocese of New York voted in favor of changing the site unless an "immediate guarantee" of a nonsegregated meeting was given.[10] A group of black Episcopalians, including Supreme Court Justice Thurgood Marshall, the Reverend Tollie L. Caution, and the chief counsel for the NAACP, met with Bishop Sherrill and urged a change in the convention site.

Protests increased over the anticipated segregation in Houston, particularly when Bishop Quin of Texas was not able to give Sherrill assurances that hotel and eating facilities for deputies would be integrated. The presiding bishop announced the decision to move the General Convention from Houston on September 8, following a meeting of the convention's Arrangements Committee. Citing a constitutional provision which gave him the authority to do so, Sherrill said, ". . . This has been the most painful and difficult decision I have ever been called upon to make. I am certain that the witness of our church must be so clear that it need not be explained."[11] About a month later, Sherrill announced that arrangements had been made to hold the 1955 convention in Honolulu, Hawaii.

Any choice Bishop Sherrill made could not have avoided controversy. "Letters began to pour in upon me, expressing approval and strong vituperation," he commented. "Both support and dissent came at times from the most unexpected quarters. All in all it was an unhappy period for me."[12]

After this incident, the 1955 General Convention issued the strongest statement the church had made to that date on the racial issue. The convention urged Episcopalians to:

accept and support the ruling of the Supreme Court and, . . . anticipate contructively the local implementation of this ruling as the law of the land.

Stating that "discrimination and segregation are contrary to the mind of Christ and the will of God," the action resolved that,

. . . in the work of the church we should welcome people of any race at any service conducted by a priest or layman of any ethnic origin, and bring them into the full fellowship of the congregation and its organizations.[13]

A year later in Montgomery, Alabama, Rosa Parks left her job at Montgomery Fair Department Store where she worked as a seamstress. It was a cold dark evening on Thursday, December 1, 1956, when she took a seat on the city bus. A few minutes later, a white man asked her for her seat, and she said "No." He complained to the bus driver, who told her "If you don't move, I'll call the police and have you arrested." She refused, saying, "Have me arrested, I'm not going to move."

The police arrested her and she was later convicted for violating a city code requiring segregated seating on city buses. Indignant members of the black community went into action, and planned a boycott of city buses. The new pastor of Dexter Avenue Baptist church, an unknown twenty-six year-old who had a way with words, was asked to be the spokesman for the protest. His name was Martin Luther King, Jr. That boycott lasted 381 days, and Martin Luther King, Jr. soon became a household name across the country.[14]

The ferment in the Episcopal Church over racial integration only reflected the unrest throughout American society. However, despite the conventions' laudable statements, incidents of segregation and prejudice continued to occur among Episcopalians.

At a press conference on September 18, 1956, Presiding Bishop Sherrill stated that, "Integration in the whole church is inevitable; it is fundamental to the heart of the Gospel." It had been decided at the House of Bishops meeting at Sewanee the preceding week that a press conference would be held instead of issuing a pastoral letter. Sherrill reaffirmed the stand of the 1955 General Convention, stating, "The House of Bishops is in agreement on the morality of integration; the question of pronouncements is one of timing, not of principles."[15]

At the 1958 General Convention, Arthur C. Lichtenberger, Bishop of Missouri, was elected to succeed Henry Knox Sherrill as presiding bishop. Lichtenberger had been a teacher in China, a parish priest, and faculty member at General Theological Seminary in New York City prior to becoming Bishop of Missouri in 1952. He said at the time of his election that human rights "to vote, to eat a hamburger where you want, to have a decent job, to live in a house fit for habitation are not rights to be litigated or negotiated." In succeeding years, he assumed a courageous leadership role in supporting the church's civil rights stands.

The Episcopal Society for Cultural and Racial Unity

The Episcopal Society for Cultural and Racial Unity organized in 1958 and for twelve years played an active and sometimes confrontive role in the Episcopal Church. The Reverend John L. Kater, Jr., who wrote a doctoral dissertation on the organization's history, describes its beginning:

> Prior to the General Convention of 1958, a conference of interested churchmen met at Eaton Centre, New Hampshire to consider means for the church to respond to the [racial] crisis. . . . It led to the suggestion that an unofficial church organization might be effective in combating segregation . . .[16]

After a favorable response to starting such a group at the 1958 General Convention, an organizational meeting was held at St. Augustine's College in Raleigh, North Carolina in December of 1959. "We commit ourselves to establish total participation in the church for all persons without regard to race, class, or national origin," read the statement of purpose adopted at the meeting.

A national office for the society was subsequently established in Atlanta and the Reverend John B. Morris, twenty-nine years old and white, was named executive director. A nationwide campaign for membership and contributions met with considerable success. In an August, 1960 report, Morris announced that membership stood at more than 1,000, with 24 percent of its members in the South. At its peak, there were ESCRU chapters in twenty-six cities.

A 1961 "Prayer Pilgrimage" that stretched from New Orleans to Detroit was one of ESCRU's most publicized events. The bus trip, made by a group of interracial clergy ended at that year's General Convention. In inviting applications, Morris warned that no one should apply unless they were "willing to undergo a period in jail."

The twenty-eight priests determined not to submit to "immoral laws" requiring them to segregate along racial lines. However, the group decided that some of its members would try to avoid arrest in order to complete the pilgrimage, while others would not. After leaving New Orleans in a chartered bus on September 12, the group's first stop was at Vicksburg, Mississippi. Here, they spent three hours with administrators discussing the segregated status of All Saints' School, an Episcopal school of girls.

The next—and most publicized—stop was at the Trailways bus terminal in Jackson, Mississippi. Twelve white and three black priests attempted to eat in the "whites-only" restaurant at the terminal. Jackson police subsequently arrested and jailed the clergymen. The Reverend Robert L. Pierson,

son-in-law of Nelson Rockefeller, and the Reverend Malcolm Boyd were among those arrested. An Episcopal judge in Jackson found them guilty of a "breach of the peace" and accused them of violating a church tenet by "disobeying a civil authority."[17] All fifteen were jailed, but thirteen were later released when they posted $500 appeal bonds. Two remained in jail to represent the group while the others proceeded on to Detroit.

After a stop in Tennessee to protest a segregated restaurant near the University of the South's campus, and a stop in Dearborn, Michigan, to protest segregated housing, the group arrived at the General Convention. On September 20, ESCRU sponsored a dinner where they welcomed the pilgrims and issued a statement:

> We affirm that the Gospel must be preached even when the word of God is sharp and cutting . . . We remind the laity of the South that no loyalty to the secular community in which they live or its traditional way of life can rightfully oppose the just claims of their brothers in Christ.[18]

The convention itself endorsed a resolution approving the pilgrims' mission to "bear witness to their Christian convictions about justice for all people," but refused to endorse their action:

> These men have chosen the Prayer Pilgrimage as a means of bringing this stated position of the church before our people. They are doing the right as they see the right. Whether they have chosen the right way to bear witness to their convictions, time alone will tell.[19]

However, the convention did adopt another determined resolution condemning segregation:

> WHEREAS, prejudice is inconsistent with the Gospel of Jesus Christ; and
> WHEREAS, God in His providence is leading this country towards a desegregated society,
> RESOLVED, that this church, expressing penitence for marks of racial discrimination and segregation both in her past and present life and structure, take what steps she can to conform herself to the reconciling comprehensiveness of the body of Christ . . ."[20]

In 1970, John M. Burgess became the first black elected as a diocesan bishop for a predominantly white diocese. He was first elected suffragan bishop (assistant) of Massachusetts in 1962 and then bishop in 1970. He held that post until 1975. John T. Walker was elected suffragan bishop of Washington (D.C.) in 1971, and became bishop in 1977.

Among other "firsts" for blacks in the Episcopal Church, the Reverend Birney W. Smith, Jr. was elected a member of the church's National Council in 1963. At the time, he was serving as rector of St. Augustine's Church in Kansas City, Missouri. In 1969, the Reverend Dillard Robinson, III, became dean of Trinity Cathedral in Newark, New Jersey, thus becoming the first black dean of a cathedral. Charles Lawrence, Ph.D., a sociology professor at Brooklyn College in New York, became the first black president of the General Convention's House of Deputies in 1976.

The Lovett School Incident

One problem which received extensive national attention centered around the Lovett Episcopal Day School in Atlanta, more commonly known as the Lovett School. Its whites-only admission policy was brought forcibly to public attention in 1963 when it refused to admit Martin Luther King, III, the five-year-old son of the civil rights leader.

The school's trustees argued that they were not in defiance of the church since the school was not "officially" an Episcopal school. However, fourteen of its trustees were Episcopalians, its constitution made the dean of St. Philip's Cathedral their chairman, and the school's charter required religious teaching according to the precepts of the *Book of Common Prayer*. A retired Lovett teacher explained some of the thinking that occurred within the community: "I think that the board was worried that the school would be cut off from the financial community of Atlanta . . ."[21]

Ralph McGill was editor of *The Atlanta Constitution* and a member of St. Philip's Cathedral at the time. In a published interview, he stated "To say that this is not a church-related school is complete hypocrisy . . . although the bishop has said it isn't a church school, it remains one just the same . . . the cathedral leadership has acted with hypocrisy!"[22]

Eventually, the Diocese of Atlanta severed official connections with the school. Bishop Randall Claiborne of Atlanta later stated that the action had "removed the school from the orbit of discipline of the Episcopal Church . . ." The bishop also stated that Episcopal priests in the diocese could no longer serve as headmaster. This resulted in the resignation of the Reverend James McDowell.[23] Less than a year later, the Board of Trustees changed the policy to allow the admission of black students. Nevertheless, Martin Luther King, III found his education elsewhere. Episcopal priests were re-instated as headmasters, but it remained an independent school with only semi-official church connections.

The Presiding Bishop's Leadership

Presiding Bishop Arthur Lichtenberger was noted for his civil rights leadership, and served a term as chairman of the National Council of Churches' Commission on Religion and Race. In a 1963 statement titled "A Time to Act," Lichtenberger stressed that the church's mission in human rights went beyond proclamation.

> It is not enough for the church to exhort men to be good . . . [People] today are risking their livelihood and their lives in protesting for their rights. We must support and strengthen their protest in every way possible.[24]

The presiding bishop called upon Episcopalians to involve themselves in social change and contribute both money and personal involvement to the struggle. John Hines, who succeeded Lichtenberger as presiding bishop, described him this way:

He was strongly committed to civil rights. He was a gentle person, but he had a great capacity for indignation.[25]

The Episcopal Church was saddened with Lichtenberger's early retirement due to a disabling illness. In March 1963, the first announcement was made that Bishop Lichtenberger was suffering from the preliminary stages of Parkinson's disease. A year later, on March 30, 1964, he announced his intention to resign in a letter to all bishops: "I regret very much to tell you that the difficulties do persist and evidently will continue. I have been working constantly and steadily to overcome this disability, but I have made little progress . . ."[26]

Bishop Lichtenberger died four years later at his summer home in Bethel, Vermont. During the four years between his resignation and death, he served as a visiting professor of pastoral theology at the Episcopal Theological School in Cambridge, Massachusetts. In addition to his strong civil rights leadership, Lichtenberger was known as the first presiding bishop to visit the pope. He made an unofficial call on Pope John XXIII, while en route to the Third Assembly of the World Council of Churches in New Delhi, India, in 1961.

In an August, 1963 meeting in Toronto, the House of Bishops adopted a statement supporting the legislative proposal that later became the Civil Rights Act of 1964. Their resolution called for:

The Congress of the United States to pass such civil rights legislation as shall fairly and effectively implement both the established rights and needs of all minority groups in education, voting rights, housing, employment, and access to places of public accommodation.

The bishops' statement also supported the "March on Washington for Jobs and Freedom," planned as a massive demonstration on August 28th. Their statement recognized, "Not only the right of free citizens to peaceful assemblage, but also that participation in such assemblages is a proper expression of Christian witness and obedience."

After the Civil Rights Bill was passed in June of 1964, Lichtenberger issued a public statement. While he admitted that "legislation cannot change attitudes," he stressed:

. . . law does influence the way in which men and women treat one another; and more than just relationships do provide a social climate in which attitudes change . . . We must commit ourselves without reservation to the full support of civil rights.[27]

The 1964 General Convention

The 1964 General Convention gave its blessing to Episcopalians who worked for civil rights change:

. . . since areas of racial and social conflict affecting all minorities continue to multiply . . . this convention and the whole church gives unwavering material and moral support to those members . . . who obey the mandate of Christ by personal involvement in these areas of conflict.

This convention also elected John Elbridge Hines, Bishop of Texas, as its next presiding bishop. At fifty-four, Hines was the youngest man ever elected to the church's highest post. At thirty-four, he had been one of the youngest men ever elected bishop when he became Coadjutor Bishop of Texas. From the beginning, Hines was firmly committed to social and racial justice. Three years after his election, he was to lead the church into the General Convention Special Program—the boldest step in its history to deal with racial and social injustice.

The most significant civil rights statement of the 1964 convention came in the form of a resolution which, in effect, approved of interracial marriage within the church. The broad statement on race said that the exclusion of any person because of race from the "rites and sacraments" of the church is "contrary to the mind of Christ and the church." Since Holy Matrimony is listed as a rite of the Episcopal Church, the effect was not ambiguous. Commenting on the action, *The Christian Century* wrote,

While not encouraging miscegenation, the affirmation . . . puts the Episcopal Church on record as recognizing that persons of different racial backgrounds may marry with her blessing. The boat has at least been slightly rocked.[28]

Violence Escalates

The summer of 1964 brought riots, not only in the South, but in New York City, Detroit, and elsewhere. In Chester, Pennsylvania, demonstrations against inadequate schools provoked police action as violent as that which occurred in Birmingham and Montgomery. Commenting on the summer of 1964, John L. Kater, Jr. wrote that it "frightened many people who had been uncommitted or even sympathetic to the civil rights movement. This fear was exploited by politicians for whom 'crime in the streets' and 'law and order' became code phrases for Negro rioting and police repression."[29]

Martin Luther King, Jr. called his first march from Selma to Montgomery on behalf of black voting rights on March 7, 1965. The march turned into chaos as "state troopers and deputy sheriffs smashed into the Negro columns with nightsticks, whips, and teargas, sending about seventeen persons to hospitals."[30]

A second march was held three days later in which King had invited clergymen from throughout the country to participate. The Reverend David R. Hunter, head of the Episcopal Church's Christian Education Department, led a ten-man delegation from the National Council of Churches. The Reverend Arthur E. Walmsley, executive secretary of the Department of Christian

Social Relations, led a delegation of Episcopal priests. Through its newsletter, *Church and Race,* this department both prodded and encouraged the church to participate in the struggle for racial justice.

The Episcopal Church and the nation was shocked and dismayed with news on August 19, 1965, that an Episcopal seminarian had been shot and killed in Haynesville, Alabama. Jonathan Daniels, a white, second-year student at the Episcopal Theological School in Cambridge, had spent the summer in Alabama teaching remedial reading to black children. He was killed by a shotgun blast from a local white man who later claimed "self-defense." The Reverend Richard Morrisroe, a white Roman Catholic priest from Chicago, was also shot and critically wounded. The two men were approaching a country store when the shooting took place. The accused killer was later tried and acquitted by an all-white jury.

The Black Power Movement

The Civil Rights Act of 1964 brought legal equality in public accommodations and employment to blacks, and addressed most types of overt discrimination to which American blacks had been subjected. The legal ramifications brought immediate and continued changes in American society. It was probably this milestone as much as anything that brought a change in the focus of the civil rights movement, as well as in the Episcopal Church's response.

Beginning in the mid 1960s, black empowerment as epitomized in the slogan "black power" came to be the predominant theme in the civil rights movement. The term "black power" was first introduced by Stokely Carmichael at a rally in Greenwood, Mississippi, in 1966. The emergence of the concept of black power changed the goals and strategy of the civil rights movement in visible and permanent ways. One of the earliest results of this change was the rejection of the word "Negro" as a "white invention" and its replacement by the more forthright term "black."

John L. Kater, Jr. wrote in an article in the *Historical Magazine of the Protestant Episcopal Church:*

Integration had been pursued in personal terms, understood as the removal of barriers to individual advancement and the forging of bonds across racial lines. The black power movement pointed out that the institutional structures of American society oppresses blacks quite apart from the vagaries of personal attitude.[31]

The term "black power" had different meanings for different people. A report adopted and later published by the Executive Council suggested several different interpretations:

a) Black power may represent the nurturing of pride among Negroes in their cultural heritage, in their *negritude*—a drive for self-realization, self-identity, and dignity through consciousness of group history . . .

b) Black power may mean the effort within the black ghetto to build communal solidarity, to create a power force capable of changing the conditions of urban life.

c) Black power may mean repudiation of the theory of non-violence and a call to all Negroes to defend themselves against their oppressors.

d) Black power may mean rejection of integration as a goal of a strategy, brought on by the realization among ghetto people that the methods of white-dominated civil rights organizations will not improve the conditions of their lives.

e) Black power may be seen as an attempt to show the black masses that they must express themselves militantly, aggressively, and in their own ways . . .

f) Black power may mean racial supremacy, black nationalism, violent insurrection, and "burn, baby, burn."[32]

"As the implications of Black Power began to dawn upon the Episcopal Church, it became clear that the theological underpinnings of the church's role in the civil rights movement were called into question," said John L. Kater, Jr. in an *Historical Magazine* piece:

Furthermore, not only did its advocates generally refuse to concede a special place to the church as God's instrument of unity; many of them saw it as, at best, irrelevant, and at worst, as an enemy, one among many racist institutions which must be defeated if black power was to become a reality.[33]

The reaction from leaders in the church to the changing mood was, at best, mixed. One bishop stated in his diocesan paper, "There is no place in the church for the thinking of the Klan or the philosophy of black power." John B. Morris, executive director of ESCRU, wrote in 1966:

I view the catapulting to prominence of 'Black Power' as I discern it in the main—as tragic historically, practically untenable, morally and theo-logically unacceptable, but probably inevitable and possibly necessary.[34]

This change in focus was to have two main effects on the infrastructures of the Episcopal Church. One was the eventual decline of the Episcopal Society for Cultural and Racial Unity. This developed partly from internal dissension between those who advocated the earlier goals of the civil rights movement and those who thought ESCRU should shift its focus towards black power and the struggle against institutional racism.

The larger effect was the establishment and development of the General Convention Special Program (GCSP) by Presiding Bishop Hines in 1967. Its main thrust was the empowerment of blacks and minority groups through grants to help these groups achieve their purposes. Many ESCRU members felt that the Episcopal Church had responded to ESCRU's goals by the establishment of GCSP, and there was no longer a need for the organization.

Union of Black Episcopalians

The Union of Black Clergy and Laity, later to become the Union of Black Episcopalians, was formed at a meeting on February 8, 1968 at St. Philip's Church in Harlem, New York. The union's predecessor was the "Conference of Church Workers Among Colored People" which was organized in 1882 by John Peterson, a teacher and deacon at St. Philip's Church. The conference met annually and its meetings were highly organized with festive services, preaching, lectures, reports, and debates. Every third year it met at General Convention and appointed lobbyists to press for the goals of black Episcopalians.

The conference sponsored a monthly newspaper, *The Afro-American Churchman,* and later *The Church Advocate,* edited by George Freeman Bragg, Jr. The Rev. J. Carleton Hayden wrote:

> Over the years, the Conference achieved many goals. Segregation was never written into national policy or canon law. Another national commission to evangelize and educate southern blacks was established . . . The Conference continued until the mid-1960s, although it gradually gave way to the Episcopal Society for Cultural and Racial Unity (ESCRU) . . .[35]

The genesis of the Union of Black Clergy and Laity began in April, 1967, when 145 black priests took out a two-page advertisement in *The Episcopalian* and other church periodicals to protest discrimination in the hiring, placement, and deployment of black clergy. Citing the "systematic denial of participation by Negro men and women in all aspects of the life of the church," the advertisement said qualified black clergymen were not called to white parishes, and were excluded from the faculties of seminaries and private schools. Black Episcopal clergy "have been made to feel the chagrin of an 'invisible people' within the body of Christ," the advertisement stated.[36]

Black leaders saw the need for a new organization to serve the interests of black Episcopalians. This led to the formation of the Union of Black Clergy and Laity in 1968, later named the Union of Black Episcopalians (UBE). Today, the Union of Black Episcopalians is a confederation of twenty chapters and ten interest groups that are linked throughout the United States. UBE's official statement of purpose affirms ". . . the involvement of black people in the total life of the church, on every level and in every way: mission, stewardship, evangelism, education, sharing, liberation, empowerment, leadership, governance, and politics . . . The church is not whole unless all of God's people are an integral part of it."

5

Civil Rights: The General Convention Special Program

TOWARD THE LATTER PART OF THE 1960s, the civil rights turmoil in the United States worsened. In the summer of 1967, new and bitter violence erupted in ghettos across the country. The severest toll of death and destruction was felt in Newark, New Jersey and Detroit. For six days between July 12 and 17 in Newark, twenty-six people were killed, 1,500 were injured, and 1,000 were arrested. A week later in Detroit, at least forty people died, 2,000 were injured, and 5,000 were left homeless as a result of rioting, looting and burning in the city's black ghetto. Violence subsided only with the help of 4,700 federal paratroopers and 8,000 National Guardsmen.

Nineteen hundred sixty-seven was a critical year for the United States and for the Episcopal Church. The church's membership showed a slight increase, but it was to be the last increase for fifteen years. Baptisms took the biggest dip since 1962. The "Doctrine Debaters," Bishop James Pike in the United States and Bishop John A. T. Robinson in England were challenging the basic tenets of the Christian faith, while Thomas J. J. Altizer and William Hamilton were proclaiming "the death of God."

The year began with the death of three astronauts as they rehearsed the Apollo flight. By the end of the year, the United States had 475,000 troops in Vietnam and protests were mounting on campuses around the country. Moved by reports of the race rioting, Presiding Bishop John Hines made trips into ghetto areas to survey the mood and people. He toured Bedford-Stuyvesant, a depressed area of Brooklyn, as well as the slums of Detroit. In each of these areas, he spent a day walking around, unrecognized, talking, asking questions and listening. Leon Modeste, a black church leader who would later work closely with Hines, said of him: "You really felt this was a guy with a real mission who felt the church had to do something about the injustices in this country." A few days later, Hines spoke to the Emergency Convocation of the Urban Coalition. In his remarks, Hines said, "We are part of the problem inasmuch as the sickness of our society is our sickness

46

also." In identifying himself among the oppressors, Hines stressed that he was aware that the problem itself would have to be redefined before a solution could be found.

As the 1967 General Convention approached, the stage was set for one of the most radical proposals ever presented to the Episcopal Church. In his September 17 opening address in Seattle, Washington, Presiding Bishop Hines made this declaration:

> As at least the beginning of this church's response to the deep human need dramatized by the conflict in the cities, I am recommending the development of a program to be extended over the next triennium, by which the church can take its place humbly and boldly alongside of, and in support of, the dispossessed and oppressed peoples of this country . . .
>
> It will encourage the use of political and economic power to support justice and self-determination for all men. It will make available skilled personnel assistance, and request the appropriation of substantial sums of money to community organizations involved in the betterment of depressed urban areas.[1]

Hines went on to state that he was requesting a sum of $3 million annually, to come from the general budget and the United Thank Offering. The convention responded with little dissent and voted to appropriate $1.9 million from the general budget. By a vote of 447 to 20, the Triennial Meeting of the Episcopal Church Women voted to suspend the rules of order and give the $2 million remaining in its 1967 United Thank Offering to the special program. The women also made the special program their first priority for future thank offerings.

In "A Minority Report to the General Convention," one member of the Program and Budget Committee dissented. J. L. Caldwell McFaddin of Texas objected to the $500,000 earmarked specifically for groups seeking "black economic and political power." He warned that "this is a most divisive proposal and most dangerous. It will alienate thousands of members of our church, and, we fear, seriously endanger our program." While he did not object to the remaining money in the special program proposal, he stated, "Our offerings should not be diverted to achieve economic and political power for any group, white or black."[2]

However, the convention rejected the amendment to eliminate $500,000 appropriation. Mr. McFaddin's objections went unheeded, but his words were prophetic of the way the program would be perceived by many Episcopalians.

"The Episcopal Church was seen by many people as friendly but somewhat aloof and represented a more mature tradition than most institutions on the American scene," wrote Vine Deloria, Jr., in a *Historical Magazine* article. "Its entrance into the Civil Rights Movement was one of the signals . . . that the moral and ethical issues which civil rights symbolized were substantial and serious."[3] Deloria was a member of the Executive Council and the GCSP Screening and Review Committee.

After playing its overture at General Convention, GCSP enacted its drama over the next six years in perhaps the Episcopal Church's most controversial era. The history of civil rights between 1967 and 1973 is in large measure the history of the General Convention Special Program.

In 1968, an organization called Southern Media of Jackson, Mississippi, received a $24,000 grant to produce low budget films, made by blacks, "to help create a new self image for oppressed people." The Avondale Community Council of Cincinnati received $42,000 for its effort to mobilize black residents to act on educational, housing, and welfare issues. Tribal Industries of Reno, Nevada, received a grant to help develop small businesses and other enterprises for the benefit of Nevada Indians. The "Drum and Speak" bookstore in Washington, D.C., received a $30,000 grant for the "initiation of betterment programs for the black community."

These are examples of the kinds of programs aided by GCSP, and grants-making was the main thrust of its functions. Any group or individual was eligible to supply for a GCSP grant. Those making applications were required to meet "one or more" of the following criteria:

a) Community organization on a national, metropolitan or neighbor-hood level; the basic purpose here is to gain social, political, or economic power.

b) Service to the poor based on programs designed and controlled by the poor themselves. These would include training in the skills necessary to assure the effective conduct of such programs.

c) Community leadership training and experience in specific areas of need identified by the applicant.

d) It must also be based on the fundamental principle of assisting the poor to organize themselves to have an effective share in determining their own destiny.[4]

The criteria also stated, "No funds received can be used in connection with any individual or group which advocates violence." The bishop of the diocese in which a program requesting a grant was located was required to be consulted for an opinion. An Executive Council report stated, "No bishop, however, has veto power over funding." It was these two issues—the use of nonviolence and the local bishop's lack of veto power—that proved crucial in the controversies which later developed.

The GCSP had three goals:

a) To help the poor and disenfranchised—particularly the black and brown communities gain social, political and economic power in order to have an effective voice . . . in the decisions which affect their lives.

b) To provide initiative and support for the development of church and community organizations which are attempting to eliminate racist practices within the church and other institutions.

c) To assist in the use of the church's influence and economic power, separately and in coalition, in order to support justice and self-determination for the poor and powerless.[5]

GCSP staff members first screened all grant applications before passing them on to the Screening and Review Committee. This committee, a sub-unit of the Executive Council, met three times a year. The presiding bishop was chairman. Other committee members included two representatives from the General Division of Women's Work, two representatives of the Union of Black Clergy and Laymen, and seven representatives of minority groups to whom GCSP addressed itself. A broad representation of black, Puerto Rican, American Indian, Mexican American, and Appalachian residents were included.

Presiding Bishop Hines appointed Mr. Leon Modeste, an accredited social worker, as GCSP Director. He had worked at the Episcopal Church Center as Associate for Community Services in the Department of Christian Social Relations, and was primarily responsible for evaluating the community service programs of the department.

Hines gave Modeste full control in selecting and organizing the GCSP staff. Modeste stated:

I requested that I have a free hand in being able to put the staff together. I felt it had to be people who knew something about what the whole struggle was about. I got people who had been with CORE [Congress of Racial Equality] and SNCC [Student Nonviolent Coordinating Committee]. At the time, the church didn't have any kind of network with the black community. That's why we set up a different kind of criteria for getting the staff. They were community organizers and people who had been part of 'the movement.' The only Episcopalians I had that I know of were Barry Menuez and the Reverend Quinland Gordon.

Modeste admits that many of these staff members were not often sympathetic to the traditional aims of the church:

There were some [on the staff] who felt 'this was the time to do something black' and the church was just playing the game. They thought it was a kind of political move by the church and it would end soon. There was a distinction among them between Hines and the Episcopal Church. Some really respected him, but they didn't seem to have a lot of respect for the church.[6]

From its beginning, many clergy and laity perceived GCSP as something which was not really a part of the Episcopal Church. The grants it gave went to groups whose aims many perceived to be at variance with Christian principles.

By the end of its first year, more than $1 million had been allocated to community organizations and groups throughout the nation. At the same time, however, GCSP had begun to develop suspicions among local parishes and dioceses who responded by withholding their financial pledges to the church. In 1969, ten dioceses failed to meet their quota to the national church. In 1970, that number rose to forty-seven, or almost half. Bishop Hines was disappointed when he told the December 1968 Executive Council meeting, "Doubtless we have made some mistakes in handling and interpreting the GCSP . . . We should not permit our pride to blind us to our faults and failures."

After reporting on the "rewarding response" of $170,000 in gifts for a Biafra Hunger Appeal, Hines said,

There may be a curious relationship between some aspects of the generous outpouring of support in the Biafran appeal and, in some places, the indifference or occasional outright hostility with which some of our people have met the General Convention Special Program. It may mean that a need which costs us nothing more than money . . . fares much better with us than a need which threatens not our money, but our traditional assumptions, or our prejudices . . .[7]

Controversial Grants

While support for GCSP was generally widespread among national church leaders—if not "the folks back home"—some controversial grants aroused criticism. In 1969, $30,000 went to Malcolm X Liberation University in Durham, North Carolina, and aroused considerable opposition from the bishop and diocesan leaders there. In a statement in the diocesan newspaper, the Right Reverend Thomas Fraser said, "Let it be clearly understood that there is no place in the church for the thinking of the Klan or the philosophy of black power."[8] Later the Diocese of North Carolina cut its pledge to the national church by $160,000.

Shortly before the 1970 General Convention in Houston, the Executive Council voted 21-6 to give $25,000 in GCSP funds to the Black Awareness Coordinating Committee in Denmark, South Carolina. The two South Carolina bishops, John Pinckney of Columbia and Gray Temple of Charleston, pleaded in vain with the Council to deny the funds, pointing out that the previous year the group had seized the campus of the Episcopal Church's Voorhees College in Denmark, disrupting classes.

Several of the Black Awareness Committee's leaders had been convicted and sentenced to prison terms by predominantly black juries. The group had also been denounced by two of South Carolina's leading civil rights organizations for "forcing certain goals and ideas on community blacks, rather than letting those blacks determine their own goals."

Probably the most controversial GCSP grant was given in November 1968 to the Alianza, a Hispanic organization in New Mexico. Its leader, Ruis Lopez Tarjirina, was serving a jail term at the time the grant was made. The Bishop of New Mexico, C.U. Kinsolving, III, asked that the grant be denied because the group "advocated violence in making its claim to thirty-five million acres of New Mexico state land." Overriding his objection, the Council approved $40,000 for the group.

The founder of the Alianza, Federal de Mercedes, laid claim to most of the land in the American Southwest (including parts of Texas) and launched a virtual guerilla war in New Mexico to attempt to take the land. During their activities, two unarmed forest rangers were assaulted and their trucks were seized. A judge sentenced the Alianza's leader and four of his men to prison terms ranging from sixty days to three years. While they were out on bail, a courthouse was seized, two law officers were shot and a third was pistol whipped. The National Guard was called to restrain the groups, some members of which received long prison terms.[9]

In reacting to the Council's decision, Bishop Kinsolving announced that his diocese would halt its support of the national Episcopal Church and would not pay its $82,365 quota in 1969.

Dr. Clifford Morehouse, then president of the House of Deputies, later told the 1970 General Convention:

"We were assured by the GCSP staff and Screening and Review Committee that, however violent the Alianza might seem to be, there is nothing in their corporate declarations to say that they *advocate* violence—so, we were told, they qualify under our criteria. Thus, despite strenuous objections and documented arguments by the Bishop and diocesan leaders of New Mexico . . . we granted the Alianza $40,000 with no strings attached."[10]

"GCSP has never promoted the use of violence," Leon Modeste later wrote. "However, as a part of the black experience, we understood the reasons why those blacks who did preach the use of force did so. We did not disassociate ourselves from the people who did advocate the use of armed struggle.[11]

The Black Manifesto

"We are demanding $500 million from the Christian white churches and Jewish synagogues . . . to pay reparations to black people in this country." This was the essence of *The Black Manifesto,* first announced when James Forman, a "black power" leader walked into services at Riverside Church, New York City on May 3, 1969.

"This total comes to $15 per nigger," he said. "Only a beginning of the reparations due us as people who have been exploited and degraded, brutalized, killed and persecuted."[12]

Forman, who wrote the *Manifesto,* had first presented it to the Black Economic Development Conference (BEDC), which met a week earlier in Detroit on April 26. BEDC adopted the manifesto as its own statement of purpose and principle. A week later, the public first heard the statement when Forman interrupted the Riverside Church service. The "reparations" were to be used for a southern bank, four major publishing and printing industries, four audiovisual centers, technical training centers, a research center, a welfare rights organization, a university, and a labor strike and defense fund for blacks.

The next Sunday black civil rights leaders presented the demands for reparations demands in churches throughout the country. On May 13 in New York, a delegation of twenty-seven blacks arranged a meeting and presented Episcopal Church leaders with its list of demands. They asked for $60 million, plus 60 percent a year of the income from all assets of the Church.[13]

Presiding Bishop Hines later called the manifesto language:

. . . revolutionary . . . inflammatory . . . and violent, so as to shock, challenge, frighten, and if possible, overwhelm the institutions to which it is directed. It was no surprise then that the immediate response . . . of the white establishment was—with few exceptions—one of outrage and furious hostility.[14]

The Executive Council appointed a ten person committee to prepare a response to the demands. Adopted on May 20, 1969, the committee's report acknowledged continuing racism and injustice in America, but did "not accept" the manifesto as it was presented. The response, contained in nine articles, cited present programs of the church that sought to eliminate racial injustice, including several GCSP-supported programs and the deposit of nearly $1 million of church funds in ghetto banks.

1969 Special General Convention

In responding to pressure to include a wider range of participation, the 1967 General Convention in Seattle approved a "special session" of the convention for 1969. The Executive Council later scheduled this for August 31 through September 5 at the University of Notre Dame in South Bend, Indiana. Although not all were deputies, this was the first time in General Convention history that women, ethnic minorities and young people were included in large numbers. It was also the first time that the convention was held on a college campus, and that time was scheduled for conference functions, as well as traditional legislative functions.

On the second day, Daniel T. Carroll, a Chicago lay deputy, was speaking on a deployment plan when his remarks were interrupted. The Reverend Paul Washington, a Pennsylvania deputy, and Muhammed Kenyatta, also from Philadelphia, seized the microphone and said they would not let Carroll continue.

After a mild tussle between Presiding Bishop Hines and Kenyatta, the black leader gave a speech demanding $200,000 from the Episcopalians as a response to the Black Manifesto and to fund the Black Economic

Development Conference (BEDC). The Reverend Mr. Washington proceeded to explain that none of the $200,000 should come from GCSP funds.

After a couple of days of open hearings, the convention opened debate on the demands on Tuesday evening. It continued throughout the evening, with a lot of parliamentary wrangling. The greatest concern of the deputies seemed to be "what the people back home" would do and say if the convention acceded to the reparations demands. Later a vote was taken and the measure was defeated. Immediately, Canon Junius Carter of Pittsburgh stood up and said:

> I'm sick of you . . . It hurts me terribly to know I'm in this Episcopal Church which is afraid to take a stand. You talk about fighting for salvation, but I don't know what that is now . . . You talk about resurrection. There's no resurrection at all. We just finished a crucifixion.[15]

The convention was thrown into an uproar. The House of Deputies voted to reconsider its action, and following a night of intense lobbying, another vote was taken and the proposal was adopted. The resolution authorizing the financial commitment read:

> . . . while rejecting much of the ideology of the Black Manifesto, we recognize that the Black Economic Development Conference is a movement which is an expression of self-determination for the organizing of the black community in America.[16]

Parishes began to protest the Notre Dame convention's decision to give $200,000 to BEDC. St. Dunstan's in Seattle, Washington staged a "giver's revolt." The parish decided to withhold a percentage of their diocesan contribution and send it to "some worthwhile Christian mission which is struggling because of the loss of funds on account of these unwise appropriations."

Two Chicago churches, St. Paul's by the Lake and St. Chrysostom's, issued statements protesting the Notre Dame allocation of funds. Members of the vestry of St. Paul's informed diocesan officials that they "oppose, resent, and to the extent of canon law reject the election to pledge any contributions to . . . the Black Economic Development Conference."[17]

Other parishes and dioceses announced similar actions. A 1970 Diocesan Press Service release stated that, "A budget voted by the church's Executive Council at its February meeting is more than one million dollars under [that of] 1969 and has been brought about by a decline in giving of the dioceses of the church." The same news release said that would mean reducing by forty the staff of the Episcopal Church Center in New York City.

A year later, the situation became worse. In a move that took the church by surprise, the new forty-one member Executive Council decided to cut the staff at the Episcopal Church Center by one half: from 204 persons to 110.

Executive Council member Vine Deloria, Jr., became a sharp critic of GCSP. He wrote in the *Historical Magazine:*

I resigned in total disgust with the GCSP and the Executive Council in the fall of 1969 just after the Notre Dame convention. The pain involved in these decisions reflects more than intellectual disagreement since my family had been prominently involved in the mission of the Episcopal Church to the American Indian community since the 1870s.[18]

Deloria charged that GCSP did not seek input from American minorities other than blacks:

The original guidelines of GCSP called for representation of the poor although it was no secret that the program had been called forth by the activities of the black community alone. Indians and Chicanos and the unorganized white poor had as yet played no major role in American politics and were unrecognized as forces which had to be placated.[19]

The 1970 General Convention: The Tide Rescinds

"It is a disturbed Episcopal Church which gathers in Houston today," read a convention news release. "On the eve of convention, the GCSP is rated 'Topic A' wherever early-comers gather this weekend in hotel lobbies, coffee shops, and convention center corridors."

In his opening address, Presiding Bishop Hines asserted that the many objections to the special program and to his leadership reflected a deeper problem involving "the meaning of mission in Christ's name . . . [and] the cost we are willing to pay in response to God's call." While he called for unity, Hines' sermon made it clear that he believed social justice was more important than church unity.

In a later session, Leon Modeste, GCSP director, explained that the program had an average annual budget of $1.7 million, and had aided more than 250 minority groups in its three year history. Critics and supporters alike had their say. "I rejoiced when my staid old Episcopal Church decided to put its money where its mouth had always been," said the Reverend Canon Gordon Gillett of New Hampshire.

Criticisms focused on two main points: First, the support or practice of violence by groups receiving GCSP money. About ten grants made between 1967 and 1970 were controversial for this reason. Second, the lack of in-put or veto power from dioceses where grants were made aroused considerable ill-feeling. Several grants had been made in communities over the objections of the local bishop.

Dr. Clifford Morehouse, president of the House of Deputies, told a later session, "I confess that my enthusiasm for the *administration* of the program, as distinguished from its *aims,* has been considerably tarnished by my three years of often traumatic service on the Executive Council." He cited three results of some of the "dubious" grants:

First, they have antagonized thousands of church people, many of whom have retaliated in the only way they know—by cutting their pledges to the national church. Second, they have escalated a sizeable credibility gap between the presiding bishop and the Executive Council, on the one hand, and the dioceses, parishes, and individual church members on the other hand. Third, they have placed the future of GCSP itself in serious jeopardy, because if the funds for support of the church's program are further reduced, neither GCSP nor other important aspects of that program can long survive.[20]

The convention finally voted a compromise resolution on GCSP. The program would continue, but with certain restrictions. Funds would be denied to any organization which "advocates the use of violence" in carrying out its program, or if any member was convicted of a crime involving "physical violence" in carrying out its program.

More importantly, no grant could be given without the approval of the local bishop. If the bishop vetoed a grant proposal, the Executive Council could override it with a majority vote. The compromise brought a surprising unanimity. One of its fiercist critics, the Right Reverend William Moody of Lexington, Kentucky, later told the House of Bishops: "I recognize the time has come when sensible people must compromise and I support the document as it stands." Bishop C. U. Kinsolving of New Mexico voiced his support as well. Bishop Archie Crowley, Suffragan Bishop of Michigan, said he was "amazed and delighted . . . and didn't think it could have been done as well as it was."

Under the stricter guidelines adopted by the 1970 General Convention, GCSP continued its grants-making process throughout 1971 and 1972 with less public dispute than in earlier years. There were, at least, none of the controversial grants that had brought so much attention in earlier years.

Vine Deloria, however, wrote in the *Historical Magazine* that protests declined because those who criticized GCSP were often considered "racist":

Protests by local bishops and informed churchmen in various dioceses were turned aside with hints that the protest was generated by racial considerations. Since no one wished to be tagged as a racist when he was simply demanding accountability, protests declined and this lack of friction was cited as evidence that the program was working.[21]

In the fall of 1972, the Executive Council sent teams of representatives to every diocese to meet and talk with diocesan leaders. These teams, totaling over one hundred people, consisted of Executive Council members, Episcopal Church Center staff, and other selected lay and clergy leaders. More than 6,000 Episcopalians attended these meetings.

"There has never been a greater effort to hear the church express her concerns," their final report read. It further stated:

There is a clear demand for major revision in the empowerment grant programs. The greatest dissatisfaction is with GCSP as it is presently administered . . . This program as it presently exists ranked in the lower end of the church's . . . priorities.[22]

Complaints within the Executive Council erupted in late 1972 when Bishop Wilburn Campbell of the Diocese of West Virginia resigned from the Screening and Review Committee (although he remained an Executive Council member). Citing "personal, emotional frustrations" he charged a number of irregularities in program administration. He told the December Executive Council meeting: "Many of the members of the Screening and Review Committee are basically hostile to the church. There have been moments when I felt I was in a meeting of Black Muslims and not Christians."[23]

Following Bishop Campbell's resignation, Presiding Bishop Hines called for an investigative committee review of GCSP. Hines presented a summary of the committee's report at the February meeting of the Executive Council in 1973. He stated that GCSP had been "administered not faultlessly, but with integrity" and that the "staff had done a tremendous job and has rendered an enduring service to the church."[24] At the same meeting, Philip Masqualette, a Texas layman, also resigned from the Screening and Review Committee. He had previously filed a list of eighteen proposals for the improvement of GCSP's administrative procedures. Subsequently at the Executive Council meeting in May, Masqualette proposed a series of resolutions for revision of the Screening and Review Committee's charter.

The council voted to adopt Masqualette's resolution to set a quorum of eight or more of the fourteen members of the Screening and Review Committee, and to prohibit votes by mail, telegram, or telephone. The council also adopted his resolution which requested a statement of criteria and procedures for grants to coalitions. Three other resolutions proposed by Masqualettes were either defeated or tabled.[25]

There was a great irony to this particular meeting of the Executive Council meeting. While the Executive Council was performing surgery on GCSP with Masqualette's changes, it was also digging its grave. At this same meeting, the council approved a recommendation to establish a new staff section that would in effect terminate GCSP as a separate program of the Episcopal Church. The May 2, 1973 Diocesan Press Release stated:

The Executive Council . . . adopted a resolution to establish a new staff section on grants to racial and ethnic minorities, to coordinate the administrative grants currently managed by three existing agencies . . .

The establishment of the new staff section followed a summary report after the council visited ninety-one of the dioceses of the church which indicated "widespread support" for the separate grant programs "to be consolidated into a single agency."

The current agencies which administer grants to racial and ethnic minorities are the General Convention Special Program (GCSP), the

National Committee on Indian Work (NCIW), and the National Commission on Hispanic Affairs (NCHA).

A new Committee for Community Action and Human Development (CAHD) will replace the Screening and Review Committee of the GCSP and it will fund community-oriented projects for the black community. The new ministry with black Episcopalians will be committed to Episcopal Church-oriented work.

The final approval for this proposal came at the 1973 General Convention in Louisville, Kentucky. The convention spent little time debating the proposal. Under its new title "Committee for Community Action and Development," the same activities under GCSP were continued at a reduced funding level of $650,000 per year (the 1973 level was $1 million). At the same time, funds for Indian work were increased from $46,000 to $376,000, and funds for Hispanic work were increased from $80,000 to $400,000. "With a surprising lack of controversy, both houses passed a 1974 national church budget of $13,625,732," read an official convention news release.

Evaluating the GCSP

Clearly the GCSP had positive results that are difficult to measure. Leon Modeste stated in a 1982 interview, "It really opened the church in a lot of ways. It gave the church insights it didn't have before, along with new ideas and new approaches." The same 1970 convention that had voted to place restrictions on GCSP also voted to allow women to be ordained as deacons, and seated women deputies for the first time. Six years later, women were allowed to become priests. The concepts of equality that the Civil Rights movement promoted opened the eyes of the church to new concepts of ministry among all people.

In 1976, the General Convention also voted to establish a program called "Venture in Mission." This program raised over $150 million to fund domestic and overseas mission projects and was called "the most successful capital funds drive in the history of American Christianity" by some Episcopal Church leaders. While the two shouldn't be compared, GCSP doubtlessly helped pave the way for the mission-consciousness needed for Venture in Mission to be so successful.

On the other hand, the Episcopal Church was generally unprepared to cope with the change in mood and focus of the Civil Rights movement which occurred after 1965. The shift moved towards combating institutional racism rather than individual discrimination, and indeed the church was an institution that could not plead innocence. The GCSP was a bold response to this change, and the only program of this nature and magnitude undertaken by any denomination.

"The Episcopal Church had embraced the shades of Rudyard Kipling and the styles of imperialistic England for too long to make a sudden, sophisticated, and substantial move into America of the sixties," wrote Deloria. "When it did move, the Episcopal Church chose the most tangible but least sophisticated weapon in its institutional arsenal. Money."[26]

Both John Hines and Leon Modeste attribute most of GCSP's problems to their failure to communicate its aims to the whole church. "The failure of the General Convention Special Program, where it failed, was that it could not communicate its motivations and hopes effectively to the whole of the church," said John Hines in a 1978 interview.[27]

Throughout the duration of GCSP, few ever criticized its aims or intentions. Episcopalians held a wide degree of consensus about racial injustice, and GCSP was initially seen as an attempt to address it. The problems developed from adverse publicity when grants went to groups involved in violence. When this began to occur, local bishops demanded more control over the grants-making process. John Hines said in a 1982 interview that he believes this was the "beginning of the end" for GCSP:

> The biggest problem, as I look back on it, and one we never did solve was that it sort of floundered on the sacred, so-called 'Episcopal principle' of the Episcopal Church. That is, that the bishop is the boss. If anything ever happened in the Episcopal Church, if the bishop was for it, it was going to happen; if the bishop was against it, it wasn't . . .

Speaking of the revised GCSP criteria requiring a majority vote by the Executive Council to override a local bishop's objection to a grant in his diocese, Hines said:

> Well, that killed the thing. Not only because Houston [where the 1970 General Convention was held] had reduced the amount of money for the grants . . . . but now the Executive Council was more likely to turn out with a dissenting point of view among its members to thwart the progress in this way. Then, the GCSP couldn't get past the 'Episcopal principle.'[28]

Since 1973, General Conventions have been relatively silent on civil rights matters. That isn't to say, however, that nothing is being done. The Union of Black Episcopalians continues as the major network to speak for the concerns of black clergy and laity. The Coalition for Human Need at the Episcopal Church Center continues making similar grants as those made by GCSP, although to wider minority constituency. The 1973 General Convention also created the Episcopal Commission for Black Ministries and a position for a commission staff officer at the Episcopal Church Center in New York City. The purpose of the commission and its staff officer is to work with black Episcopalians to:

— make the church more responsive to the needs of black communicants.
— assist black Episcopalians in their efforts for self-determination and development.
— enable black Episcopalians to contribute to the entire church their unique gifts of ministry.

There is still a long way to go. Black congregations are usually small and struggling, and most predominantly white congregations have only a small percentage of black members. Many have none, particularly in small communities.

The observance of the birthday of Martin Luther King, Jr. each January brings to memory his eloquent and stirring vision of "I have a dream." The Episcopal Church has made some progress in fulfilling that dream for its own black members. Within the United States, however, most blacks believe it is a dream yet unfulfilled.

6

The Church in Society: More Tough Issues

A TWENTY-TWO YEAR OLD CHURCH ORGANIST in Pennsylvania announced one Sunday in 1972 that "In light of President Nixon's invasion of Cambodia, we'll sing a hymn of peace today."

"No we won't," replied the officiating priest, "We'll sing 'Onward Christian Soldiers'." The organist refused and was told to leave the church.

A church doesn't always choose to "confront the issues" of society, because more often than not the issues confront the church. Church members hold jobs, go to school, and live in the same world we hear about on the news every night. Among Episcopalians, there are Vietnam veterans, peace activists, homosexuals, and those who have had abortions. They bring these same concerns to church every Sunday.

And "issues" don't always come in intellectual terms—they come in living and breathing through the doors every Sunday. Regardless of how the church states its "position," people deal with it at different levels. The Civil Rights movement and the womens' rights movement were the major forces to confront the Episcopal Church in the decades after World War II, but there were others as well.

The Vietnam War, the gay liberation movement, abortion, apartheid in South Africa and the peace movement engaged the church in debate at all levels. The consensus on any of these issues was never unanimous, but one point was certain: If you had an opinion on any issue, you could find an Episcopalian somewhere to agree with you. The advantage of the Episcopal Church's "comprehensiveness" is that it usually doesn't force an opinion on its members. It could not even always reach enough of a consensus to formulate a clear resolution at its conventions. Nowhere was this seen more clearly than in debate on the Vietnam War.

The Vietnam War

Philip Deemer in *Episcopal Year 1970* wrote, "The Episcopal Church is divided from top to bottom over the Vietnam War."[1] That pretty well sums

60

up the position of the Episcopal Church on the most controversial war in United States history.

In 1961, fourteen Americans died in Vietnam; in 1963, the toll had reached 489. By 1966, 4,000 soldiers had been killed, and there were nearly 500,000 American soldiers fighting in Vietnam. One historian describes the quagmire this way:

> For more than seven years . . . American combat forces remained bogged down in a war that the United States was never able either to win or fully to understand. Combating a foe whose strength lay not in weaponry but in a pervasive infiltration of the population, the United States responded with the kind of heavy-handed technological warfare designed for conventional battles against conventional armies.[2]

The only resolution the 1967 General Convention in Seattle, Washington, was able to agree upon said that Episcopalians couldn't agree on the subject. It stated in part:

> Differences are painfully evident within our church and at this convention. Indeed, no small part of our existential agony lies in our inability to agree among ourselves on an issue. We take comfort from the knowledge that the whole truth is known only to God.[3]

During the debate, an attempt to gain approval for a strong anti-bombing resolution was soundly defeated, as well as one stating unqualified support for United States government military policies.

"You let us down, but we love you," read placards held by young people at the convention as they started a quiet parade through the Seattle Convention Center after the vote. Throughout the convention, the young people continued to work for passage of the anti-bombing resolution.

Debate on the Vietnam issue took place again at the 1970 General Convention, but the House of Deputies could not agree with a resolution passed by the bishops. The resolution stated that the "present regime in Vietnam by its actions seems to be a hindrance to the achievement of peace," and urged the United States government "to cease immediately and finally the bombing of the people and country of Vietnam; and to withdraw all American forces . . . by December, 1971." The bishops had passed the resolution by a vote of eighty-six to thirty-seven.

The House of Deputies saw it differently. A deputy from South Carolina said, "Our advising the president on this is like the administration' in Washington advising us on Prayer Book revision."

"This war has proved to be the most tragic mistake our country has ever made," asserted a deputy from Pennsylvania. "This resolution will not stop the shooting but it will serve to put the conscience of the church on record." Despite the arguments, the House of Deputies reached a stalemate and defeated the resolution by a slight majority.[4]

The Vietnam War brought increasing numbers of young men applying for conscientious objector status—not because they were pacifists—but because they objected to the Vietnam War. In 1943, the General Convention recognized the numbers of conscientious objectors within the church, and passed a resolution assuring them "of the continuing fellowship of the church with them and care for them." The matter of objection to a "specific" war raised more complex questions, both for the church and the nation.

Neither the United States Selective Service nor the courts would recognize these specific objections to this particular war worthy of conscientious objector status. Many fled to Sweden or Canada rather than fight in Vietnam. Church debate on the subject was crystalized with a statement adopted by the 1968 meeting of the House of Bishops in Augusta, Georgia. In this statement, the bishops supported the right of a man to object to a particular war:

> . . . We, as bishops, recognize the right of a man to object on grounds of conscience, provided he has made every effort to know all the relevant factors involved, to participation in a particular war, even though he may not embrace a position of pacifism in relation to all war . . .[5]

After the conflict in Vietnam had ended in 1973, the bishops also adopted a statement urging a general amnesty for all who had left the country rather than be drafted. Adopted in October of 1973, the statement urged appropriate governmental authorities to "grant to Vietnam veterans every benefit it has given to veterans of past wars," and that "general amnesty be granted to all who refused to participate in the conflict in Indochina."

In 1974, President Ford adopted a program of "earned reentry" for draft resistors. The Episcopal bishops found this policy less than satisfactory, and responded by adopting another resolution in October of 1974. They stated that President Ford's plan "falls short of accomplishing the human goal of healing divisions resulting from United States involvement in Vietnam" and called again for "general amnesty." A general amnesty for Vietnam War evaders was not granted until 1977 by President Carter, shortly after the beginning of his term.

A Bishop for the Armed Forces

One of the troubling issues of the modern era was whether the church should have a bishop for ministry in the armed forces. The General Convention of 1949 changed the canons to allow a bishop for the armed forces, but the church took no immediate action. At its 1956 meeting, the House of Bishops approved a statement that a bishop for the armed forces was "neither necessary nor expedient at the present time." The statement indicated that the office of a bishop "indicates territorial jurisdiction. We might well be initiating a dangerous precedent in electing and consecrating a bishop to serve any special interest group . . ."[6]

At the time of the 1956 statement, more than one hundred Episcopal chaplains had served in the armed forces, and many more had served in World War II. The Armed Forces Division of the Episcopal Church Center in New York coordinated their work.

However, the House of Bishops at the 1964 General Convention elected a current bishop, Arnold Lewis of the missionary district of Western Kansas, as a suffragan bishop for the armed forces. Six years later, Bishop Clarence Hobgood, a career military chaplain and lieutenant colonel, was elected solely to become a suffragan bishop for the armed forces.

Bishop Hobgood was consecrated on February 2, 1971, at the Cathedral of Saint Peter and Saint Paul in Washington, D.C., in an impressive ceremony attended by hundreds of military and church officials. The 'fly in the ointment' was the nearly 150 clerical and lay members of the Episcopal Peace Fellowship (EPF) assembled in the nave to challenge the holy procedures. While their objections did not affect the outcome, Presiding Bishop Hines did agree to permit Peace Fellowship representatives to voice their dissent during the proceedings at the cathedral.

Hines invited the Reverend Edward Lee, a spokesperson and Temple University chaplain to read EPF's formal protest to the congregation. Father Lee said that in consecrating a bishop solely for the armed forces, the Episcopal Church was "in serious error and blasphemous violation of the peace-making imperative of the Gospel of Jesus." While he said that the church should have a ministry to the armed forces, "We are dissatisfied with the existing and establishing arrangements for the support and criteria of that ministry."

Later in the service, the congregation was asked about the bishop-elect, "Is he worthy?" At that point, the 150 EPF members rose in the nave and together shouted: "He is worthy, but not for this office."[7]

A similar enactment occurred seven years later when Hobgood's successor, the Reverend Charles Burgreen, was consecrated Suffragan Bishop for the Armed Services at the Cathedral of the Incarnation in Garden City, Long Island in 1978. Burgreen was a career Army chaplain and colonel who retired from active duty in 1978. Between 1973 and 1978, he served as executive assistant to Bishop Hobgood.

When Presiding Bishop Allin asked if anyone knew of a reason why the consecration should not proceed, two members of the Episcopal Peace Fellowship asked to be allowed to speak. The Reverend Nathaniel Pierce of the Diocese of Idaho stepped forward and stated that the church had chosen to "legitimize that which is illegitimate, to sanctify that which is unchristian, to bless that which is not of God." He said that the church had sold out to the Gospel itself, and become a partner in a "scheme that contemplates the wholesale destruction of human life."[8] While the protests were heard, the tradition was already established. The Episcopal Church had a bishop for the armed forces, and had already had one for fourteen years.

Homosexuality

Upon learning that a scheduled service of an Episcopal congregation was to include the wedding of two men, an Episcopal bishop invoked a seldom used article of canon law to have the group locked out of a Washington, D.C. church. When Bishop William Creighton ordered the sanctuary of St. Stephen and the Incarnation Church locked in 1971, he cited Canon 24, a rule citing the authority of the bishop to determine who may use the facilities of an Episcopal church building. While the church's rector had given permission for the service, a minister of another denomination was officiating at the service.[9]

Homosexual issues in the Episcopal Church reflected the wider gay liberation movement that gained momentum in the United States beginning in the early 1970s. The beginning of the movement is generally dated as 1969 in an incident during which New York City police raided a Greenwich Village gay bar. The aggressive response against the police received wide media attention and signalled the beginning of an era of demand for gay rights.

The gay liberation movement challenged all of the traditional assumptions about homosexuality being sinful and contrary to Christian norms. Homosexuality becomes widely heralded as an "alternative lifestyle," as opposed to an abnormal or inferior one.

Integrity was founded as an organization for gay Episcopalians in 1974 by Dr. Louis Crew, a college English professor. Described officially as an organization for "gay Episcopalians and their friends," chapters quickly opened in most metropolitan areas of the country. The first Integrity chapter was started in Chicago, and by mid-1976, the national organization reported twenty-six chapters, with twelve more in the formative stages. The national president reported in an Integrity newsletter, "Some of our chapters—about half—meet at parish churches, and all of them have a significant program of worship together. Many celebrate Holy Communion together before each meeting."

The first national Integrity convention was held in August, 1975, at the Cathedral of St. James in Chicago. Dr. W. Norman Pittenger, retired professor from the General Theological Seminary, gave the keynote address titled 'Making a Case for Gays in the Church and in the Ministry.' The address was a harbinger of things to come. James Wickliff of Chicago and Ellen Barrett of New York City were elected as Integrity's first co-presidents. James Wickliff had been employed in Peace Corps training and research, and Ellen Barrett was a recent graduate of the General Theological Seminary.

The Very Reverend James E. Carroll, dean of the Cathedral of St. James in Chicago, told the local press that Integrity was a "group of loyal churchmen who want to be part of the church and who want to come to terms with their own sexuality as churchmen and not (as) pariahs and untouchables." *The Living Church,* a generally conservative magazine, commented on this first convention in a favorable editorial:

The "straights" and the "gays" within the church have a vast amount of unfinished business between them to which both must address themselves openly, honestly, frankly, and lovingly. The whole question of what is morally right or wrong in anybody's sexual behavior must be faced by both groups within the church—and together.

In addition to its otherwise charged agenda, the 1976 General Convention was the first to address the homosexual issue. Without much apparent controversy, it passed a resolution stating that "It is the sense of this General Convention that homosexual persons are children of God who have a full and equal claim with all other persons upon love, acceptance and pastoral concern and care of the church."

The second part of the resolution stated: "This General Convention expresses its conviction that homosexual persons are entitled to equal protection of the law with all other citizens and calls upon our society to see that such protection is granted."

In December of 1975, not long after her election as co-president of Integrity, Ellen Barrett was the focus of some controversy when she was ordained to the diaconate by Bishop Paul Moore of New York City. Two years later, she was ordained to the priesthood. Controversy erupted in the Diocese of New York and throughout the Episcopal Church. In his book, *Take a Bishop Like Me,* Bishop Moore reports quite openly and courageously about his experiences: "My misjudgment was that Ellen's ordination would make a splash only in my own diocese . . . (but) the news of the ordination was published in every little paper in the country. It was a human interest story no self-respecting city editor could pass up, sex and religion all tied up in a titillating little story . . ."

Bishop Moore reports receiving one letter that read, "Sir: I am so disgusted with you (believe me, the Holy Apostles must be turning in their graves) and the whole city of New York. With a bishop like you, small wonder there is so much rottenness, crime and everything terrible in your city."[10]

Prior to the ordination, Bishop William Frey of the Diocese of Colorado wired Moore and said, "There are far more constructive ways to show pastoral concern for homosexuals than by attempting to bless that which God offers to redeem." Bishop Robert Rusack of Los Angeles told Moore in a telegram that the ordination of a homosexual is "totally improper, reflective of contemptible impatience." Moore reports that he received letters from forty-two bishops, "Ten positive . . . and thirty-two negative ones."

Later the matter was brought up at the House of Bishops in its 1977 meeting at Port St. Lucie, Florida. The House was asked to express its "strong disapproval of the unilateral action of the bishop, the Standing Committee and the Commission of Ministry in the Diocese of New York in conferring Holy Orders upon a person who is a professed homosexual and who advocates homosexuality as a legitimate lifestyle."

Speaking in his own defense, Bishop Moore told the House of Bishops, "I remind you that the ordination itself had nothing to do with homosexual practice but only with admitted orientation . . ." He said later, "The statement was well received. At last my main point, that I had ordained an admitted, not practicing, homosexual seemed to have gotten through."[11]

The motion of disapproval was tabled by a vote of 66 to 48 after Bishop Moore was asked if Miss Barrett advocated and practiced homosexuality at the time she was ordained. He said she did not openly advocate it at the time she was ordained, and "whether she has since is open to question."

The bishops later adopted—almost unanimously—a statement from their theology committee which stated that, pending further inquiry and study by the church, the ordination of "advocating and/or practicing homosexuals was inadmissible."

The ordination of Ellen Barrett, as well as the mood of the church, brought increasing pressure from all sides for the General Convention to adopt a policy on the ordination of homosexuals. Advocates for the ordination of homosexuals frequently cited the matter of honesty and integrity in ordination procedures. Many argued that since it was widely recognized there were already many gay priests, others should not have to be dishonest and lie about their sexual orientation while going through the selection process. Opponents of the ordination of homosexuals usually cited scriptural statements, Christian tradition, and the "wholesome example" necessary for parish leadership.

Diocesan resolutions and statements reflected the diversity of viewpoint within the Episcopal Church. The Diocese of Michigan adopted a statement in 1974 calling for "opening ministries, professions, and occupations to homosexuals." The Diocese of Indianapolis stated that sexuality "is one significant factor in the choice of persons for Holy Orders, but it is only a portion of the full range of human potential . . ." A Wisconsin diocese said it opposed "the ordination of an avowed, practicing homosexual person; and . . . the ordination of those advocating homosexuality as a legitimate, normative, alternative lifestyle."[12]

The national church's Standing Commission on Human Affairs and Health brought a proposed statement on the ordination of homosexuals to the 1979 General Convention. Chaired by the Right Reverend Robert R. Spears, Bishop of Rochester, the commission presented a comprehensive report and recommended that homosexuality should not be "an absolute barrier to ordination." The Spears Report affirmed that "There should be no barrier to the ordination of homosexual persons who are able and willing to conform their behavior to that which the church affirms as wholesome."

Prior to the General Convention vote, more than thirty people in the Denver Convention Theater testified before a crowd of 1,500 during an open hearing on human sexuality. Discussion centered around the Spears Report.

"We are everywhere," said one Integrity member. "There are gay laypeople, gay priests, gay deputies, and (gasp!) gay bishops." He and other gays declared that their homosexuality and their Christian commitment were not incompatible, but both allowed spiritual growth. Members of King's Ministries, a Denver-based group of former homosexuals, were the only representatives who spoke against homosexuality at the hearing, and insisted that homosexual practice was not compatible with Christian teaching.

Ultimately the proposal from Bishop Spears' committee was not adopted. Instead, the convention passed a substitute resolution from the Ministry Committee of the House of Bishops which took a stand against the ordination of practicing homosexuals. The final paragraph read:

We reaffirm the traditional teaching of the church on marriage, marital fidelity and sexual chastity as the standard of Christian sexual morality. Candidates for ordination are expected to conform to this standard. Therefore, we believe it isn't appropriate for this church to ordain a practicing homosexual, or any person who is engaged in heterosexual relations outside of marriage.

Shortly after the convention passed the resolution, a group of twenty-one bishops led by Bishop John Krumm of the Diocese of Southern Ohio signed a "conscience statement" which said they couldn't abide by the restrictive resolution. Their dissenting statement recognized that:

. . . there is a minority of persons who have clearly not been called to the married state . . . who are incapable in the very nature of their formed personalities of conforming to the predominant mode of behavior . . . We are deeply conscious of, and grateful for, the profoundly valuable ministries of ordained persons, known to us to be homosexual, formerly and presently engaged in the service of this church.[13]

Following the 1979 General Convention, there was little heard on the sexuality issue—at least formally—for several years. No resolutions on homosexuality were debated or adopted at the church's 1982 convention in New Orleans, although the issue did arise again at the 1985 convention in Anaheim, California. In proposed canonical changes to Title III, both Houses passed a resolution stating that "No one shall be denied rights or status in this church because of race, color, ethnic origin, sex, *sexual orientation* [italics added], physical disabilities, or age . . ."

The question of "sexual orientation" wasn't debated when it came to "rights or status," but a similar resolution proposing equal access to the "selection process for ordination" was another matter: "No one shall be denied access to the selection process for ordination because of race, color, ethnic origin, sex, *sexual orientation* [italics added], physical disabilities, or age, except as otherwise specified by canon."

This proposed canonical change was passed by the House of Bishops, but defeated by a narrow majority in the lay order of the House of Deputies. It brought perhaps the most heated debate of an otherwise placid convention.

The AIDS crisis received substantive attention from the deputies and bishops at the 1985 convention. In a resolution which received quick and unanimous support in both Houses, the convention voiced its prayers and support for AIDS victims. A resolution repudiated "any and all indiscriminate statements which condemn or reject AIDS victims" and called upon the presiding bishop "to establish and lead a National Day of Prayer and Healing" for AIDS victims. The resolution asked dioceses and parishes to establish programs of AIDS prevention education, as well as to promote general education and awareness of the disease.

Abortion

"I've had two abortions," one woman said during a diocesan convention debate in 1979 on a 'pro choice' resolution. "I do not want to see my church do anything to restrict my right to reach an informed choice about this most crucial decision."

A few years later during a Washington, D.C. ordination, five came forward from the congregation when Bishop John Walker asked ". . . if any of you know any impediment or crime because of which we should not proceed, come forward now, and make it known."[14]

The group protested the ordination of the woman who "admitted her personal support" of abortion and was the wife of a physician who owned and operated several abortion clinics in the Washington area. Bishop Walker interrupted the service to retire for a conversation with a spokesperson for the group, but later continued the ordination. The objectors based their stand on No. 20 of the Articles of Religion of the Episcopal Church that "it is not lawful for the church to ordain anything that is contrary to God's word."[15]

Since the 1973 *Roe vs. Wade* Supreme Court decision permitting legalized abortion, probably no issue has engendered more deeply held convictions on both sides of a controversial issue. On no other issue have churches of all denominations held such divergent, and often opposing, views. Not simply a religious or moral issue, the discussions cut across legal, medical, and public policy questions, and sometimes became a major topic of debate in political elections.

Before the Episcopal Church first considered the question of abortion at its 1967 General Convention, the Lambeth Conference of bishops had issued its opinions. This worldwide conference of Anglican bishops, held every ten years, has no legislative authority over member churches, but seeks to provide guidance and teaching through its resolutions and reports.

At the 1958 Lambeth Conference, the bishops issued a lengthy committee report on "The Family in Contemporary Society," affirming:

In the strongest terms, Christians reject the practice of induced abortion or infanticide, which involves the killing of a life already conceived (as well as a violation of the personality of the mother), save at the dictate of strict and undeniable medical necessity . . . the sacredness of life is, in Christian eyes, an absolute which should not be violated.[16]

The 1968 Lambeth Conference reaffirmed this report, while the 1978 Lambeth Conference did not make a statement on the abortion issue.

The 1967 General Convention in Seattle was the first to consider the abortion issue. By this time, abortion law reform had become a legislative issue in virtually all of the fifty states. In a resolution titled "Abortion Law Reform," the convention adopted a resolution supporting abortion law reform to allow abortions where "the physical or mental health of the mother is threatened seriously" or where the pregnancy resulted from rape or incest.

Statements in the same resolution, however, "condemned . . . abortions of convenience" where the child was conceived out of wedlock, or if the family could not afford the baby, or if the pregnancy "might prove difficult" or if the birth of the child "would be inconvenient or socially embarrassing."

This 1967 resolution was the predecessor of a 1976 resolution that would be subsequently reaffirmed at the 1979 and 1982 General Conventions. The resolution was a compromise that sought to accommodate divergent viewpoints. On the one hand, it expressed "unequivocal opposition" to any state or national legislation "which would abridge or deny the right of individuals to reach informed decisions."

On the other hand, the resolution urged church members to seek "other preferable courses of action" when considering an abortion. It also said that those who seek abortions for other than acceptable reasons, may need to "seek the advice and counsel of a priest of this church, and where appropriate, penance." The resolution read as follows:

WHEREAS, it is imperative for the church as a body of Christ to provide clear guidelines for human behavior which reflect both the love and judgment of God, now therefore be it,

RESOLVED, that the following principles and guidelines reflect the mind of the church meeting in this . . . General Convention:

1. That the beginning of new human life, because it is a gift of the power of God's love for his people, and thereby sacred, should not and must not be undertaken unadvisedly or lightly but in full accordance of the understanding for which this power to conceive and give birth is bestowed by God.

2. Such understanding includes the responsibility for Christians to limit the size of their families and to practice responsible birth control. Such means for moral limitations do not include abortions for convenience.

3. That the position of this church, stated at the sixty-second General Convention of the church in Seattle in 1967 which declared support for the "termination of pregnancy" particularly in cases where "the physical or mental health of the mother is threatened seriously, or where there is substantial reason to believe that the child would be badly deformed

in mind or body, or where the pregnancy has resulted from rape or incest" is reaffirmed. Termination of pregnancy for these reasons is permissible. 4. That in those cases where it is firmly and deeply believed by the person or persons concerned that pregnancy should be terminated for causes other than the above, members of this church are urged to seek the advice and counsel of a priest of this church, and, where appropriate, penance. 5. That whenever members of this church are consulted with regard to proposed termination of pregnancy, they are to explore with the person or persons seeking advice and counsel other preferable courses of action. 6. That the Episcopal Church express its unequivocal opposition to any legislation on the part of national or state governments which would abridge or deny the right of individuals to reach informed decisions in this matter and to act upon them.

The abortion question is yet unresolved, both in the United States and in the Episcopal Church. A "pro life" group of Episcopalians was formed in 1966 by Bishop Joseph M. Harte of the Diocese of Arizona. Following the 1973 Supreme Court decision legalizing abortion, chapters of Episcopalians for Life began to develop around the country. The group's name was changed to *National Organization of Episcopalians for Life* (NOEL) in 1982. By 1985, there were more than forty NOEL chapters in twenty-six dioceses of the Episcopal Church, with a membership of more than 10,000.

NOEL along with several individuals and dioceses presented a number of "pro life" resolutions to the 1985 General Convention, all urging the Episcopal Church to modify its position on this issue. None of the resolutions reached the floor for debate. However, recognizing the intensity of increasing abortion debate in the mid-1980s, the convention adapted a resolution urging parishes and dioceses to study the issue further. The resolution urged dioceses to initiate "study and discussion of the personal, sociological, and theological implications of abortion" by appointing commissions to "oversee a process reaching into every local congregation willing to be involved."

Corporate Ethics

The Episcopal Church's Executive Council began dealing with the apartheid issue in May 1968. That year Anglican Bishop Robert Mize was notified by the South African government that he could neither reside nor minister in his own diocese, the Diocese of Damarland and Ovamboland in what is now Namibia. The government's decision prompted a resolution condemning the action at the Executive Council's May meeting.

At its December meeting that year, the council passed a resolution which defined certain criteria for church investment decisions in South Africa, based on a company's provision of salary, pensions, and equality for blacks in the workplace. Since that time, each General Convention and many Executive Council meetings have dealt with issues of apartheid or investment criteria in some fashion.

In 1971, the Episcopal Church and five other Protestant church groups challenged twelve American companies about their involvement with South African investments. "United States churches have long been concerned about the oppression of millions of black people by a white minority in southern Africa . . . The time is past when United States companies can operate without questions being asked about their role and their operations in South Africa," said the Reverend W. Sterling Cary, newly-elected president of the National Council of Churches and a spokesperson for the action.

The six church groups filed stockholders resolutions for placement in annual meeting proxy statements with the twelve targeted corporations. The purpose of the action, they said, was to bring to the companies' attention church concern about apartheid in South Africa. The resolutions asked the companies to disclose the history of their involvement in South Africa, comparative statistics on numbers of workers, wages paid, trade union contracts, and compliance with apartheid laws.

"The Episcopal Church is *incarnate* in a broad spectrum of economic and business activity," wrote the Reverend David Dillon in the Massachusetts diocesan newspaper. Perhaps the least-publicized ministry of the church over the past twenty years has been its quiet engagement with various corporations over questions of social responsibility.

John Goodbody, who served as the Episcopal Church's communications executive between 1971 and 1980, summarized the church's involvement in social ministry in a lengthy article that appeared in the June, 1985 issue of *The Episcopalian*. "Over the past twenty years, efforts have been made both by proxy resolutions and by a direct approach to corporate boardrooms to encourage business firms to use their financial influence to foster equal opportunity policies and community responsibility," he wrote.

"Proxy fights were sometimes regarded as unnecessarily divisive by some Episcopal leaders, both business and clergy. Others, however, vigorously supported this intervention. The involvement and commitment of the church has become increasingly recognized and respected . . ." he pointed out.[17]

The church was represented in a well-publicized proxy struggle with General Motors in 1971 to urge new initiatives against apartheid in South Africa. In such proxy representation, the Episcopal Church often acted as a partner with an ecumenical consortium, the Inter-Faith Center on Corporate Responsibility. The Washington-based Investor Responsibility Research Center reports that churches have been responsible for at least two thirds of the shareholder resolutions on social responsibility.

The Most Reverend Desmond Tutu captured the attention of the world in 1984 when he received the Nobel Peace Prize, but the outspoken South African leader had already endeared himself to many American Episcopalians. Tutu brought applause and standing ovations when he addressed a joint session at the 1982 General Convention. The Anglican archbishop called South Africa a "third world country" with a first world economy. "Third world unemployment and poverty exist alongside first world abundance," he said, asking the industrial West to recognize its responsibility to share resources and "end its corporations' economic exploitation in Africa."

The first convention to call for disinvestment came at Anaheim in 1985. That resolution, noting that proxy voting "had not proved effective in promoting change either in the companies or in the South African system," mandated the Executive Council and Church Pension Fund "to divest all holdings of companies doing business in South Africa and Namibia." The resolution also urged all dioceses and parishes to consider similar action.

The Peace Movement

After Ronald Reagan became president in 1981, the peace movement began to develop as an opposition force to large increases in the United States defense budget. "Your bishops perceive the nuclear arms race as the most compelling issue in the world public order," said the pastoral letter from the House of Bishops in 1982. "The arms race summons all morally serious people to action. Christians and Jews and all religious people are joined by multitudes of no religious allegiance," the bishops declared.

The 1982 convention endorsed a bilateral nuclear freeze and asked the president to propose a United States/Soviet verifiable agreement to halt the testing, production, and further development of all nuclear weapons. Dozens of churches and church-related groups passed similar resolutions as a protest against President Reagan's staunch insistence on increased military expenditures, as well as increased U.S. / Soviet tensions during the early 1980s.

The momentum among mainline church leaders on this issue continued to develop during the early 1980s. "In the world today a concept called 'national security' has been allowed to become an earth-shadowing idol," Presiding Bishop John Allin said in a farewell address to deputies and bishops at the 1985 General Convention. "The resources of earth needed for the support and development of life and just living conditions among the peoples of earth are increasingly mortgaged for an illusive defense depending upon destructive weapons."

This convention echoed the presiding bishop's message with several resolutions on the peace theme. One resolution called for "support and work for a verifiable, bilateral nuclear freeze, and continuation of the SALT II accords." The same resolution designated the first Wednesday of each month "as a day of reflection and action on peace-making." Another resolution expressed the convention's opposition to President Reagan's Strategic Defense Initiative, popularly known as "Star Wars." The resolution asked Congress to withhold funds from the project.

The convention also established a Standing Commission on Peace and Justice and charged it with developing "recommendations and strategies which will be of concrete assistance to this church in furthering the work on issues of peace and justice." The commission had been established as a temporary "Joint Commission" by the 1979 convention, but this action made it a permanent commission of the Episcopal Church.

Other Social Issues

The issues with which the church has been involved are many. The National Episcopal Coalition on Alcohol was formed in the early 1980s to provide education, publicity, and training on alcoholism issues for Episcopalians. The Episcopal Society for Ministry on Aging has carried out its work by educating the church on issues involving its senior citizens. Refugee resettlement became a major concern as Vietnamese, Afghans and Central Americans, particularly, were displaced by economic and military conditions in their homelands. The "sanctuary movement," while not addressed by the Episcopal Church as much as some other denominations, brought to light the enormously complex problems in Central America.

The problems faced by the church and society as a whole aren't solved by panel discussions, conferences, or occasional gifts to the United Thank Offering. In one sense, the church never solves the "issues." For, as we have said, the "issues" will exist as long as the church's doors are open.

7

Educating the Church

"WE ARE NOT ONLY ACCEPTING religious illiteracy for our children, we have at the present time no serious intention of doing anything about it. By and large our church's Sunday schools are a disgrace."[1]

These words were uttered by the Bishop of Western Michigan at the diocesan convention on February 24, 1946. Bishops' addresses sometimes go no further than dusty diocesan journals, but this one helped change the course of Christian education in the Episcopal Church, and Bishop Lewis Whittemore became a leader in the movement of the 1940s and 1950s which revitalized the national church's Christian education program.

Bishop Whittemore went on to say, "We must face the fact that today the church, on the national scene, at least, is neurotic if not schizophrenic. It is turned in on itself and its own morbidness . . . With all the capacity in the world to make an enormous contribution, it loses itself in its own shadows . . . The Episcopal Church needs to get excited about a whole new set of issues and leave some others to the junk pile of history . . . The real issue with which the church ought to be concerning itself is Christian education," he said.[2] In his remark about letting go of certain issues, the bishop was referring to the years of division and debate over the Presbyterian merger negotiations. What made his role historic was that he had made his point at exactly the right time for a reconstruction of the church's educational system. The church was ready and needed it badly.

Church school attendance had dropped from 510,000 to 388,000 between 1933 and 1943, a decrease of over 20 percent. This was the lowest figure for church school attendance since before the turn of the century. While communicant strength tripled between 1890 and 1945, church school enrollment was approximately the same at the beginning and end of those fifty-five years. But no Christian education curriculum had been prepared by the national church.

At the 1945 meeting of the House of Bishops, Bishop Whittemore had already made a fervent plea for a stronger program of Christian education:

74

We are giving up our responsibility if we continue to teach less and less. The trend has been in that direction for some time . . . Instruction in the doctrine and discipline of the church has been reduced to an alarming extent.[3]

Bishop Whittemore and Bishop Malcolm Peabody of Central New York prepared a resolution, later passed by the House of Bishops, which called "the attention of the National Council to the church's current failure to properly instruct the people in her essential teachings." They requested the council to prepare "a corpus of instructional material to be acquired by every child by the time of confirmation, and by the time of leaving high school."[4] Thus began Whittemore's vital role in the drama which was to unfold in a unique way during the next twelve years. Throughout 1946, Bishop Whittemore's ideas were already being discussed in the church. Portions of his diocesan convention address were published in various church magazines and diocesan newspapers. The General Convention that year made this statement about Christian education:

"Experience gathered in every realm of the church's work has indicated increasingly that church education of all ages is of utmost significance. A generation has grown up with almost no knowledge of the Bible, and a minimum knowledge of the church."[5]

With these words, the convention passed a resolution making Christian education a "department" instead of a "division" in the national church and increased its budget by $28,000. It also instructed the National Council to direct the department to prepare curriculum materials for use by the entire church.

The problem with Christian education in the church could be partly traced to a declining birth rate, and partly to the Depression, with its severe economic effects on the church. Bishop Whittemore said that "some of it could be traced to the neurotic preoccupation of the church with its churchmanship differences."

During this era following the Presbyterian merger negotiations, tensions between "high church" and "low church" parties were intensified, much more so than in later decades. Thus leaders felt it would be impossible to prepare new Sunday school materials acceptable to both "high church" and "low church" parishes and members.

It did not, however, prove to be an impossible task. After his election as presiding bishop, one of the first tasks Henry Knox Sherrill approached was finding the best person to head the Department of Christian Education. In 1947, he chose the Reverend John Heuss, who had come to national attention as rector of St. Matthew's Church in Evanston, Illinois. During the ten years he was rector, Father Heuss had developed an outstanding program of Christian education, and the church had tripled in size to 1,200 communicants.

In November of 1947, Father Heuss' work in the new department began. His first job was to "sell" Christian education to the Episcopal Church. Heuss began a national speaking campaign with two purposes in mind. First, he wanted to bring before the church the vital need of a good educational program. Secondly, he needed to persuade church leaders to provide the funds to carry out such a program. He was successful.

At the 1949 convention in San Francisco, Father Heuss gave an address called "Let Us Strike Off These Ignoble Chains." He recited the shocking statistics of the drop in Sunday school attendance, outlined plans for the revitalization of the church's educational program, and challenged the church to support his efforts. The response was more than he expected. As a result of Heuss's speech, the convention approved the budget of $341,500 which he requested, an increase of $217,148 over the original appropriation of $124,352. In approving his request, the Joint Committee on Program and Budget had this to say:

> No clearer mandate has come to your committee than the demand for a truly adequate program of Christian education. Diocese after diocese has urged us to give this matter high priority. We believe that the plans developed by the department of Christian Education are most promising . . . This ($341,500) is a large sum of money, but we believe it will be well invested and will earn generous dividends in better educated and therefore more effective laity.[6]

Heuss, in a later article, described four new directions in which the church had to move in order to make Sunday school effective. He indicated that these would constitute the major emphases of the department:

1. *Educational needs of the small school.* Father Heuss pointed out that a survey revealed that the majority of Episcopal church schools were very small and that many of the teachers in those schools "will never be adequately trained. Therefore, the teaching materials prepared for them must of necessity be very simplified and practical."

2. *A new emphasis on facts.* "The task ahead of us is to see that the beliefs of the Christian religion in general and of the Prayer Book in particular are clearly and intelligently set forth in the curriculum we have been requested to prepare."

3. *A workable and realistic curriculum.* "The first task of curriculum development is to publish a manual of instruction, which shall contain a clear statement of these things . . . It was early decided that the first step in this work was to get a clearcut idea of what a child should be expected to know . . ."

4. *Teaching function of the home rediscovered.* "The new curriculum must be aimed at the home. It must be prepared for use in the home and great emphasis must be placed upon the whole planning of adult education in areas other than in curriculum . . . I do not believe that our Sunday schools will ever be really effective until we find the way to create again truly religious homes."[7]

In 1948, the year before Heuss had articulated to the convention the four points for the department to focus on, he had presented a report on the church's educational plight and a proposed plan of action. The report, titled *The Future Development of Christian Education,* was subsequently adopted by the council.

The Church's Teaching Series

The well-known *Church's Teaching Series* became the first result of this plan. Skeptics had said it wouldn't be possible to form a consensus about "what the church teaches" on any subject. But the success of this book series proved them wrong. Aimed at lay people, the series summarized the beliefs of the church in six basic areas—Scripture, church history, doctrine, worship, ethics and canon law.

The Bible was the first subject in the series. Dr. Robert C. Dentan, professor of Old Testament at Berkeley Divinity School in New Haven, Connecticut, was chosen to write *The Holy Scriptures.* His first manuscript was mimeographed and sent to church people of all persuasions for comments, criticisms, and suggestions. As comments arrived, he made revisions and sent out copies for more suggestions. Soon a consensus began to develop. When *The Holy Scriptures* was published by Seabury Press in 1949, it became an immediate success and went through several printings over the next two decades.

The Reverend Norman Pittenger, professor of apologetics at General Theological Seminary, and the Reverend James Pike, chairman of the Department of Religion at Columbia University, wrote the second book of the series titled *The Faith of the Church.* It became a success as well and sold over 100,000 copies. Later volumes of the series dealt with worship, Christian living, church history, and the Episcopal Church and its work. The total series sold over 500,000 copies before it was revised in 1979.

With its publication, the Episcopal Church became the only branch of the Anglican Communion with a current collection of basic teaching about its beliefs and work, representing the best in corporate scholarship that the church had to offer. George E. Demille, author of *The Episcopal Church Since 1900,* wrote, "If Father Heuss' tenure of office had produced nothing more than *The Church's Teaching Series,* it would have been the most notable achievement in the field of Christian education made by the Episcopal Church in the twentieth century."[8]

Leadership Training

The primary thrust of the Department of Christian Education, initially, was the development of an eleven-year curriculum plan that could be used by any parish Sunday school. While it was being written, the department engaged in a program to develop a new interest in Christian education, as well as to train parish and diocesan leaders.

In order to equip the Episcopal Church for this new educational task, the Department of Christian Education prepared a diversified leadership training program. Recognizing that most clergy had received little, if any, training in Christian education, the new field program began with them.

In the fall of 1949, the department began a unique in-service training program for clergy which continued for three and a half years. Using the facilities of the College of Preachers in Washington, D.C., they invited twenty-five clergy per week to attend a conference on Christian education. In a doctoral dissertation, Dorothy Braun described the conferences:

> Here they considered together the goals of the parish, learned something of child development and how the Gospel speaks to each age level, and were intoduced to some of the insights of group dynamics and to a wider use of visual aids. In addition, the department sought to clarify for them its unique theory . . . of curriculum development which involved the entire parish . . .[9]

As the demand for the conferences increased, teams of three members carried the program to all parts of the country. Holding one to five day conferences, the teams met separately with clergy and vestries, members of diocesan departments of Christian education, Women's Auxiliaries, youth leaders and young people. At night, they conducted a series of meetings for clergy and lay people.

In April, 1952, Father Heuss accepted a call to become rector of Trinity Church in New York City. That same month, the Reverend David R. Hunter, director of the Department of Christian Education for the Diocese of Massachusetts, succeeded him as director of the entire department. Church leaders recognized the outstanding contributions made by Father Heuss during his five years as head of the department. The National Council expressed its appreciation with these words:

> With vigor and self-abnegating devotion, Dr. Heuss has done far more than set up a new curriculum. He has given a vitality and unifying force to the entire educational life of the church and, with the gifted staff of the department, has led us to the rediscovery of the redemptive power of a truly Christian education.[10]

In 1954, under Hunter's direction, the department developed another popular vehicle for leadership training. Known as Parish Life Conferences, staff members conducted weekend retreats for groups of up to forty parish leaders—about five from each parish. Dorothy Braun comments, "Together they faced realistically the true purpose of the parish, the deepest human needs and how they can be met, and their own responsibility to help the parish become a redemptive community."[11]

The department held the Parish Life Conferences in three quarters of the dioceses of the Episcopal Church. Sunday school teachers were urged to attend the conferences so that they could "relate their church school teaching to the redemptive life of the parish." Teacher training was made available through workshops. Almost every diocesan Department of Christian Education participated. The conferences were followed by parish workshops, running from four to eight evenings, with leadership supplied by teachers who had attended the regional meetings.

In 1954, the department met with diocesan leaders throughout the country and conducted a five hour curriculum demonstration with local church school teachers. Diocesan leaders then discussed and evaluated the program, which was used to train teachers during 1954-55. Thus they were prepared to use the new curriculum materials that became available in mid-1955.

The Seabury Series

During the development of the new curriculum by the Department of Christian Education, there was internal friction over the educational philosophy of the approach. Stated simply, some advocated the "content approach" emphasizing the basic doctrines and teachings of the church. Others emphasized a "relational" approach, teaching students to deal with the issues in everyday life through class discussions and relationships. The latter philosophy prevailed in the series.

Despite many difficulties—including a complete turn-over in editorial staff—the Department of Christian Education succeeded in keeping its promise to have curriculum materials published by the 1955 General Convention. By May of 1955, nine books were ready for distribution to the church.

These included teaching manuals for grades one, four, and seven; student readers for these grades, and a manual for parents' classes. The contents reflected the department's earnest efforts to relate recent findings in the fields of child development, psychology, and sociology to the teachings of the church. Conscious of the newness of its approach to teaching, the staff endeavored to prepare the church to receive the new curriculum and use it with skill and satisfaction.

The *Seabury Series* published a total of seventy-eight student readers, teacher's manuals, and other leadership aids between 1955 and 1967. There was a curriculum for nursery and kindergarten children, and for the first through eleventh grades.

The Department of Christian Education listed "four necessary conditions" it considered so important that parishes were not encouraged to use the *Seabury Series* unless they were met:

1) An ever-widening group of individuals within the congregation "genuinely concerned about the redemptive task of the parish"—that is, the life-changing impact of the Gospel on the lives of people.

2) An emphasis on family worship. "This is necessary to the religious life of the home and it is also a significant factor in the Christian education of both the children and their parents," department literature stated.

3) A weekly class for parents and godparents. "Learning is as important for adults as for children."

4) Religious and educational preparation of teachers. "Their relationship with the source of power must be strengthened and they must be introduced adequately to the purpose and methods of the new courses."

Peter Day, editor of *The Living Church,* contrasted the emphasis between the *Seabury Series* and Morehouse-Barlow's *Episcopal Church Fellowship Series,* another popular series used by many parishes. He wrote:

[In the *Seabury Series*] . . . Continunity is supplied by the group; the class is a family within the parish family, within the larger church family; exploring together the implications of the church's doctrine and practice for themselves.

[In the *Episcopal Church Fellowship Series*] . . . Continuity is supplied by the course; the class meets together to explore a predetermined area of church doctrine and practice, attempting to learn what its implications are for themselves.

He adds:

From the standpoint of the teacher, the first few weeks under the *Seabury Series* would be the hardest; once the class got rolling, it would carry its own momentum. The Church Fellowship Series would probably get off to a smoother start, but would run into dead spots from time to time when the subject matter refused to "come alive" in a particular week."[12]

From the beginning, the *Seabury Series* met with a mixed reaction from the church at large. An editorial in *The Living Church* stated, ". . . The series has by no means won the universal support of parishes and missions and it is quite possible that General Convention will be asked to call for a return to a more familiar Sunday school plan."

A showdown on Christian education was in the making for the 1958 General Convention. Peter Day wrote in *The Living Church:*

But this year, at Miami Beach, after three years of actual experience, both friends and foes of the *Seabury Series* felt that it was time for General Convention to say what it thought about the *Seabury Series* without compromise or ambiguity. The department deserved to have either a go-ahead signal or a stop signal.

A number of resolutions asking for revision of the series passed the House of Deputies, but the House of Bishops failed to concur. Before developing and presenting a resolution on the floor, the Christian Education Committee invited interested deputies to an open hearing. Twenty-two priests and laypersons came and spoke before the committee—and all supported the *Seabury Series.* Day comments:

It was evident that the supporters of the department's program were much more organized than the opponents, although the latter included some of the most powerful personalities in the House of Deputies.[13]

One of the main criticisms of the *Seabury Series* was its scattered use. Only one-third of the parishes—representing a little less than half of the church's Sunday school children—were using it. Critics said it was unfair for the church to fund materials and training that only a portion of its members were using.

The Reverend Don Frank Fenn, one of the series' strongest critics, argued, "It is quite evident that the *Seabury Series* predominates in larger parishes where there are larger sums of money available and where there are more full time directors of religious education."[14]

Another criticism was that the content of the lessons lacked teaching in the doctrinal essentials of the Christian faith and the Episcopal Church. Instead, there was a lot of emphasis on the problems, interests, and concerns of the children. "Too much 'method' and not enough 'content,' " the critics maintained. An editorial in *The Living Church* commented, "One frequently repeated charge . . . is that the department has adopted the philosophy of progressive education just at the time when the public schools are abandoning it."

Nonetheless, the *Seabury Series* and the Department of Christian Education survived the 1958 General Convention. The 1958 General Convention passed a resolution commending the Department of Christian Education for its work on the series, although not without some heated debate. The resolution also called for "continued study and development by the department to bring into existence an increasingly useful set of materials and methods for the whole church."

While this convention had offered a clear-cut endorsement of the program, it had become equally clear "that about one-third of the clergy supported the department's program, one-third opposed, and one-third supported while not being involved with it," as reported by the Reverend Ann McElligott in a thesis for the General Theological Seminary.[15]

The year 1958 seemed to mark a turning point for the *Seabury Series*—it had reached the top of the hill and seemed headed on a downhill course after the convention. This was partly due to the mixed reception of the series and partly due to changing social conditions and the mood of the church. As a result, the department changed its thrust.

After 1958, the department sought to change its relationship to the dioceses. It no longer focused on offering a product; rather its approach shifted to serving as consultants, asking, "how can we help you?" Department officers had to face the fact that their program was only being accepted by about one-third of the churches. Since a number of critics clearly favored the "content" approach to Christian education, the department had to find ways to serve that constituency as well.

In 1963, the Reverend David Hunter resigned to become associate general secretary of the National Council of Churches. Carmen St. John Wolff, Hunter's associate director, was appointed to replace him. During this time, the program orientation was also changing from "educating for the church" to educating for ministry in the world.

The End of an Era in Christian Education

The sixties challenged traditional models of authority in society, and brought an end to what some called the church's "curricular imperialism." The "I have the answer for you" attitude was vigorously challenged as a new mood of grassroots participation, "ownership," and leadership collaboration began to grow.

In an interview with the Reverend Ann McElligott, the Reverend George Peabody, who was director of the department's leadership training division, said that this older "medical model" no longer worked:

This is the medical model where the patient has nothing to say about it. I believe the sixties was a challenge to this medical model throughout all our institutions—namely that father knows best, parent knows best, priest knows best, men know best, whites know best, top management knows best. In that model all the subordinates have to do is accommodate her or himself.[16]

The Department of Christian Education was reorganized and, for all practical purposes, abandoned in 1967 (as a separate department). When the Executive Council met prior to the General Convention that year, it voted for "a sweeping staff reorganization" and called for "a more flexible form of organization" than departmental assignment of staff. Within this structure, former Christian Education officers were primarily assigned to the "Unit of Services to Dioceses." By 1970, sweeping changes reduced the total Executive Council staff to thirty-one officers, eliminating all but one of the members involved in an educational ministry.

George Peabody summarized the impact of the sixties mentality on the church:

As the needs of the church transformed, and were transformed by the events of the sixties, the rationale for departmentalization and for the continued existence of a separate department assigned the task of Christian education was lost.[17]

The year 1967 was, of course, the beginning of the General Convention Special Program—an effort that would preoccupy the church's attention and money for the next six years. It signalled the end of an era for Christian education in the Episcopal Church.

Other Educational Programs

After the decline of the *Seabury Series* the national church provided no curriculum materials for parish Sunday schools. Parishes were left on their own to locate curriculum materials, and often used those from other denominations or from independent publishers.

In 1977, however, the Diocese of Colorado developed a series called *Living the Good News,* which became widely used throughout the church. The concept began with a small group of people in Denver that year. Their original goal was to develop lessons for churches in the Diocese of Colorado based on the new three-year lectionary. *Living the Good News,* or "the Colorado Curriculum," as it became popularly known, was based on a unifying theme from each Sunday's Scripture readings. Providing material for kindergarten through adult classes, more than one-third of all parishes in the country were using it by 1985.

The *Education for Ministry* (EFM) program developed by the University of the South became another successful program for lay education in the Episcopal Church. However, it was not intended for use in parish church schools. Developed in 1975, the program centered around a seminar group of six to ten students and a specially trained leader. The groups met once a week, usually on a week night. By 1984, there was 3,700 students in 525 groups, as well as 900 students in Australia, the Bahamas, Canada, Mexico and New Zealand.

The purpose of the four-year program was to provide persons "with the education to carry out the ministry to which every baptized person is called." EFM leaders, called "mentors," attended training sessions on the Sewanee campus and returned to their own communities to lead the seminar groups. EFM seminars provided training in Scriptures, church history, ethics, moral and systematic theology. "While the academic material is substantial, the focus is on seeing one's life as ministry, and reflecting on that ministry," said Dr. Charles Winters, founder of the program.[18]

The Seabury Press

For the past fifty years, two official publishing ventures have provided the church with general books and literature: The Seabury Press and Forward Movement Publications. Seabury Press was a result of the church's renewed interest in Christian education in the late 1940s. During that time, a number of people were urging the church to establish its own publishing house.

Originally, the National Council developed a plan to create a Division of Publications within the Department of Christian Education. But October of 1951, the National Council had rescinded the action and instead decided to create a separate organization which would be closely associated with the department. Named Seabury Press after the first bishop of the Episcopal

Church, it was incorporated as a non-profit enterprise under the laws of Connecticut, responsible to the National Council through the Department of Christian Education.[19]

Leon McCauley, who was manager of the religious department of Oxford University Press, was appointed as its first general manager. Seabury Press officially opened January 1, 1952. Initially set up to publish Christian education materials, Seabury Press soon expanded into several other areas.

Financed partly by loans from official church sources and in substantial part by gifts and loans of interested laypersons, Seabury Press' goal was to become a self-sustaining operation. The backbone of the press' initial operation was the later volumes of the *Church's Teaching Series.* By the end of 1951, Seabury Press had published its first books—the adult study courses for the first three books of the *Church's Teaching Series.* Later, it would add Prayer Books and hymnals, the volumes of the *Church's Teaching Series,* an expanding list of general books on church subjects, and, when it was ready, the new curriculum. With the publication of the first three church school courses in May, 1955, the press entered full-scale operation for the first time.

Seabury Press continued to publish with varying degrees of success for thirty-two years, until it was finally sold in 1983 to Winston Press in Minneapolis. About two years later, Winston Press sold it to Harper and Row Publishers. Financial losses that had averaged $250,000 in each of the previous four years had led to the Executive Council's decision to make the sale. In agreeing to sell the company, the council authorized an interest-free loan of $500,000 to help meet transitional expenses towards closing.

Throughout its history, Seabury Press competed with Morehouse-Barlow Company and the Church Hymnal Corporation in the Episcopal church market. The Hymnal Corporation is a wholly-owned subsidiary of the Church Pension Fund and publishes hymnals, pew editions of the Prayer Book, and resource books such as the *Episcopal Clerical Directory* and *Lay Leadership Directory.* Morehouse-Barlow Corporation is a privately owned corporation based in Wilton, Connecticut, and has a long history of publishing books and materials for the Episcopal Church.

Forward Movement

Few organizations have made as strong an impact on the Episcopal Church in the twentieth century as Forward Movement Publications. Known best for its *Forward Day by Day* devotional booklet, the work of Forward Movement has enriched the lives of Episcopalians for over fifty years.

The Forward Movement venture began at the 1934 General Convention in Atlantic City, New Jersey. Still in the midst of the Depression, many dioceses and parishes were deeply in debt. Overseas and home missionary programs were crippled. While the previous General Convention had instructed the national church staff and executive council not to go into debt under any circumstances, it couldn't be avoided. Morale was low and dissension was high as delegates gathered in Atlantic City.

With the theme "Hold the Line," a small group of church leaders organized an "Everyman's Offering" to help the national church pay off its debts. One report has it that a Tennessee deputy stated, "This church needs more than a campaign to hold the line; we need to move forward."

The Program and Budget Committee subsequently proposed the appointment of a Joint Commission on a Forward Movement. The commission's charge was "to prepare and carry out definite plans . . . for an organized effort to reinvigorate the life of the church and to rehabilitate its general, diocesan, and parochial work."[20]

Under the leadership of Bishop Henry Hobson of Southern Ohio, the commission, based in Cincinnati, sponsored conferences, mass meetings, and Bible study groups. Commission members visited diocesan conventions and summer conferences. A Lenten manual titled *Discipleship* was the commission's first publication in 1935. It was written by the Reverend Gilbert P. Symons, who became Forward Movement's first editor. *Discipleship* was such a success that volunteers came from all over Cincinnati to pack and mail 672,000 copies during the weeks just before Lent.[21]

The first issue of *Forward Day by Day* was published during Lent of 1935, and has been published four times yearly ever since. The success of *Discipleship* and *Forward Day by Day* led to Forward Movement's expansion in publishing other works. The titles of the early publications reflect Forward Movement's mission to the church: *Come to Confirmation, Prayers New and Old, Call in Your Laity, An Act of Affirmation,* and *Building a Parish Program.* Since then, Forward Movement has published hundreds of titles which have provided both education and spiritual renewal in the life of the Episcopal Church.

The quarterly publication, *Forward Day by Day,* remains its most popular publication with a current circulation of over 500,000. More than 90 million copies have been distributed since 1935, and editions have been published in Japanese, Chinese, Spanish, and Portuguese. The basic format for each day remains the same: a scripture reading, a brief comment or meditation, and a suggestion for personal prayer.

Forward Movement is a self-sustaining publishing house, independent of the national church budget. Bishop Hobson personally raised most of the money to get the publication program started. The Diocese of Southern Ohio donated rent-free space for many years, as well as the services of the first editor. Over the years, Forward Movement has had five editors, all who were ordained priests: Gilbert P. Symons, 1935-50; Francis J. Moore, 1950-57, 1963-64; Clement W. Welsh, 1957-63; James W. Kennedy, 1964-77; and Charles H. Long, Jr., since 1978. Bishop Henry Hobson retired as board chairman in 1976 after forty-two years of service, and was succeeded by Bishop John M. Krumm of the Diocese of Southern Ohio.

The Reverend James Kennedy came to Forward Movement from the parish ministry, but also had a wide-ranging ecumenical background. He had helped establish the Joint Commission on Ecumenical Relations in 1949, and served as its secretary for twenty-five years. Kennedy was responsible for expanding Forward Movement into book publishing, and was also the first person to hold the title of both editor and directòr. Charles Long came to Forward Movement in 1978 from the post of director of the North American office of the World Council of Churches. One of his most important contributions was consolidating all printing, mailing and distribution services in Cincinnati. For years, the editorial and business offices had to deal with a single printer in Buffalo, New York, who also maintained the inventory and filled all orders. The result of the consolidation of operations was increased efficiency and the highest level of financial stability in Forward Movement's history.

But curriculums and publishing houses do not tell the true story of Christian education in the Episcopal Church. The true story is never recorded because it takes place in thousands of parishes across the country every Sunday morning. It is the story of unheralded, unknown Sunday school teachers, dedicated parish priests and faithful parents. Presiding Bishop Edmond Lee Browning honored his sixth grade Sunday school teacher Gladys L. Hall, an eighty-eight year-old deacon, by having her read the Gospel at his 1986 installation service. Few, however, ever receive such prominent recognition.

The Rt. Rev. and Mrs. Henry Knox Sherrill
Presiding Bishop, 1946-1958

The Rt. Rev. and Mrs. Henry Knox Sherrill prior to departure to 1958 Lambeth Conference. Presiding Bishop Sherrill was elected at the 1946 General Convention in Philadelphia, and served in the office until 1958.

A photo of three presiding bishops taken at the 1964 General Convention in St. Louis: Arthur Lichtenberger (1958-1964); John M. Hines (1965-1974); and Henry Knox Sherrill (1947-1958). Presiding Bishop Lichtenberger died in 1968 and Presiding Bishop Sherrill died in 1980.　　　　　　　　　　　DPS PHOTO

The Episcopal Church Center at 815 Second Avenue, New York. The building, owned by the Episcopal Church, was completed in 1962.

Eleven women deacons were ordained priest at Philadelphia's Church of the Advocate on July 29, 1974. Two years later at the 1976 General Convention, the Episcopal Church made its historic decision to canonically allow the ordination of women to the priesthood. **DPS PHOTO**

Three nominees for presiding bishop greet a jubilant Edmond Browning following his election at the 1985 General Convention in Anaheim, California. l-r: The Rt. Rev. Furman Stough, Bishop of Alabama; The Rt. Rev. William Frey, Bishop of Colorado; The Rt. Rev. John T. Walker, Bishop of Washington; Presiding Bishop Browning; and former Presiding Bishop John M. Allin. **DPS PHOTO**

Jeanette Piccard, 81, reacts jubilantly to the 1976 convention's vote to endorse the ordination of women to the priesthood. Mrs. Piccard was one of the "Philadelphia 11" irregularly ordained in 1974. She died in 1981.

James Pike
Bishop of California from 1958-66.

Archbishop of Canterbury Donald Coggan at the 1976 General Convention, Minneapolis.

Archbishop of Canterbury Donald Coggan (left) with Presiding Bishop John M. Allin at the 1976 General Convention in Minneapolis. DPS PHOTO

The Rt. Rev. John Coburn delayed his consecration as Bishop of Massachusetts in order to preside at the 1976 General Convention as president of the House of Deputies. He was president of the House of Deputies from 1967-1976. DPS PHOTO

Charles R. Lawrence, II
1915-1986

Charles Lawrence was elected the first black president of the House of Deputies at the 1976 General Convention, and served in that capacity until 1985. His death in 1986 ended years of distinguished service as a lay church leader.　DPS PHOTO

Robert A. K. Runcie (left) was selected Archbishop of Canterbury in 1980. Here he chats with John M. Allin, who served as presiding bishop of the Episcopal Church from 1974-1986.　DPS PHOTO

All bishops of the Anglican communion gather every ten years at the Lambeth Conference, hosted by the Archbishop of Canterbury. This shot was taken of a procession at the 1978 Lambeth Conference, held at the University of Kent near Canterbury.

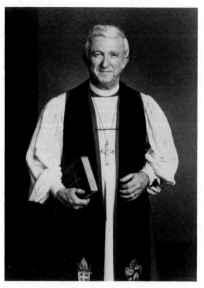

Presiding Bishop
Edmond Lee Browning
KARSH, OTTAWA

The Rev. Everett Fullam, rector of St. Paul's Church, Darien, CT and a major leader in the charismatic renewal movement.

Archbishop of Canterbury Robert A. K. Runcie presents a basket of fruit upon his arrival in Lagos, Nigeria, in 1984 for the Anglican Consultative Council meeting. Standing in rear is Terry Waite, who gained worldwide attention in 1986, for his role in the release of American hostages from Lebanon. Next to him is Timothy Olufosoye, Archbishop of Nigeria.

The Most Rev. Desmond Tutu first learned of his selection as Nobel Peace Prize winner while serving as visiting professor at New York's General Theological Seminary in 1984. Here he laughs with Archbishop of Canterbury Robert A. K. Runcie during a visit to Lambeth Palace a few months later. DPS PHOTO

8

The Clergy and the Seminaries

"DURING MY YEARS AS DEAN of the theological seminary rarely a week went by that I did not receive a letter or phone call the gist of which could be boiled down to 'Your seminary doesn't teach enough _____,' " said the Very Reverend Frederick H. Borsch at a 1985 conference on seminaries in Cambridge, Massachusetts. Borsch was dean of the Church Divinity School of the Pacific in Berkeley, California, between 1972 and 1981.

He continued, ". . . Your seminary doesn't teach enough spirituality, church administration . . . Bible, fund-raising, educational skills, preaching . . . how to develop the gifts of others, pastoral ability, ethics. The list could be extended. Although I developed some fairly sophisticated rejoinders, my private response to these charges was to beat myself upon the breast and to say, 'Yes, they're right. We aren't teaching our students enough about _____.' "[1]

The demands upon seminaries from their many constituencies are always numerous: spoken and unspoken expectations come from many quarters. Yet seminaries, if they are doing their job properly, rarely "make history." They educate—in quiet, sustained, and effective ways—the future leaders who themselves move the currents of the church's history. Since 1970, one of the major problems the Episcopal Church faced was too many men and women who wanted to become its ordained leaders.

"If the current trends of clergy oversupply and church membership decline continue, there will be an Episcopal priest for every lay member of that denomination in the year 2004." That shocking prediction came in 1978 when the results of a study were presented at a meeting of church and seminary leaders at Duke University. The study also pointed out a serious oversupply of clergy in the United Church of Christ, the United Methodist Church, and the two major Presbyterian bodies.[2]

A slight decrease in the number of parishes coupled with a tremendous increase in the number of clergy created the problem. In 1950, the *Episcopal*

Church Annual reported that there were 7,784 parishes and organized missions, and 6,654 ordained clergy. By 1956, the first year that the number of clergy surpassed the number of parishes, there was 7,200 parishes and 7,889 ordained clergy. But that didn't yet mean a "surplus" of clergy, since a number of ordained persons were serving in hospitals, institutional chaplaincies, secular work, or retired.

By the 1970s, however, the situation became serious. More than 11,000 ordained clergy served the church, while the number of parishes had actually declined to 7,464. In 1975, there were 400 fewer parishes than there were in 1950, while the number of ordained clergy had more than doubled. Bishops and dioceses sought ways to limit the number of people accepted for ordination and seminary training. Job mobility for older clergy also became more difficult. Upon retirement in 1985, an Ohio priest was asked why he had stayed in the same parish for twenty-three years. He replied, "When it came time to look around for another parish, there just weren't any jobs available. So I decided this must be where God wanted me to be for the rest of my ministry."

The reason for the surplus situation can be explained partly by demographics. During the "baby boom" of the 1950s, the population was growing rapidly. Churches also grew rapidly to meet the needs of the expanding population. From 1950 to 1960, the number of Episcopalians increased from 2.5 million to 3.4 million. Many of the small "mission" (diocesan-aided) congregations found in almost any diocese were started during this time. Clergy couldn't be recruited and trained quickly enough to serve the growing congregations.

By the 1970s, the population growth had levelled off and churches stopped growing. However, the "baby boomers" who filled Sunday schools in the 1950s were now seeking jobs, careers, and vocations. Not only that, but many of these "baby boomers" were products of the ambience of the sixties era. They rejected traditional careers in business or law to seek livelihoods in areas that provided greater human service and "meaning." For many, that meant the Episcopal priesthood.

Fortunately, a more moderate situation began to prevail in the 1980s. There were almost 400 more "parishes and organized missions" in 1984 than in 1975, according to the *Episcopal Church Annual*. Church membership, which had decreased successively for fifteen years, began to level off and show some increases around 1982. By 1985, many of the clergy who went to seminary after World War II were now of retirement age. Around 400 retired each year, while the number of ordinations was averaging around 300 per year.

At a 1986 diocesan clergy conference in Dallas, Texas, the Reverend Preston T. Kelsey II, director of the Board for Theological Education, stated that the 1978 prediction of one priest for every lay member in 2004 was "now very much out of date, terribly misleading, and nothing upon which we should depend for future projections." He even suggested that the Episcopal Church might be entering another period of clergy shortage.[3]

Seminary Enrollment Trends

Among the seminaries, three major enrollment trends took place in the 1970s and 1980s: more women, older students, and more laity seeking a theological education. The eleven accredited seminaries had a total enrollment of 1,128 in the fall of 1985.

The number of women in Episcopal seminaries increased from 4 percent in 1970 to 14 percent of total enrollment in 1976-77. Female enrollment climbed to 30 percent in 1982-83 and remained around that level for the next few years. This increase in female students occurred in all Protestant seminaries. Among the Protestant seminaries, the number of female students increased from 3,300 (10 percent) in 1975 to over 14,400 (26 percent) in 1985. That ranged from a low of 14 percent in Southern Baptist seminaries to 53 percent in United Church of Christ seminaries.[4]

Much of this increase reflected the changing social and professional roles available to women. The year 1963 is sometimes cited as the beginning of the women's movement in the United States. However, United Methodist, Presbyterian, and Lutheran churches began ordaining women for parish leadership roles seven years earlier in 1956. As mentioned in Chapter 3, the Episcopal Theological School in Cambridge, Massachusetts, began admitting women to its bachelor of divinity program in 1958, while Virginia Theological Seminary followed in 1963.

In January of 1984, forty-eight students and faculty from eight seminaries attended "A Celebration of the Ministry of the Laity" at the College of Preachers in Washington, D.C. This was the third conference sponsored by the Network of Seminarians with Lay Vocations. The Network, established in 1980, served a two-fold purpose: to encourage lay theological education, and to support students with lay vocations in seminaries.[5]

The statistics reflected the increasing emphasis on theological education for the laity. The number of students enrolled in non-master of divinity programs, or non-degree programs, increased from ninety in 1970 to 210 in 1980. By 1985, this figure had increased another 15 percent to 275. Again, this trend merely reflects what was occurring among all Protestant seminaries. "Sometime in the 1970s, the churches' perception of ministry began to change," said Dr. Leon Pacala, executive director of the Association of Theological Schools. "Churches began to see ministry as belonging to the entire people of God, not just clergy. The seminaries had to expand their constituencies to meet those needs."

Finally, an increasingly older population was entering the Episcopal seminaries. By the 1970s, the recent college graduate who immediately went to seminary became the exception rather than the norm. In 1985, the typical student entering an Episcopal seminary was around forty years of age.

The Right Reverend William E. Swing, Bishop of California, lamented the situation in a 1985 article titled "Where Have All the Young Men Gone?" After noting statistics on increases in the average age of male seminary students, and increases among female students, he observed that "what has happened to us is what has happened in the Roman Catholic Church, that is, we are in the midst of a crisis in vocations among young men."[6]

This troubling situation is not one that can be explained away with demographics; it's one that the church must actively address. However, it should be noted that the age eighteen to twenty-five group is currently (as of 1987) at one of its lowest levels in fifty years, according to United States census statistics. Colleges and universities must compete against each other for students. In the meantime, the Episcopal Church must consider its outreach and ministry on college campuses and question whether it's as effective as it could be.

The Church Deployment Office

In the 1970s, "the computer" became one of the most talked about tools among ordained clergy and parishes seeking new staff members. "The computer" was a computerized data bank at the Clergy Deployment Office, which matched clergy job skills to parish needs. The Development Office had been authorized by action of the 1969 General Convention (Notre Dame) and put into operation at the Episcopal Church Center in New York by 1971.

This office and its computerized data bank were meant to solve a problem described in a 1969 report to the General Convention by the Board for Clergy Deployment:

Many clergymen 'don't know where to turn' when they want to move. Some areas of the nation are oversupplied. Others have difficulty filling vacancies. All bishops have difficulty in evaluating credentials. Vestries and calling committees have few guides to aid them. Finally, clergymen's jobs are so ill-defined that they often operate on assumptions that are not related to the assumptions of their parish . . .[7]

"The computer" could match detailed descriptions of a clergy man or woman's talents and experience with descriptions of the expectations and needs of each parish for each vacancy. By 1972, more than half of the ordained clergy had filed profiles with the Deployment Office. "This is a most encouraging start toward meeting that age-old problem of the church world, matching the right person with the right job," said the Reverend Roddey Reid Jr., executive director of the Deployment Office during its first decade. In later years, the Deployment Office added lay church professionals to its data bank.

Bishop John Burt of the Diocese of Ohio, who served as board chairman of the Board for Clergy Deployment said, "This plan serves church and ministry alike by means of a great technological step forward. I think we can be proud of the response of our clergy in view of the purely voluntary nature of the project . . . I think that our friends in the business world would call these results 'phenomenal.' "[8]

Seminary Finances

With picket signs reading "Take this job and sanctify it" and "Inflation hits everyone," faculty members at an Iowa Presbyterian seminary went on strike in 1980. One faculty member said "A friend of mine . . . who makes $25,000 a year lifting carcasses at the local meat-packing plant was shocked to discover he was making more than a college professor." As far as anyone knew, the strike by University of Dubuque faculty members was the first in United States history.

The incident, reported in a *Christian Century* article, illustrates one of the major dilemmas faced by all seminaries in the modern era—finances. The author of the article reported, "The economic conditions that forced professors to the picket lines in Dubuque are being felt by every one of the 193 seminaries currently on the roster of the Association of Theological Schools."[9]

Theological education in the Episcopal Church is unique in one way. The Episcopal Church is the only major denomination that, until 1982, provided no systematic means of support for its seminaries. That year, however, the General Convention asked parishes to give one percent of their annual budget to a seminary of their choice. Even today, the seminaries receive no aid through the national church budget.

Seminaries are independent educational institutions and do not fall under the jurisdiction of the national church. James Fenhagen, dean of the General Theological Seminary in New York, commented in 1981 that "It was clearly the intent of the founders to establish the seminaries as strong, independent institutions, free to be prophetic without fear of being controlled by the church, and they established generous endowments to establish and protect their autonomy."[10]

Since 1949, the "Theological Education Offering" was one means by which parishes supported the seminaries. The 1949 General Convention had established a "Theological Education Sunday," and asked each parish to receive an offering during January for the seminary of its choice. At its peak in the late 1960s, the offering produced more than a million dollars for the seminaries, or almost one-fifth of their total revenue. Eventually, the money provided by the Theological Education Sunday Offering declined to five percent of the seminaries' total revenue. A 1976 General Convention report from the Board for Theological Education cited its lack of continued success: "The story of the decline of the offering is too soon told. One-third of the congregations participate in it. The average annual gift per communicant is the price of a morning newspaper."[11]

In 1970, Episcopal seminaries enrolled the smallest number of students—an average of eighty-seven—of any denomination, and at the highest per capita costs, as the Board for Theological Education reported to the 1970 General Convention. [12] The report pointed out that the United Methodists, with two more seminaries, educated four times as many students. The Disciples of

Christ, with six fewer schools, educated a hundred fewer students. In 1985, the situation was unchanged. It cost Episcopal seminaries twice as much to educate a student as it did seminaries from any other denomination. In 1984-85, the average cost per student was $14,526 at Episcopal seminaries, $7,657 at Presbyterian seminaries, $7,566 at Roman Catholic seminaries, $7,052 at Lutheran seminaries, and less than $7,000 at all other seminaries.[13]

In 1979, the General Convention directed the Board for Theological Education to propose legislation that would result in a new system for parishes to provide additional funds for the seminaries. The board retained a private firm to undertake a comprehensive study of the current seminary financing. According to this report, six of the ten accredited Episcopal seminaries experienced operating deficits in fiscal years between 1977 and 1980. The deans reported a high turnover among clerical and support personnel, and salaries for faculty and staff which did not keep pace with inflation. Deferred maintenance (upkeep of buildings) ranged from twenty thousand dollars at the Episcopal Theological Seminary of the Southwest in Austin, Texas, to more than $7 million at General Theological Seminary in New York City.[14]

The resolution prepared by the board—and passed by the 1982 General Convention—asked that parishes donate one percent of their annual budget to the seminary of their choice. Although the "jury is still out" on the long-range effects, preliminary signs indicate that the plan was a success. All the seminary deans agreed that the plan had brought a marked improvement in seminary finances. Only three years after passage of the one percent legislation, Richard Reid, dean of the Virginia Theological Seminary reported that "We have had a significant increase in giving from parishes . . ." James Fenhagen, dean of New York's General Theological Seminary also reported, "We have found that we are receiving gifts from churches that we have never received from before, and it has opened up a whole new and broader connection with the churches."[15]

New Degrees

Besides finances, a change in degree structure and titles was another major issue for Episcopal and non-Episcopal seminaries alike. Up until the 1950s, seminaries of all denominations offered the bachelor of divinity degree for the three-year program of preparation. In the late 1960s, many clergy began asking if the first professional degree from seminaries shouldn't be a doctorate. Some argued that ministers spend as much time in preparation as doctors and dentists, and their degree should be a doctorate as well. Even law schools began offering the doctor of jurisprudence instead of bachelor of law degrees during this time.

Eventually, the Association of Theological Schools recommended that seminaries change the degree title to master of divinity. Douglass Lewis wrote in an article for *The Christian Century:* "Uneasy with the whole affair and fearful that all seminaries would be stampeded into four-year doctorates, the Association of Theological Schools decided to call the three-year professional degree a Master of Divinity, but opened the door to those who would add a fourth year and call the degree a Doctor of Ministry."[16] This change occurred around 1970 and all Episcopal seminaries soon followed suit. The seminaries invited their graduates who had received the bachelor of divinity to return their diplomas in exchange for the new master's degrees.

Soon after, many seminaries added the doctor of ministry (D.Min.) as a graduate degree program. The initial doctor of ministry programs were completed with a year of residency on campus. Now, the vast majority of the ninety-eight programs (among all seminaries) are programs where parish clergy complete the courses over several years while retaining their full-time posts. Enrollment in doctor of ministry programs increased from 688 in 1971 (at all seminaries) to more than 6,300 in 1985. Doctor of Ministry enrollment in Episcopal seminaries was 110 in 1985.

The School of Theology at the University of the South began a summer doctor of ministry program with Vanderbilt Divinity School in Nashville, Tennessee, in 1974. Virginia Theological Seminary began its program around the same time, as did General Theological Seminary in New York. The Episcopal Divinity School in Cambridge, Massachusetts, added one a few years later. The Church Divinity School of the Pacific participated in a doctor of ministry program offered by the Graduate Theological Union in Berkeley, California. Nashotah House Seminary in Nashotah, Wisconsin, offers the Master of Sacred Theology degree, a one-year graduate degree. Besides that, General Theological Seminary is the only Episcopal seminary with a year-round graduate program, and the only seminary offering the Doctor of Theology (Th.D.) degree.

The Board for Theological Education

Dr. Nathan M. Pusey, an Episcopalian and then president of Harvard University, reported the findings of a study of theological education to the 1967 General Convention. In a hard-hitting address he stated, "There has resulted a gradual weakening of the church just at a time when it required vigorous leadership and increased strength . . ." The results of the far-ranging study, Dr. Pusey said, were disturbing and sometimes shocking. Citing "dozens of causes" for the weakening of the seminaries' training and the disillusionment of many of the practicing clergy, the report revealed that almost one-third of the clergy did not have a college and seminary education, and only 60 percent had received degrees from one of the eleven accredited Episcopal seminaries.[17]

The report also uncovered substandard salaries, outdated teaching methods, inadequate field education and training that was "too remote from the present world." In the report's foreword, Pusey charged the Episcopal Church with "a long debilitating lack of concern for theological education."

The report was based on data gathered by a theological education study commission which Pusey chaired, and was written by commission member

Dr. Charles L. Taylor. Taylor was dean of the Episcopal Theological School in Cambridge, Massachusetts, from 1944 to 1957. The report's major recommendation was the establishment of a Board for Theological Education. The report further stated, "Until now, although the Joint Commission on Education for Holy Orders and the periodic meetings of the seminary deans have brought a semblance of unity to theological education, essentially each seminary has faced its own needs and problems."

The convention approved the commission's recommendation. The new board was subsequently charged with maintenance of educational standards, research into the changing needs of theological education, fostering cooperation with universities and other seminaries, and discovering new ways to meet the financial needs of the seminaries.

The Very Reverend Almus Thorp Sr., dean of Bexley Hall Seminary in Rochester, New York, became the first director of the board in 1969 and served in that post until 1977. Dr. Fredrica Thompsett, a laywoman, was director of the board from 1977 to 1984, when she was succeeded by the Reverend Preston T. Kelsey, II.

Seminary Mergers

Between 1945 and 1974, there were four mergers among the Episcopal seminaries. The first came in 1949 with the closing of the church's only seminary for training black priests. Since 1878, Bishop Payne Divinity School in Petersburg, Virginia, operated as a predominantly black seminary. (See also Chapter 4.) Faced with financial problems and difficulties in recruiting qualified students, pressure also increased against maintaining a segregated institution. The seminary closed in 1949, and its assets were merged with Virginia Theological Seminary in 1953.

In 1968, Bexley Hall Seminary moved from its Gambier, Ohio, campus to affiliate with Colgate Rochester Divinity School and Crozer Theological Seminary in Rochester, New York. Formerly the divinity school of Kenyon College, an Episcopal college, Bexley Hall Seminary moved to affiliate with the predominantly Baptist coalition of seminaries. The Very Reverend Almus Thorp, Sr., served as dean during those transition years between 1959-69.

The president of Kenyon College, F. Edward Lund, cited the "Pusey Report" in the college's December 1967 decision to move Bexley Hall seminary. Lund said, "The Pusey report revealed that seminarians want scholarship, but want it 'closer to where the world is, both in physical location, and habits of thinking.' Episcopal divinity schools are 'too many, too small, and in a few instances, too inadvantageously located.' "[18]

The Berkeley Divinity School in New Haven, Connecticut, merged with Yale Divinity School in 1971. Under the terms of the agreement, Berkeley retained its own dean, board of trustees, and constitution. Berkeley and Yale agreed to a single admissions process, a united curriculum and faculty, and the granting of Yale degrees to all students. Episcopal students receive a Berkeley certificate as well.

In 1974, the Philadelphia Divinity School in Philadelphia, Pennsylvania, merged with the Episcopal Theological School (E.T.S.) in Cambridge, Massachusetts. Although the school retained its location on the Cambridge campus, the resulting institution—Episcopal Divinity School—had a new name, a new board of trustees, and new articles of organization. The University of Pennsylvania bought the old campus of Philadelphia Divinity School.

The New Schools

The Episcopal Theological Seminary of the Southwest was established in 1953 in Austin, Texas, by the Diocese of Texas. Primary leadership came from Bishop Clinton Quin and Coadjutor Bishop John M. Hines, who oversaw the project. At the time, the diocese was located more than 1,000 miles from the nearest Episcopal seminary. Diocesan leaders saw a clear need for a seminary to serve the fast-growing area, which included Houston and Austin.

In a 1952 address to the diocesan convention, Bishop Hines made the proposal for a new seminary: "We are not looking simply for a diocesan seminary. We want a theological school which the Southwest can share in, and claim pride for our church . . . It has been sixty years since a new seminary has been created and lived to tell the tale."[19]

The 1952 convention of the diocese approved the establishment of the seminary and elected a board of trustees, with Bishop Hines serving as chairman of the board. Soon the canons were changed to allow trustees to be elected from other dioceses. The seminary graduated its first class in 1954. Its first dean was the Very Reverend Gray M. Blandy, who served in that post from 1952-1967.

Not without skeptics, another seminary was opened in 1976—the Trinity Episcopal School for Ministry in Ambridge, Pennsylvania. Trinity was founded in 1975 by the Fellowship of Witness, an organization devoted to promoting the evangelical tradition in the Episcopal Church. Like the Fellowship of Witness, the goal of the seminary was to provide an evangelical, biblically-based education, within the context of the Anglican tradition.

The Right Reverend Alfred Stanway, an Australian bishop, agreed to become the school's first dean and president, and help the school get started. Bishop Stanway had spent twenty years as a missionary bishop in Tanzania with an outstanding record of accomplishment. After leaving Africa, he returned to Australia to become Deputy Principal of Ridley Theological College in Melbourne and was there prior to coming to Trinity. The seminary opened its doors on September 25, 1976 at a temporary site near Pittsburgh. That year, the Reverend Dr. John Rodgers left Virginia Theological Seminary where he was chaplain and professor of systematic theology to become the senior professor for the new seminary. In 1978, he was named its second dean and president about the same time the seminary established its permanent campus in Ambridge.

The seminary was to enjoy a remarkable success. Enrollment quickly reached a comparable level with other Episcopal seminaries, and most of its graduates passed the church's General Ordination Exam. By June of 1985, the seminary had received full accreditation from the Association of Theological Schools in the United States and Canada.

The Episcopal Seminary of the Caribbean was established by the church's Executive Council in 1960 to serve the needs of the dioceses in the Caribbean and in Central and South America. Located in Carolina, Puerto Rico, it was heavily subsidized by the Executive Council from the beginning, but its financial position became precarious. This unique outpost of theological education was forced to close for financial reasons in 1978.

The Absalom Jones Theological Institute in Atlanta, Georgia, was founded in 1971 for Episcopal students attending the Interdenominational Theological Center. The latter is an accredited seminary that had been formed earlier from six small seminaries that served predominantly black denominations. The Absalom Jones Institute, while not a separate seminary, supported a dean and faculty member, provided a few courses for the Episcopal students, and offered continuing education for Atlanta-area clergy and laity. It is named after the first black priest in the Episcopal Church, Absalom Jones, who was ordained in 1804.

Diocesan Seminaries

The financial difficulties faced by residential, accredited seminaries have been made more difficult by competition from a proliferating number of diocesan training programs and seminaries. While four dioceses established formal campus programs, more than thirty-five dioceses established procedures to enable ordination candidates to "read for Holy Orders." A report on theological education made to the 1976 General Convention noted, "One of the most striking developments in recent years has been the increasing utilization of programs of preparation other than the accredited seminaries."

The Mercer School of Theology, serving the Diocese of Long Island, was establishing in 1955 to serve persons with "late vocations," enabling them to continue secular employment while going to school. All classes for the four-year program were scheduled for evenings and Saturdays.

The Bloy School of Theology began in 1958 through a Church Divinity School of the Pacific (CDSP) extension program. CDSP started the program in the Diocese of Los Angeles for those students who could not move 500 miles north to study in Berkeley. After 1962, CDSP did not feel it could economically maintain the Los Angeles campus. The Diocese of Los Angeles took it over and changed its name to "Bloy House" after its bishop, Frances E. Bloy. The diocesan seminary moved from Los Angeles to Claremont, California, in 1970 to share resources with the Claremont School of Theology, a large accredited seminary with which it maintained close relations. At that time, the name was changed to the Episcopal Theological School at Claremont. It continues under the leadership of the bishop of Los Angeles as chairman of the board.

The Episcopal Theological Seminary in Kentucky was originally founded in 1832 in Lexington, and operated for about twenty years. The Right Reverend William Moody, then Bishop of Lexington, re-opened the seminary in 1951 to train students from his diocese. In later years, an increasing number of students came from outside the Diocese of Lexington and it moved away from its identification as a diocesan-centered institution. Although it sought to become nationally recognized, the seminary never received accreditation. In 1986 under the Right Reverend Don Wimberly, who became Bishop of Lexington in 1985, the Episcopal Theological Seminary in Kentucky changed its focus from training for ordination to continuing education and education for the laity.

The Diocese of Dallas began its "Diocesan Ordination Course" in 1971 as a program of study for those candidates who could not attend a residential seminary. In 1975, the school expanded into a five-year program and changed its name to the Anglican School of Theology. Two years later, it moved to the campus of the University of Dallas, a Roman Catholic school. The Anglican School of Theology shares facilities, programs, and faculty with the University of Dallas. However, with its weekend schedule of classes, its educational thrust is towards part-time students who hold full-time jobs during the week.

In addition to the schools mentioned above, more than thirty dioceses maintain training programs of one kind or another. Although generally intended for persons planning a "non-stipendiary" ministry (a part-time ministry while maintaining a full-time secular job), an increasing number of graduates of these programs were laity who felt the need for theological training. A report to the 1979 General Convention identified 2,400 students enrolled in thirty-eight programs, but stated "no more than 440 of these persons are intending ordination."[20]

Part of the reason for the rapid increase in diocesan training programs and seminaries could be attributed to demand from increasingly older candidates for ordination. These older students, both men and women, were often married with children and full-time jobs. They could not move off and enroll in a residential seminary as easily as a twenty-five-year-old single person could. Another reason for the diocesan seminaries can be attributed to the rapidly increasing cost of a seminary education. Older students, especially, could not maintain families and at the same time pay thousands of dollars in tuition and travel required for a year in a residential seminary. The demand created by these students was met by bishops and diocesan leaders who—in many cases—felt distrustful of accredited seminaries, which they perceived as too liberal, too high, or too low.

The increasing number of diocesan training programs was not without a number of critics. "What corporation would build new factories to produce a certain product when the market for it was glutted?" wrote O. C. Edwards, dean of Seabury-Western Theological Seminary in a 1980 article that appeared in *The Christian Century.*[21] On the other hand, defenders maintained the need for the schools. "We have long needed more local and flexible institutions to bring people into deeper and broader touch with their religious tradition," wrote Edwin G. Wappler, the dean of Bloy House, in a reply to Edwards' article also published in *The Christian Century.*

Admittedly, this discussion of theological education has been limited to the economic and organizational issues of theological education, and cannot be considered a comprehensive assessment. The contribution of the seminaries to the church's life through other means, while much harder to measure and document, is profound. Whether in ecumenical relations, Prayer Book revision, or a number of other endeavors, the seminaries have contributed scholars and writers to dozens of standing commissions and committees. Faculty members from the seminaries lead hundreds of retreats and conferences in parishes and dioceses each year. The effects of published contributions from the church's theologians and scholars simply cannot be measured. For instance, the *Church's Teaching Series* has been the greatest publishing success in Episcopal Church history, and almost all of the original and revised volumes were written by seminary faculty. These volumes are used each week in hundreds of parishes across the country.

The future of the Episcopal Church's seminaries continues to be a subject of debate as they compete with one another for students, donor dollars, and public support. The "one percent plan," while offering some help, cannot save sinking ships in the theological harbor. The numerous diocesan training programs continue to compete with the accredited seminaries for students. Tough questions remain to be answered in the realm of theological education, and the answers won't come easily.

9

A New Hymnal and
Book of Common Prayer

SOME WELL-ATTENDED OPEN HEARINGS on the proposed revision of the *Book of Common Prayer* (BCP) at the 1976 General Convention "provided two evenings of good theater as a procession of gifted speakers gave impassioned—and sometimes witty—defenses of the old book and attacks on the new," according to one ecumenical observer.[1]

A Long Island deputy said that the mental health of Episcopalians might suffer if they were forced to stop using their accustomed liturgy. He cited a psychiatrist who had treated Roman Catholics for severe post-Vatican II depression related to the change from Latin to the vernacular. A Milwaukee priest spoke compellingly of the "sign value" of the old liturgy. "Traditional English speaks to us of our Anglican roots," he said. The revised book, he complained, assumes contemporary English as the norm—but "much of the contemporary languages will seem dated in fifteen to twenty years."

A women complained that the passing of the peace was a "shocking break" in the mood and continuity of the service. Besides, she added, "only the pretty ones get kissed."

On the other hand, supporters of the new Book were equally eloquent. A Pittsburgh deputy declared that "No woman should ever again have to say 'for us men and for our salvation.' " A member of a religious order testified to the experience of using the new forms daily within a religious community: "They wear amazingly well." He praised the new book's language for its "leanness, compression, tautness, simplicity, profundity and power."[2]

Unity for Episcopalians arises not so much from a common theology as from a common worship. The Episcopal Church is a *worshiping* church, and the source for that worship is its *Book of Common Prayer*. Not merely a "book of prayers," the *Book of Common Prayer* contains the services of the church—marriage, burial, ordination, Morning and Evening Prayer, and many others. So it is much more than a "prayer book." It is the book that

107

determines the liturgical practice for almost every occasion of the Episcopal Church. It is also a book for personal devotion and prayer. The Daily Offices (Morning and Evening Prayer) are said each day by thousands of Episcopalians: clergy, laity, and members of religious orders.

It is not surprising, then, that revising a prayer book would cause so much debate and concern. Many people hold the language of the Prayer Book near and dear. They go to church year after year and recite the creeds and prayers. The language is familiar, comfortable, and as much a part of their lives as are the words of the Bible. The 1928 Prayer Book itself has been praised for its theology, its similarities to the original 1662 *Book of Common Prayer*, as well as its eloquent use of the English language.

The Episcopal Church made the decision to revise its 1928 *Book of Common Prayer* in 1976. Three years later, the General Convention ratified the decision and the new book became the 1979 *Book of Common Prayer*. For many Episcopalians it brought an uncomfortable transition, but for more it was a welcome change. The change was not the result of a sudden decision, but years of preparation that went back to the early 1950s. The *tradition* of Prayer Book revision itself goes back to the historic roots of Anglicanism.

Historic Background of Prayer Book Revision

The *Book of Common Prayer* has been a part of the Church of England's tradition since the English Reformation. Thomas Cranmer wrote the first English Prayer Book in 1549, seventeen years after Henry VIII dissolved England's relationship with the Pope in 1531. The Church of England revised its Prayer Book in 1552, 1559, and again in 1662. The 1662 version remains in use in England today, with some worship and liturgical supplements. From the beginning, the *Book of Common Prayer* was a source of unity for Anglicans. At the time of Cranmer, the English Church was split between advocates of Roman Catholic and Protestant theologies. This "high" and "low" tension has been a part of Anglicanism ever since, but the Prayer Book always provided a source for common worship and loyalty.

The first *Book of Common Prayer* for the Episcopal Church was approved in 1789 at its first General Convention. But Americans needed a new version, since they could hardly be expected to pray for the King of England. Neither could they expect newly-ordained priests pledge loyalty to the King. The American version was based on the English Book and the *Book of Common Prayer* of the Episcopal Church of Scotland. Since the Church of Scotland had consecrated Samuel Seabury, our first bishop, in 1784, they expected something in return. They asked Samuel Seabury to incorporate part of the Scottish liturgy into the first American Prayer Book.

In much of the Anglican Communion, Prayer Book revision became a common practice in the twentieth century. Anglican Churches in South Africa, India, Japan, Canada and the West Indies have revised their Prayer Books since 1960. In addition, Anglicanism's historical thrust encourages its national churches to develop an Anglican identity within their particular culture. Instead of using a universal Prayer Book from the Church of England, each of the churches has developed its own Prayer Book according to its unique language, culture, and history.

In its preface, the first American Prayer Book of 1789 set the precedent for Prayer Book revision by stating that "in every church what cannot be clearly determined to belong to Doctrine must be referred to Discipline; and therefore, by common consent and authority, may be altered, abridged, enlarged, amended, or otherwise disposed of, as may seem most convenient for the edification of the people . . .''

After Prayer Book revisions in 1892 and 1928 in the United States, the General Convention of 1928 established a Revision Commission as a permanent agency. Later it was called the Standing Liturgical Commission. The commission's charge was to deal with liturgical matters, concerns, and problems developing from the use of the 1928 *Book of Common Prayer.* The Convention Journal of 1928 stated its purpose as:

. . . the preservation and study (of) all matters relating to the *Book of Common Prayer* with the idea of developing and conserving for some possible future use, the liturgical experience and scholarship of the church.

Commenting on the 1928 Book's adoption, the Reverend Bayard Jones, the vice-chairman of the Standing Liturgical Commission, wrote in 1953:

The whole years of debate had aroused widespread interest in the subject [of Prayer Book revision] and the mind of the church was more receptive of suggestions for revision when the work was brought to an end than when it began. . . . It was realized that there were some rough edges in what had been done as well as an unsatisfied demand for still further alterations.[3]

The Reverend Charles Price, professor of systematic theology at Virginia Theological Seminary, says that significant factors at work during the 1950s and 1960s produced a climate ripe for Prayer Book revision. The liturgical movement, which brought changes in the Roman Catholic and many Protestant churches, was one of these factors. The second factor was the ecumenical movement with its roots in the twentieth century understanding of the mission of the church. The revival of Biblical theology also brought a desire on the part of churches to go back to liturgical practices of the early Christian church.

After World War I, Roman Catholic scholars began to search for liturgical forms used prior to the Middle Ages. Many believed that the liturgy of the early church more clearly grasped and expressed Christian faith than did later medieval forms. Protestant Biblical theologians and authors like Hans Lietzmann and Oscar Cullman pointed out the importance of liturgical documents of these early centuries.

Charles Price wrote:

For these and perhaps other reasons, most of the churches in Western Christianity are currently involved in liturgical renewal of faith and at providing a way to worship which is at once more ancient in its roots and more ecumenical in its outreach than currently-used major liturgies.[4]

The recognition of a need for a new Prayer Book came as early as 1949 when the Standing Liturgical Commission made its report to the General Convention:

The accumulated number of these requests and suggestions has now become so great and comes from such a variety of sources, that we are forced to believe that a movement for a general revision of the Prayer Book is not far away.[5]

In 1953, the Standing Liturgical Commission reported a similar degree of dissatisfaction with the Prayer Book. The terms were even stronger:

There can be no doubt as to the dangerous degree of dissatisfaction in the church with our present service. It is not a mere question of individual idiosyncrasies. It is the distinctly ominous fact that large sections of the clergy are expressing their criticisms of the service in the absolute manner of refusing to follow the provisions of the *Book of Commom Prayer*. . . .

These various kinds of ritual disobedience of which the above [cited examples] are examples rather than an exhaustive list are no doubt serious enough since they mark the breakdown of a reasonable degree of uniformity in that essential service which is the fundamental tie of the church's unity.[6]

Perhaps the major complaint arising from the pew was that Prayer Book language differed from what most Americans used. "What does 'vouchsafe' mean?" said one communicant, referring to words from the communion prayer which asked God to "vouchsafe to bless and sanctify . . ." In the Nicene Creed, "Why will 'the quick' be judged along with the dead?" asked one new Episcopalian. Women complained about "for us men and our salvation" in the Nicene Creed, as well as giving thanks "for all men" in the prayer for the whole state of Christ's church. The 1928 services frequently used 'thee' and 'thou' when 'you' had become the accustomed form of American English.

Realizing the need for further study and development, the 1949 General Convention authorized the Standing Liturgical Commission to publish a series of *Prayer Book Studies*. Each of these studies was to deal with a particular office or feature of the Prayer Book, explaining its history and theological background, current issues and problem points, and suggestions for the church to consider. These *Studies* were not meant to be taken as proposals for immediate legislative action, but "reports to the church at large." Their purpose was to spread a general understanding of the needs and problems; elicit criticisms, suggestions, and further contributions; and finally, "produce some kind of unanimity of the mind of the church."

Prayer Book Studies I. Baptism and Confirmation was the first title published in 1950. Between 1950 and 1976, twenty-eight titles in the *Prayer Book Studies* series were published. While most of the studies dealt with various services and offices contained in the Prayer Book, two dealt with the calendar and church year. *Prayer Book Studies 15* was a commentary titled "The Problem and Method of Prayer Book Revision." The table at the end of this chapter lists the title and publication date for each of the *Studies.*

The canons of the Episcopal Church do not allow parishes to use liturgical services other than those contained in the *Book of Common Prayer.* Until 1961, "trial use" of proposed liturgies was not allowed. The Standing Liturgical Commission offered to the 1952, 1955, 1958, and 1961 General Conventions a resolution seeking to allow trial use of proposed liturgies, by amending Article X of the church's constitution. Citing "trial use" in other Anglican provinces, such as South Africa, India, Japan, and Canada, the Standing Liturgical Commission urged the American church to adopt the procedure. The 1961 General Convention finally approved the concept of "trial use." The canons were changed to allow a future General Convention to:

> Authorize for trial use throughout this church, as an alternative at any time or times to the established *Book of Common Prayer* or to any section or office thereof, a proposed revision of the whole book or of any portion thereof, duly undertaken by the General Convention.

When Presiding Bishop Arthur C. Lichtenberger called for discussion on the proposal and there was no response, he said in amazement, "Not even on this?" Since this was an amendment to the Constitution, it also had to be approved at the next General Convention in order to take effect. It passed.

After the 1961 General Convention allowed trial use, the 1964 General Convention subsequently directed the Standing Liturgical Commission to develop a plan for revising the Prayer Book and present it to the 1967 General Convention. In the resolution's words, the plan would be one "by which a revision of the *Book of Common Prayer* be undertaken . . . with a special view to making the language and the form of the services more relevant to the circumstances of the church's present ministry and life."

The Standing Liturgical Commission presented a plan for Prayer Book Revision to the 1967 General Convention which passed without significant debate. The Society for the Preservation of the *Book of Common Prayer,* later to become so vocal in its opposition, was not yet organized. The 1967 General Convention was preoccupied with Presiding Bishop John Hines' proposal for the General Convention Special Program.

The adopted plan appointed the Standing Liturgical Commission as the "instrument of revision," rather than a newly appointed body, and called for a large number of consultants to assist the commission in its task. The commission was requested to present drafts of revised portions of the Prayer Book to the 1970 General Convention for trial use consideration.

Trial use was an important part of the revision process. In its report to the 1967 convention, the Standing Liturgical Commission stressed: "The Standing Liturgical Commission is strongly committed to the principle that new forms of service should undergo such testing before they are adopted and imposed upon the church through legislation."[7] *Prayer Book Studies 15: The Problem and Method of Prayer Book Revision* stated:

There is one advantage to trial use that possibly outweighs all objections. It removes the risk of liturgical revision from the realm of purely theoretical discussion and provides a basis of judgment on proposed forms from concurrent experience.[8]

Along with the plan for a revision of the *Book of Common Prayer,* the Standing Liturgical Commission offered the first trial services for approval at the 1967 General Convention. Trial services are those which could possibly be included in a new Prayer Book. Without significant debate, the convention approved "The Liturgy of the Lord's Supper" from *Prayer Book Studies 17,* which was a revision of the eucharistic rite.

In implementing the plan for revision, some 250 consultants were appointed. They were representative of a cross section of the Episcopal Church and included bishops, priests, deacons, and laypersons. Among them were poets and writers, scholars, young people, retired priests, businessmen, housewives, lawyers, doctors, and teachers.

These consultants divided themselves into two main groups. One group served on fourteen drafting committees, operating mainly in different geographical areas. Each drafting committee was asked to produce a preliminary draft revision for a single service or section of the Prayer Book. A member of the Standing Liturgical Commission chaired each committee.

Members of the other group were "reader-consultants," who kept in touch with each other through letters and telephone calls. They received all the materials prepared by the drafting committees at all stages of the work and submitted comments, criticisms, and suggestions. To give the commission the benefit of an ecumenical perspective, a group of fourteen representatives from other denominations served as consultants. At a later stage of the work, the commission included the chair officers of diocesan liturgical commissions in the church-wide consultation.

In 1970, the first book for trial use, simply titled *Services for Trial Use,* was published. The sales of *Services for Trial Use* reached 800,000 copies, far exceeding expectations for its use. Approximately one copy for every three Episcopalians was sold.

The 1973 General Convention authorized a number of minor changes in the eucharistic rites, which were included in *Authorized Services 1973.* This was tagged the "Zebra Book" because of its striped cover.

The *Draft Proposed Book of Common Prayer* was released by the Standing Liturgical Commission of February 2, 1976. Deputies and bishops had seven months to examine the proposed book before the final vote came in

September. Approval of the proposed book was expected: it never held the same suspense as did the resolution on the ordination of women to the priesthood. Nonetheless, critics of the proposed book produced some heated debate on the subject.

The 1976 General Convention approved the *Draft Proposed Book of Common Prayer* by a majority that startled even its supporters. The House of Bishops approved it by a unanimous voice vote, while the House of Deputies vote broke down as follows:

Clerical order: 107 dioceses for, 3 against, 3 divided; Lay order: 90 dioceses for, 12 against, 9 divided.

This session had "none of the electricity and pathos that had characterized the women's ordination debate" three days earlier, according to the *General Convention Daily.* "In a business-like manner, at times testy, at times humorous, the deputies waded through three dozen last minute amendments seeking mainly to restore isolated words or phrases from the 1928 Prayer Book," according to the *Daily.*[9]

Representatives of the Society for the Preservation of the *Book of Common Prayer* (SPBCP) were shocked at the overwhelming majority that voted in favor of the proposed draft. The society, which claimed some 10,000 members, had worked hard to defeat the new book. Harold Weatherby of Nashville, the society's secretary said, "Most of the people who voted 'no' were people we knew. We won no converts."[10]

Other SPBCP members complained. Walter Sullivan, referring to the use of "you" for "thee" and "thou," said, "Now we are asked to speak to God in the same impertinent inflections we use with our business associates, our telephone operators, and with the other good but hardly deified beings with whom we daily come in contact." He also complained that "most references to Judgment Day" were omitted and that the language was an "effort to weaken the faith."[11] The Society for the Preservation of the *Book of Common Prayer,* whose name was later changed to simply the *Prayer Book Society,* continued to promote the use of the 1928 BCP in years following the adoption of the 1979 book.

Approval of the new Prayer Book was required at two successive General Conventions. The final approval in 1979 was even more one-sided. The House of Bishops approved it by a unanimous voice vote. The House of Deputies debated for twelve minutes before giving it their unanimous endorsement.

Clerical order: 107 for, 1 against, 2 divided; Lay order: 99 for, 2 against, 6 divided.

Later, the convention voted that "liturgical texts from the 1928 Prayer Book may be used in worship" under certain guidelines, as approved by the local bishop. In an effort to reconcile opponents of the change, the convention wanted to allow some continued use of the 1928 book without appearing to sanction two official Prayer Books. The resolution stated that it "in no way sanctions the existence of two authorized *Books of Common Prayer.*"

Nature of the Changes

How, then, was the Prayer Book changed? One of the major changes is the new Prayer Book's increased emphasis upon Holy Communion as the principal act of Christian Worship. The 1928 Prayer Book states in its introductory rubrics:

The Order for Holy Communion, the Order for Morning Prayer, the Order for Evening Prayer, and the Litany, as set forth in this Book are the regular services appointed for Public Worship. . . ." (p. vii)

In the 1979 Prayer Book, the corresponding rubric reads:

The Holy Eucharist, the principal act of Christian worship on the Lord's Day and other major Feasts, and Daily Morning and Evening Prayer, as set forth in this Book, are the regular services appointed for public worship in this Church . . . (BCP, page 13)

This change merely reflected the changing practice of the church. Prior to the 1950s, few parishes had weekly Holy Communion as the principal Sunday service. By the 1970s, however, Holy Communion had become the principal Sunday worship service at the majority of Episcopal parishes. The Reverend Earl Brill summarized the change in a *Christian Century* article:

If one were to identify the most persistent theme in the life of the Episcopal Church for the past twenty-five years, it would be the ascendency of the Catholic movement within the church. There was a time when the practice of celebrating the Holy Communion at the principal service every week, the adoption of eucharistic vestments, and the use of the sign of the cross in worship were all regarded as . . . exotic and controversial . . . Today such things are regarded as quite conventional . . .[12]

A second general change in the new Prayer Book is its greatly enhanced flexibility of use. Now there are two forms of the Communion service, Rite I and Rite II, instead of one. Rite I remains virtually unchanged from the communion service in the old Prayer Book, except for minor language changes, and it allows for a choice between two Eucharistic Prayers. Rite II, however, gives the priest and congregation four choices. Within Rite II, the new Book gives six choices for the "Prayers of the People."

One of the major additions in both Rite I and Rite II Communion services is the "Passing of the Peace." While some have felt it upset the "dignity" of the service, most Episcopalians have welcomed it. While it is not contained in the 1928 BCP, its addition in 1979 is actually a restoration from the earliest liturgies of the Christian Church, as well as later Eastern, Gallican, and Roman liturgies.[13]

Not only are alternate liturgies given for the Holy Communion service, the revised Book also provides Rite I and Rite II services for Morning Prayer,

Evening Prayer, and the Burial Offices. Morning and Evening Prayer offices have about a dozen more canticles for possible use. It would be tedious to list all the new degrees of flexibility introduced into the 1979 BCP, but they occur throughout the Book in almost all services.

The new *Book of Common Prayer* has also sought to incorporate wider participation by the laity, and recognize the ministry of all God's people. As we read in the directions, "Concerning the Service of the Church:"

> In all services, the entire Christian assembly participates in such a way that the members of each order within the church, lay persons, bishops, priests, and deacons, fulfill the functions proper to their respective orders, as set forth in the rubrical directions for each service. (BCP, page 13)

It is, indeed, a Prayer Book by the church and for the church. "For the first time in history, the Prayer Book has been produced by a process involving the whole church" said Leo Malania, coordinator for the Standing Liturgical Commission.

"The new Prayer Book sounded the death knell for many of the old churchmanship battles," wrote the Reverend Marion Hatchett, a member of the Standing Liturgical Commission. "Those on the one side were given an enriched liturgy of the Word; those on the other a remolded and enriched liturgy of the table."[14]

The Church Hymnal Corporation, publishers of the 1979 *Book of Common Prayer,* gave the Right Reverend Chilton Powell the first published copy of the new Prayer Book at an Albuquerque, New Mexico, meeting in November of 1979. The presentation was made at a meeting of diocesan liturgical and music commission leaders. Bishop Powell, who retired as Bishop of Oklahoma in 1977, served as chairman of the Standing Liturgical Commission from 1966 through 1979, and supervised the sometimes stormy revision process. In honoring Powell, assembled members of diocesan liturgical and music commissions also gave him the title, "father of the *Book of Common Prayer* 1979." The citation from the liturgical and music leaders read:

> For eighteen years he (Bishop Powell) served the Lord in his Church as a member, then as chairman of the commission with consummate skill, boundless patience, unwavering love, and constant prayer, justly earning the title of father of the *Book of Common Prayer* 1979.[15]

A New Hymnal

"The *Hymnal 1940* has been a widely used, almost universally respected and admired collection of liturgical music, but the time is hard upon us when we can no longer say with assurance that it is adequate to our needs." A member of the Standing Commission on Church Music, the Reverend Sherrod Albritton, wrote these words in a 1979 *Historical Magazine* article when the commission was in the midst of revising the *Hymnal 1940.*[16]

The first hymnal of the Episcopal Church and its first Prayer Book were adopted in 1789 at the second General Convention. This action marked the beginning of a close relationship between the *Book of Common Prayer* and the hymnal. The first hymnal contained words for twenty-seven hymns, but no music. Although subsequent General Conventions added more hymns to this sparse number, the first major revision did not occur until 1892. Reflecting the phenomenal growth of hymnody in England, the convention adopted a new hymnal containing 679 hymns. The 1910 convention called for a revision of this hymnal, and a new one was approved in 1916. This edition lasted twenty-four years before the *Hymnal 1940* was approved.

Up until 1970, the Joint Commission on Church Music (JCCM) could not publish materials without the approval of General Convention. While they searched for ways to meet the musical needs of the church, this roadblock stood in their way. It was removed when the 1970 convention resolved "that the Joint Commission on Church Music be authorized and directed to continue to produce materials for the music needs of the church; and that authorization be given for use of texts published by the Joint Commission on Church Music in its continuing project, *More Hymns and Spiritual Songs*."

The first group of materials was prepared in 1971 and 1972 and became available in 1973. *Songs for Liturgy and More Hymns and Spiritual Songs* was the complete title. It contained, in addition to the service music, a collection of seventy-one hymns to be used as a supplement to the hymnal.

The 1973 General Convention transformed the JCCM into the Standing Commission on Church Music (SCCM), which made it a permanent commission of the church. This convention expanded the canon on church music, Title II, Canon 6, by adding a second section. It read, in part:

> There shall be a Standing Commission on Church Music. It shall be the duty of this Commission to collaborate with the Standing Liturgical Commission as regards the musical setting of liturgical texts and rubrics; encourage the writing of new music for liturgical use . . . collect and collate material bearing upon future revisions of the church hymnal; and in general, serve the church in matters pertaining to music.

Similar in purpose to the "trial use" prayer books, the commission began publishing small, paperback pamphlets with collections of new and revised hymns. These included the *Church Hymnal Series* as well as *Songs for Celebration.*

The 1976 General Convention asked the Standing Commission on Church Music to begin collecting and studying songs, and make a subsequent recommendation about the revision of the *Hymnal 1940.* A threefold plan was developed and put into action.

First, the commission would study thoroughly all the texts of the existing hymnal to determine their continued usability. The commission appointed the Reverend Charles Price, professor of systematic theology at Virginia Theological Seminary and a member of the Standing Liturgical Commission, to form a committee to undertake this study. The committee included other theologians, poets, hymnologists, teachers, priests, and liturgiologists.

"Our first job was to review the text of existing hymns, where necessary, towards theological consistency and adequacy. A part of that, and no small part, has been to examine texts for sexist and racist language," Price said in a later inverview.[17]

Every member of the Episcopal Church had the opportunity to make suggestions to this committee. In 1978, Dr. Alec Wyton, coordinator of the Standing Commission on Church Music, sent a questionnaire to every parish and mission in the Episcopal Church. More than 10,000 replies to this survey were received. Within a year, the Church Hymnal Corporation sent a more detailed questionnaire to all clergy and musicians. They were asked whether, in consideration of the music and text, each hymn should be retained, deleted, or modified. They also asked for preferences for hymns to be added from other sources.

Using the *Hymnal 1940* and information gathered from the two questionnaires, Price's committee ranked the hymns with five categories. "I" meant the hymn should be retained without change. "II" meant the hymn was desirable, but needed some changes. "III" meant that the hymn was inoffensive, but innocuous. The committee decided that hymns in this category could be used or omitted, depending on need. "IV" was a category for hymns which should be dropped because of lack of use. "V" was a category for hymns which should be dropped because of theological inadequacy or poor quality.

Early in its work, the Standing Commission on Church Music adopted a philosophy for hymnal revision and established several precepts for its work. This led to the development of the following objectives:
— To prepare a body of texts which presents the Christian faith with clarity and integrity;
— To restore music which has lost some of its melodic, rhythmic, or harmonic vitality through prior revision;
—To reflect the nature of today's church by including the works of contemporary artists and works representing many cultures;
— To strengthen ecumenical relationships through the inclusion of texts and tunes used by other Christian traditions;
— To create a hymnal embodying both practicality and esthetic excellence.[18]

The commission emphasized that, in its view, the hymnal should be a companion for use with the *Book of Common Prayer:* it should serve as a "practical book of theology" and present the church's teaching fully and authentically; and it should use inclusive language, wherever possible, to affirm the participation of all in the body of Christ.[19]

The 1982 General Convention, which met in New Orleans, approved the hymn texts presented by the commission, with some minor changes. With some debate, the convention voted to restore nine hymns from *Hymnal 1940* which the commission had not recommended, including "My Country 'Tis of Thee," "I Sing a Song of the Saints of God", and "Eternal Father, Strong to Save." Efforts to restore "Battle Hymn of the Republic" and "Once to Every Man and Nation" failed. The latter was deleted because of its "Pelagian theology," the concept that salvation can be achieved through human effort and achievement.

Although the hymnal was not published until 1985, it was called *Hymnal 1982* because of the adoption of its texts by the 1982 General Convention. Between 1982 and 1985, the Standing Commission on Church Music, assisted by general editor Raymond Glover, was given authority to determine the music for the texts adopted in 1982.

When the United Parcel Service (UPS) packed the published hymnals for 7,700 parishes into eleven semitrailer trucks in December, 1985, it was billed as "the largest single shipment in UPS history." The new hymnal was officially dedicated at a January 16, 1986, service at the Cathedral of Saint Peter and Saint Paul in Washington Cathedral, preceding the January 17 installation of Presiding Bishop Edmond L. Browning.

The chairman of the Standing Commission on Church Music, the Very Reverend William Hale of Syracuse, New York, made these comments at the festive occasion: "We believe our reflections and decisions have resulted in a hymnal that can present the Christian faith with timeliness and clarity; a hymnal that includes the best of both old and new; a hymnal that is ecumenical and electric; a hymnal that can infuse our liturgy and enliven our worship."[20]

TABLE
The *Prayer Book Studies* Series

Prayer Book Studies No.	Title	Publication Date
1	Baptism and Confirmation	1950
2	The Liturgical Lectionary	1950
3	Ministration to the Sick	1951
4	The Eucharistic Lectionary	1953
5	The Litany	1951
6	Morning and Evening Prayer	1957
7	The Penitential Office	1957
8	The Ordinal	1957
9	The Calendar	1957
10	The Solemnization of Matrimony	1958
11	Thanksgiving for the Birth of a Child	1958
12	Propers for the Minor Holy Days	1958
13	Order for the Burial of the Dead	1959
14	An Office for the Institution of Rectors into Parishes	1959
15	The Problem and Method of Prayer Book Revision	1961
16	The Calendar and the Collects, Epistles, and Gospels for the Lesser Feasts and Fasts for Special Occasions	1963
17	The Liturgy of the Lord's Supper	1967
18	Baptism and Confirmation	1967
19	The Church Year	1970
20	The Ordination of Bishops, Priests, and Deacons	1970
21	The Holy Eucharist	1970
22	The Daily Office	1970
23	The Psalter	1970
24	The Pastoral Offices	1970
25	Prayers, Thanksgivings and Litanies	1973
26	Holy Baptism Together with a Form for Confirmation	1973
27	The Daily Offices Revised	1973
28	The Dedication and Consecration of a Church (and) Celebration of a New Ministry	1973
29	Introducing the Draft Proposed Book	1976

10

Listening to the Spirit:
The Renewal Movements

"IT SEEMS THAT 'RENEWAL' IS DIFFERENT for different people and different groups . . . I never ceased to be amazed at the number of definitions that are floating around for this term," wrote one priest in his diocesan newspaper. At times quietly and calmly, at other times with clamor, "renewal" is a term which began to invade the Episcopal Church in the early 1960s. Sometimes it meant one thing to charismatics, another to evangelicals, and perhaps something else to Anglo-Catholics.

The Cursillo movement, the charismatic movement and a number of evangelical organizations displayed a common thread of seeking a spiritual renewal in the Episcopal Church. The character and historical impact of these groups has been quite diverse. While they sometimes produced controversy, they also provided a healing force in the veins of the church's history.

The Charismatic Movement

"I didn't believe in God at all. I was a Yale man. I did it all myself. I sat on the throne of my life. I ran it with my own intellect, and after forty-four years, I had absolutely no peace at all. So now Jesus sits on the throne of my heart. . . . He lives in me."[1]

These words weren't expressed by a television evangelist, but by a communicant from Darien, Connecticut, writing in *The Episcopalian*. Probably no parish in the United States has symbolized the charismatic movement more than St.Paul's Church, Darien, and its rector, the Reverend Everett Fullam. Fullam, with an unfinished doctorate from Harvard University, was a philosophy professor at Barrington College and part-time parish priest at St. Mark's Church in Providence, Rhode Island, until he accepted the call to the Darien parish in 1972. In this wealthy suburb of New

York City, charismatic renewal took hold and the parish flourished. Its growth is partly told in its pledge budget: from $27,000 in 1966, to more than $500,000 in 1976 under Fullam's leadership.

One of Fullam's gifts as a parish priest was teaching, and especially teaching the Bible. His popularity began to spread beyond his church as he was invited to speak at conferences and seminars through the country. The parish subsequently released him to spend as much as 70 percent of his time on these travels to preach, teach, and speak at conferences. Later, he began traveling to such countries as Jordan, Turkey, Greece, England, and several African nations. Presiding Bishop John Allin once said he believed Fullam carried out more preaching missions in a year than anyone in the Episcopal Church.

However, the real "father" of charismatic renewal in the Episcopal Church is the Reverend Dennis Bennett. His influence in the movement began following publicity about his resignation from St. Mark's Episcopal Church in Van Nuys, California, in 1960. The resignation came after a storm of controversy in the parish after he had the baptism in the Holy Spirit and spoke in tongues. One commentator defines the experience this way: "Common to all pentecostals is the one basic belief that 'the baptism in the Holy Spirit' is an experience subsequent to conversion—all believers should have it, and the initial physical evidence of this baptism or in-filling is the speaking of tongues."[2]

Dennis Bennett, who was born in London, England, moved to the United States with his family at the age of ten with his family. After graduation from San Jose State College in 1944, he worked as an electronics salesman for two years before entering the University of Chicago Divinity School. He graduated and was ordained as a Congregational minister in 1949. In 1951, Bennett converted to the Episcopal Church and was ordained in 1952 in the Diocese of Los Angeles.

In 1953, he accepted a call to become rector of St. Mark's Episcopal Church, Van Nuys, a church of about five hundred members. At the time, St. Mark's was recovering from serious financial difficulties and Dennis Bennett proved to be a successful leader. By 1960, St. Mark's membership stood at 2,500, and the rector had three curates on his staff.[3]

Bennett first became interested in the baptism in the Holy Spirit by talking with John and Joan Baker, two Episcopalians from a neighboring parish. In 1960, he prayed that he would receive the Holy Spirit. "I had a puzzled interest," he recalled. "I was impressed with the obvious experience they had had and the way it had changed their lives on a spiritual level."[4]

Following the experience, he began to lead other members of the parish to pray in a similar manner. Several small "prayer and praise" groups were formed. By April 1960, some seventy members of St. Mark's Episcopal Church had reportedly prayed for and received the baptism in the Holy Spirit.[5]

Steadily increasing rumors and strife in the parish led Bennett to explain the experiences he'd had to the congregation at the Palm Sunday sermon in 1960. During the sermon, one of the curates took off his vestments and publicly resigned while walking down the center aisle. Later, the church treasurer demanded Bennett's resignation, and a number of other parish leaders were unhappy with the turn in character of their rector's ministry. Two days later, Bennett resigned. The events were reported in *Time* and *Newsweek,* as well as throughout the church press. In his letter of resignation, he stated:

> I am sorry for the furor, and for the pain that has been caused. I ask every person in St. Mark's whether they be for me or against me, not to leave this parish or cancel their pledge . . .
>
> Any rumors that reach your ears that in any way imply that I am leaving the Episcopal Church are false. . . . What I am standing for is to be found within the Episcopal Church; no one needs to leave the Episcopal Church in order to have the fullness of the Spirit. But it is important that the Spirit be allowed to work freely in the Episcopal Church, and it is to this that I bear witness, and will continue to bear witness.[6]

Dennis Bennett was without a job and found himself branded a "religious fanatic" throughout the Episcopal Church. However, he later visited the Right Reverend William F. Lewis, Bishop of Olympia in Washington state. Bishop Lewis invited him to become vicar of a small mission church near Seattle. Bennett accepted the call and arrived at St. Luke's Episcopal Church on July 1, 1960. A year later, eighty-five of its members had received the baptism in the Holy Spirit. Attendance multiplied and the building could no longer hold all the people. By the mid-1970s, over 2,000 people were attending St. Luke's and Bennett had become an international figure in the charismatic renewal movement. The church eventually gave him the time off to pursue a speaking and writing ministry that led him across the United States and to many foreign countries. Bennett retired from the parish in 1981.

The Church of the Redeemer in Houston, Texas, was another church well known for its involvement in charismatic renewal. The Reverend W. Graham Pulkingham was called to the dying inner city parish in 1963. Pulkingham recalls, "I had gone to Redeemer Church as an average Episcopal minister of the Gospel. I leaned moderately in the direction of liberal theology and had an active social conscience . . ."[7]

After receiving the baptism in the Holy Spirit, the direction and character of Pulkingham's ministry changed. He began to teach about the spiritual gifts, yet he also sought to build a spiritual community with a social impact in the inner city. By 1968, he described the church as an "entirely renewed and reformed Church of the Redeemer: charismatic in ministry, corporate in life and leadership, sacrificial in loving service, and eucharistic to its core."

By 1971, parish enrollment had risen to 1,400, with an average weekly attendance of 2,200. At that time, pledging to meet the church budget was discontinued (it was no longer necessary). As an experiment, Pulkingham and thirty members of the parish established a residential community in the inner city near the church. He described the community in this way:

For six months thirty-one people all but lived together . . . All day Saturday, and Sunday after church, were spent together in the member's homes. Although nothing formal was put forward and no convenants were signed, each family let me know that everything they had or could command was at the disposal of the ministry—savings, insurance, earnings, possessions, borrowing power, themselves; we relinquished everything in a literal way. It was made available to help the needy.[8]

The "experiment" worked as the parish continued its residential community and inner city ministry into the 1980s, well after Pulkingham's departure. The success of Pulkingham's ministry in Houston during the 1960s and early 1970s took him to Scotland in 1974 where he spent several years developing the work of charismatic renewal communities there. He returned to the United States in 1980 and in 1982 became rector of a parish in the Diocese of Colorado.

Although these examples represent the best known parishes and leaders, charismatic renewal was taking place throughout the Episcopal Church, beginning in the 1960s and continuing through the 1980s. Almost every diocese and major city had at least one parish described as "charismatic" or "renewed." As early as 1960, *The Living Church* published an editorial, which read in part: "Speaking in tongues is taking place within the Episcopal Church today. It is no longer a phenomenon of some odd sect across the street—it is in our midst, and it is being practiced by clergy and laity who have stature and good reputation within the church."[9]

With growing attention given to charismatic renewal, the House of Bishops issued a statement in 1962 that said nothing startling, except to make two "observations." First, the bishops affirmed that "new movements have, in history, enriched the body of Christ. We observe further that we are a church, not a sect, and that our spiritual home is, and should be, spacious."

Having said that, however, the bishops warned that "the danger of all new movements is self-righteousness, divisiveness, one-sidedness, and exaggeration. We call, therefore, upon all new movements to remain in the full, rich, balanced life of the historic church, and thereby protect themselves against these dangers . . ."[10]

In February of 1973, 300 Episcopal clergy who were active in charismatic renewal gathered for a conference at St. Matthew's Cathedral in Dallas, Texas. Organized by Dennis Bennett and the Reverend Ted Nelson, the conference led to the formation of the Episcopal Charismatic Fellowship. The Reverend Bob Hawn became the first executive secretary. In 1980, the name of the organization was changed to Episcopal Renewal Ministries.

In announcing the name change, Terry Fullam, who was president of the Board, commented in one of its newsletters:

Gradually . . . the word 'charismatic' has been used and abused to the point where it has become a stumbling block to many and enlightening to very few . . . The word 'fellowship' also presented us with some difficulties. From the very beginning we had decided that we were not to be a group seeking members and establishing chapters throughout the church, but providing assistance whenever and wherever we could.

While the charismatic movement was often associated with "speaking in tongues," the organization tried to promote all of the spiritual gifts, especially healing and teaching, through its resources. Its primary work has been sponsoring workshops and weekend "parish renewal conferences," as well as distributing cassette tapes and reading matter.

While several bishops were publicly sympathetic with the charismatic movement, Bishop William Frey of Colorado became the best known leader among the bishops. At the first National Episcopal Charismatic Conference held in 1973 in Dallas, he said, "Thank God we're losing our stiffness and dignity . . . Charismatics have crawled out from the rocks where they can see each other in the clear light of day." Bishop Frey predicted that the church would be shaken up by the charismatic movement. ". . . But there is no indication God is about to form a new church. He is strengthening what he has already got," said Frey.[11]

The Cursillo Movement

"In an age when 'renewal' has become a watchword in the church generally, the Cursillo movement in the Episcopal Church remains a proven instrument of the Holy Spirit for bringing about a strengthened faith and witness," reads a publication of the National Episcopal Cursillo organization.[12] By the end of 1984, the Cursillo movement was functioning in ninety-five of the ninety-seven dioceses of the Episcopal Church. Thousands of Episcopalians had participated in the three-day Cursillo weekends and come away with a stronger understanding of their Christian faith.

The Cursillo movement focuses on three-day weekends where participants hear fifteen talks from clergy and lay leaders on basic themes of the Christian faith. Derived from the Spanish word meaning "short course," the Cursillo weekends are intended to be a "short course in Christianity." The tightly structured weekends are highlighted by colorful festivities, music, and Spanish-flavored activities. After the weekends, the "Cursillistas" (Cursillo alumni) are asked to participate in the "Fourth Day"—which means the continuing activities of the movement centered around prayer and fellowship groups.

The Cursillo movement came into the Episcopal Church from the Roman Catholic church, which inherited it from Spain. In Francisco Franco's repressive Spain in the 1940s, the lay organization, Catholic Action, was searching for a way to make the Gospel a significant force in Spanish society. The church hierarchy had been co-opted by the government through a series of treaties and concordances. In Majorca, Catholic Action developed the idea of the "penetration of environments" by nuclei of dedicated Christians who, by their work and witness, would change the character of their workplaces and communities.

"The men of Catholic Action began meeting weekly in small groups to pray together, to encourage each other, and to plan for the future. As the movement grew, *Catholic Action* began holding three-day training sessions in what is fundamental to being a Christian, and how to live it out in the daily environment. Those weekends were called *Cursillos de Christiandad*— short courses in Christian living."[13]

Some Episcopalians who participated in Catholic Cursillos during the 1960s decided to bring it into the Episcopal Church. As a result, the first Episcopal Cursillo weekend was held in the Diocese of Iowa in 1970. The Diocese of West Texas began holding Cursillo weekends shortly after that. By 1974, a number of dioceses were holding Cursillo weekends. The National Episcopal Cursillo Information Center was formed to provide information and assistance to the growing movement. The first national gathering for Cursillo participants was held in Dallas in September of 1975. In 1979, by-laws were adopted for the formation of the National Episcopal Cursillo (NEC) as a national coordinating body.

Once it was clear that other denominations were interested in the Cursillo movement, the Roman Catholic Cursillo Secretariat began to closely guard the use of the word "Cursillo." The United Methodist church had developed a similar weekend activity that was initially called "Cursillo." But because its format and structure did not follow the Roman Catholic guidelines, the Methodists were prohibited from calling it a "Cursillo weekend." In early 1980, the Roman Catholic Secretariat and National Episcopal Cursillo adopted their first formal agreement. The agreement granted the National Episcopal Cursillo full use of Cursillo materials and the "Cursillo" name. It also established guidelines through which Cursillo could be initiated in churches in the Anglican Communion outside of the United States. Under this agreement, American Cursillo leaders later helped establish Cursillo weekends in England, Wales, Germany, Brazil, and the Bahamas.

PEWSACTION

Prayer, Evangelism, Witness, Study, and Action—this common thrust of ten organizations in the Episcopal Church led them to form a coalition of groups. To witness their common ministries, three fellowships—the Anglican Fellowship of Prayer, the Brotherhood of St. Andrew and the Order of the Daughters of the King—shared a booth at the 1970 General Convention in Houston. The booth was such a success that the leaders met the next year to discuss expanding the coalition and inviting other groups with similar aims to join them.

In 1972, at the invitation of Mrs. Samuel Shoemaker, executive director of the Anglican Fellowship of Prayer, leaders of nine groups met in Pittsburgh, Pennsylvania, to form the coalition to be called PEWSACTION. Mrs. Shoemaker was elected chairwoman, and the Reverend Robert B. Hall, director of the Episcopal Center for Evangelism, was elected vice chairman. By the 1973 General Convention, ten groups had joined.

The original PEWSACTION groups included the Anglican Fellowship of Prayer, Bible Reading Fellowship, Brotherhood of St. Andrew, Conference on the Religious Life, Episcopal Center for Evangelism, Faith Alive, Fellowship of Witness, Fish, The Fisherman, Inc., and the Order of the Daughters of the King.

"Unity without conformity" became the common theme for *PEWSACTION.* The coalition took no position on the ordination of women, Prayer Book revision, or any of the other divisive issues confronting the Episcopal Church at this time. The Right Reverend Allen W. Brown, Bishop of Albany, commented, "PEWSACTION membership repeatedly has resisted pressures to 'take sides' on issues which must be faced by the church. PEWSACTION believes that the real issue is in the area of conscious relationship to Jesus Christ."[14]

PEWSACTION functioned informally until by-laws were adopted in 1979. By 1984, twenty-two organizations were PEWSACTION members. In addition to those mentioned, others that joined were: The Church Army, A Christian Ministry Among Jewish People (CMJ/USA), Church Periodical Club, Episcopal Church Missionary Community, Episcopal Engaged Encounter, Episcopal Marriage Encounter, Episcopal Radio-TV Foundation, Episcopal World Mission, Inc., Evangelical Education Society, Fine Arts Contemporary Evangelism, Happening, MORE (Mission for Outreach, Renewal and Evangelism), National Episcopal Cursillo, National Institute of Christian Leadership, and the South American Missionary Society of the Episcopal Church. Three original groups had dropped membership: Fish, The Fisherman, Inc., and the Conference on the Religious Life.

The first National Episcopal Conference on Renewal was coordinated by PEWSACTION and held at St. Philip's Cathedral in Atlanta, Georgia, in 1974. The Reverend Robert Hall, conference coordinator, pointed out that the meeting brought together leaders from all the renewal movements in the church—charismatics, evangelists, and theologians of many persuasions. One of the aims of the conference, according to Hall, was to "make it plain to those who think their brand of renewal is the answer, that God is not limited to one channel."[15] More than 1,200 Episcopalians from forty-one states and four countries attended.

Some *PEWSACTION* Members

One of the oldest organizations devoted to renewal and evangelism is the Brotherhood of St. Andrew. It was founded in 1883 in a basement meeting room of what is now St. James' Cathedral in Chicago. According to tradition, the brotherhood began as a prayer and Bible study group of twelve men at St. James Episcopal Church. James L. Houghteling, a banker, was the group's leader. The church's rector, the Reverend W. H. Vibbert, asked Houghteling to have his group work with an alcoholic who had appealed to him for help. Later, Houghteling suggested the group take the name of

St. Andrew because—like St. Andrew—they were trying to reach out to their brothers to bring them to Christ. The group then took the name of the Brotherhood of St. Andrew. Their ministry initially focused on men living in rooming houses and hotels near the church.

There are now more than 450 chapters at Episcopal churches throughout the country. The brotherhood follows the rules of prayer, study, service, and focuses on evangelism. In the early 1970s, the brotherhood began to allow women to join as associate members. The brotherhood provides study courses for all members, training courses for chapter leaders, a national book library on evangelism, and publishes a national newspaper, *St. Andrew's Cross.*[16]

As the only worldwide prayer organization in the Anglican Communion, the Anglican Fellowship of Prayer (AFP) "seeks to answer that call to prayer by increasing and strengthening the companionship of prayer throughout the world," states an official description of its purpose. The Anglican Fellowship of Prayer became an official body in 1958 under the leadership of Bishop Austin Pardue of Pittsburgh and Mrs. Helen Shoemaker. It grew out of interest in prayer groups and annual conferences on prayer that had been held at Calvary Church in Pittsburgh during the 1950s under the leadership of its rector, the Reverend Samuel Shoemaker.

From that beginning, the Anglican Fellowship of Prayer grew into the only worldwide prayer organization in the Anglican Communion. It now has diocesan representatives in almost every American diocese and in many places around the world. The AFP encourages prayer life through books, pamphlets, a monthly newsletter, and an annual conference. Through its diocesan representatives, it also helps parishes to start prayer groups and sponsors parish schools of prayer, retreats and "quiet days."

The Fellowship of Witness is the American affiliate of the worldwide Evangelical Fellowship in the Anglican Communion (EFAC). Formed in 1961, EFAC seeks to encourage evangelical Anglicans throughout the world through literature, conferences, and prayer support. The fellowship's major purpose "is to encourage and help evangelical Episcopalians," wrote the Reverend Peter R. Rodgers, one of its members. He stated that:

The Fellowship of Witness is also concerned to bear witness to the Gospel. We seek to see the scripture restored to its rightful place in the life of the church, as the final court to appeal in matters of belief and practice . . .[17]

Beyond its annual conferences and its magazine, *Kerygma,* the most noted accomplishment of the Fellowship of Witness was establishing the Trinity Episcopal School for Ministry in Ambridge, Pennsylvania (see chapter 8).

The Daughters of the King, a lay organization for women, has more than 8,000 members in 600 parish chapters throughout the United States. Established in 1885, the order provides a framework of fellowship to assist women in maintaining a regular discipline for daily prayer and service. In dioceses where there are three or more chapters, diocesan assemblies have been established. Chapters and assemblies also send delegates to a national convention which meets every three years just prior to the General Convention.

Daughters of the King find many avenues for service by following their motto: "I am but one, but I am one. I cannot do everything, but I can do something. What I can do, I ought to do. What I ought to do, by the grace of God, I will do. Lord, what wilt thou have me do?"

Faith Alive weekends were first organized in 1970 to stimulate renewal and evangelism at the parish level. Fred Gore, a Delaware layman, and a group of men from the Brotherhood of St. Andrew, adapted the weekend format from a Methodist program called Lay Witness Mission. In a parish Faith Alive weekend, a group of lay people from other parishes in the diocese, as well as neighboring states, come and give personal testimonies of their faith. The visiting Episcopalians also lead small groups to stimulate discusssion about parish renewal.

The Right Reverend Maurice Benitez, Bishop of Texas, commented, "For myself, the single most exciting . . . event of my twenty-five years as a priest was a Faith Alive Weekend at Christ Church in San Antonio. That weekend rejuvenated that parish for the Lord, and it had a powerful effect on both my ministry and on my life. I saw the tremendous, incalculable power of lay witness." By 1980, more than 1,200 weekends had been held in Episcopal churches in all parts of the country.

The Bible Reading Fellowship exists to "encourage the systematic and intelligent reading of the Bible, to emphasize its scriptural message and to take advantage of new light shed on Holy Scripture." Harry C. Griffith, a Florida attorney, started the Fellowship in 1971, patterning it after the Bible Reading Fellowship in England, which was founded in 1922. The fellowship publishes booklets of notes and study aids—written by Anglican scholars—three times yearly to assist Episcopalians in the study of Scripture.

"It is necessary to bring people to a personal knowledge of Jesus Christ before doing many of the things that the church does," said the Very Reverend Robert B. Hall shortly before he founded the Episcopal Center for Evangelism in Live Oak, Florida. Hall, the former dean of St. Paul's Cathedral in Oklahoma City, Oklahoma, retired to the northern Florida town to direct the center. Although independent of the national church, Hall has maintained close ties with church leaders in his work. The center's primary purpose has been to promote interest in evangelism in the Episcopal Church, and to develop and distribute materials on evangelism to parishes and individuals. In 1972, Hall organized the First National Episcopal Conference on Evangelism. Held at Grace-St. Luke's Church in Memphis, Tennessee, more than 500 people participated, including representatives of almost every PEWSACTION member.

No mention of "renewal" in the Episcopal Church would be complete without some mention of the religious orders. While less visible than the evangelical organizations, the prayers and service of thousands of men and women of these orders shape the Episcopal Church in numerous unseen ways.

"For a religious community, the word 'renewal' has a particular and special meaning" wrote the Reverend Clark W. Trafton of the Order of the Holy Cross in an article for *New Life.* While in some ways it means the same as it does to all Christians, "for a monastic order, renewal also means being recalled to the vision of the founder of the community," he wrote.[18]

There is a great deal of variety among the religious orders of the Episcopal Church. Some maintain a residential community of brothers or sisters, similar to traditional Anglican and Roman Catholic orders. Others require a "Rule of Life" or discipline of prayer, study, and service for members who may be geographically scattered, and married or single. Each community maintains a particular "ethos" and focus, patterned after the vision of its founder.

In 1948, leaders from three men's communities met to consider the feasibility of forming an association of religious orders. A constitution was written, and in November of 1949, the Conference on the Religious Life was officially established, comprised of nineteen communities of the Episcopal Church in the United States. Since that time, new communities have joined, while others have ceased to exist.[19]

Since 1912, a canon had existed for religious communities. However, few orders had sought the "official recognition of the church" under the provisions of the canon. The old canon required strict supervision of a religious order by its local bishop, while members of the religious communities often felt a greater loyalty to their superiors.

In 1976, the revised canon for religious communities was accepted at the Minneapolis convention. Largely written by members of the Conference on the Religious Life, the new canon required supervision by a "bishop visitor," but he did not have to be the bishop of the diocese in which the community was located. The community could choose a bishop for that position. In the year that followed, ten communities sought and obtained official recognition under the canon. At the 1982 General Convention, another revision to the canon was passed which recognized those religious communities which were not "specifically monastic" in character; that is, communities which did not require their members to be celibate nor live within the confines of a geographical community.

In the late 1970s, the Conference on the Religious Life became active in ecumenical dialogue with Roman Catholic, Protestant and Orthodox religious communities. These talks led to the founding of the Permanent International Ecumenical Consultation for Religious Communities. The aim of the consultation is to explore ways in which the religious life can contribute to the ecumenism of the church. Every three years, it issues a paper on the results of the three year talks.

One main focus of the conference has been educational. It has sought to provide the church with information about the religious life, to encourage its growth, and to foster an understanding between the communities and the church at large. "Today members of the Conference on the Religious Life . . . sees as its purposes to coordinate the interest and experience of its members, provide opportunities for mutual support and sharing and to present to the church a coherent understanding of the religious life,"[20] wrote Father Andrew Rank, chairman of the Conference on the Religious Life.

The life of the Spirit continues to work in the Episcopal Church with all of its many expressions. Only within the Anglican tradition could such diverse ministries as those found at St. Paul's in Darien, or the quiet, sustained work of the religious orders co-exist in unity. The whole church is, indeed, greater than the sum of its parts.

11

Ecumenical Relations:
An Era of Progress

"IT HAS BEEN GRANTED TO THE AMERICANS less than any other nation of the earth to realize . . . the visible unity of the church of God." Writing in an article in 1939, Dietrich Bonhoeffer made this penetrating observation after his trip to the United States that year.

Bonhoeffer was—and still is—correct. The 1985 *Yearbook of American and Canadian Churches* listed over 220 separate Christian denominations in the United States. While this is far from the Gospel mandate "that they all may be one . . . that the world may believe" (John 17:21, RSV), there have been some enormous strides in Christian unity since 1939.

Ecumenical relations in the twentieth century is a broad and complex subject. The nature of ecumenical relations itself requires that the Episcopal Church be considered in relation to other denominations. This chapter looks at the developments that have made this the most progressive century in ecumenical relations since the Reformation, and, of necessity, includes a summary of major ecumenical developments among other denominations. What follows is a discussion of major unity attempts in the twentieth century, and the three major ecumenical organizations in which the Episcopal Church has participated: the World Council of Churches, the National Council of Churches, and the Consultation on Church Union. All three of these organizations have developed since World War II.

Chapter 12 will summarize the Episcopal Church's dialogues with churches of other denominations, especially Roman Catholics, Lutherans, and Orthodox churches, and the results of these dialogues. It will also explain the developments, policies, and "infrastructure" of the Episcopal Church which have enabled its response to the modern ecumenical movement.

The most complete source of information on Episcopal Church ecumenical relations since 1950 is *A Communion of Communions: One Eucharistic Fellowship,* edited by J. Robert Wright and published by Seabury Press in 1979. This book contains the results of the three years of ecumenical study

131

mandated by the 1976 General Convention. The study culminated in the 1979 "Detroit Consultation." With its many primary documents and contributors, the book is an invaluable reference source for scholars and historians of the Episcopal Church.

For a century, the search for unity in the Episcopal Church has been guided by criteria set forth in the "Chicago-Lambeth Quadrilateral of 1886, 1888" (see *The Book of Common Prayer,* page 876). Meeting in Chicago in 1886, the Episcopal bishops approved the four principles contained in the Quadrilateral as "the principles we believe to be the substantial deposit of Christian Faith and Order committed by Christ and his Apostles to the Church . . . and therefore incapable of compromise or surrender." They also declared the principles as "essential to the restoration of unity among the divided branches of Christendom."

These four principles, adopted by the American bishops in 1886, are:

1. The Holy Scriptures of the Old and New Testament as the revealed Word of God.

2. The Nicene Creed as the sufficient statement of the Christian faith.

3. The two sacraments,—Baptism and the Supper of the Lord,—ministered with unfailing use of Christ's words of institution and of the elements ordained by him.

4. The Historic Episcopate, locally adapted in the methods of its administration, to the varying needs of the nations and peoples called of God into the unity of his church.

Two years later, 145 bishops assembled in England for the Third Lambeth Conference in July, 1888. Before the sessions ended, all the bishops voted for a declaration nearly identical with that set forth at Chicago. The first and second points were slightly amended to read:

"1. The Holy Scriptures of the Old and New Testaments, as 'containing all things necessary to salvation,' and as being the rule and ultimate standard of faith;

2. The Apostles' Creed as the Baptismal Symbol; and the Nicene Creed, as the sufficient statement of the Christian faith."

The Chicago-Lambeth Quadrilateral has been interpreted differently from time to time, especially as to the meaning of the fourth point, but it still expresses the official position of the Episcopal Church in ecumenical dialogues with Protestant bodies.

Developments Among Other Denominations

An old Haggadic tale tells this legend: "I was walking in the mist at evening, when suddenly I saw a monster looming in the mist. As the apparition drew closer, I saw that he was a human being; and when we came face to face, I saw that he was my brother."

Ecumenical progress in the twentieth century enabled a number of Christian churches to discover they were, indeed, brothers and sisters. In the years following Bonhoeffer's visit, several churches within denominational families merged. In 1939, the Methodist church grew out of a merger between the Methodist Episcopal church, the Methodist Episcopal church, South, and the Methodist Protestant church. Subsequently in 1968, the United Methodist church formed through a merger of the Methodist church and the Evangelical United Brethern.

The United Presbyterian Church in the U.S.A. (Northern branch) developed in 1956 through a merger of the United Presbyterian Church of North America and the Presbyterian Church in the United States. It subsequently reunited with the Presbyterian Church, United States (Southern branch) in 1983 to form the Presbyterian Church (U.S.A.).

The United Church of Christ was created in 1957 through a merger of the Congregational Christian church and the Evangelical and Reformed churches. The American Lutheran church originated in 1960 through a merger of the American Lutheran church, the Evangelical Lutheran church and the United Evangelical Lutheran church. The Lutheran Church in America was formed in 1962 through a merger of four bodies: The United Lutheran Church in America, Augustana Lutheran church, American Evangelical Lutheran church, and the Finnish Lutheran church.

Lutherans continued their quest for unity with their historic decision in 1982 to unite the American Lutheran church, the Lutheran Church in America, and the Association of Evangelical Lutheran Churches. Eventual union for these three Lutheran bodies is planned in 1988.

While the modern ecumenical era brought these closely-related churches into formal unity, the mood among all Christians was generally one of warmth, charity, and cooperation. Henry Knox Sherrill, presiding bishop of the Episcopal Church from 1946 to 1958, wrote in his autobiography:

> It is safe to assert that not since the Reformation has there been such wholehearted cooperation between churches as there is today. It is spotty, at times shallow and sentimental, but nevertheless, it is also deep, real, and often goes much deeper than organizational matters.[1]

The ecumenical movement is a child of the twentieth century, developing as an outgrowth of missionary work carried out early in the century. Missionaries were the first to call attention to the absurdity and inefficiency of Christian division, not to mention its unfaithfulness to the Gospel. They saw first-hand the confusion of native converts who observed the "Presbyterian Christians," "Methodist Christians" and many more, all claiming to believe in the same God and the same Christian faith. At a practical level, missionaries realized it was easier for two denominations to sponsor one school than it was for each to try to maintain separate facilities in the same town or city.

Episcopal Bishop Charles Henry Brent was one of those early missionary leaders and the first great Episcopal ecumenical leader of the twentieth century. As first Missionary Bishop of the Philippine Islands (1901-1918), Bishop Brent developed his work in areas untouched by the Roman Catholic church—among the Igorots of the Mountain Province of Luzon and the

Tirurays of the southern islands. It was Bishop Brent who laid the foundations for the present work of the Episcopal Church in the Philippines. He was elected Bishop of Western New York and served there from 1918 to 1929.

At a worldwide missionary conference in Edinburgh in 1910, Bishop Brent conceived the idea that unity might burgeon with more inter-church understanding. He urged the 1910 General Convention to convene a World Conference on Faith and Order. As a consequence of his initiative, the convention appointed a Joint Commission "to bring about a conference for the consideration of questions touching Faith and Order" and invite "All Christian communions throughout the world which confess our Lord Jesus Christ as God and Savior to unite with us in arranging for and conducting such a conference." This historic meeting was held in Lausanne, Switzerland, in 1927. At the conference, Bishop Brent shared his vision:

> In our hearts most of us are devoted to the cult of the incomplete—sectarianism. The Christ in one church often categorically denies the Christ in a neighboring church. It would be ludicrous were it not tragic . . . Let us keep the purpose of unity firm in our hearts, and look upon all Christians as brothers beloved. It is thus by practicing unity that we shall gain unity."[2]

In addition to a series of "Faith and Order" conferences inspired by Bishop Brent, the 1910 Edinburgh Conference inspired two other currents of cooperation. One was the International Missionary Council, which encouraged cooperation among Protestant missionaries. The other, known as "Life and Work," brought Protestant and Orthodox leaders together to see what they could do about social, economic and political problems. It was led by Sweden's Archbishop Nathan Soderblom. The "Faith and Order" and "Life and Work" efforts eventually moved together, resulting in the formation of the World Council of Churches in 1948.

Efforts Toward Unity

Prior to 1960, there were three attempts to unite American churches. In 1918, representatives from nineteen Protestant communions met at Philadelphia and authorized the Philadelphia Plan of Union. The Philadelphia Plan intended to bring the churches into a federation, which would be the first step toward full corporate union. The plan failed in 1920 when the Presbyterian Church in the U.S.A.—which, incidentally, had initiated the movement—also rejected it.

Methodist evangelist Dr. E. Stanley Jones conceived of another plan in the 1930s while he was a missionary in India. Dr. Jones' plan for a "union with a federal structure" was modeled after the American federal system. His goal was "The United Church in America," a centralized organization from which the various denominations would maintain their identity as branches. The Reverend Paul A. Crow, Jr. comments on the book, *Church*

Union at Midpoint, "This plan benefited from the charismatic leadership of Jones, but never claimed a place on the official agenda of churches."[3]

A more ambitious attempt developed in the late 1940s when the Federal Council of Churches convened a plenary of its members to explore the possibility of union. The Conference on Church Union, with nine participating churches, convened at Greenwich, Connecticut, in 1949 and created high hopes and expectations for reaching a consensus. In 1951, the conference released a document called "A Plan for a United Church in the United States," popularly called the "Greenwich Plan." Its primary author was Charles Clayton Morrison, Disciples theologian and editor of *The Christian Century.*

The Conference on Church Union eventually terminated in 1958. The Presbyterian Church in the United States had withdrawn in 1953. Two of the plan's participating churches, the Congregational Christian church and the Evangelical and Reformed churches, united to form the United Church of Christ in 1957. Among other factors, these two decisions slowed its momentum to a halt.

The World Council of Churches

The World Council of Churches (WCC) was organized at an assembly which convened in Amsterdam, Holland from August 22 through September 4, 1948. Plans for the organization had begun years earlier, but its creation was delayed by World War II. The Episcopal Church endorsed the proposal for a World Council of Churches at its 1937 General Convention. The principal actors at Amsterdam were the official delegates: 352 of them representing 135 churches from forty-two countries. The World Council itself never intended to unite churches into an homogenous whole; its purpose rather was to call the churches to work for unity and encourage cooperation in various program efforts. Essentially, the World Council sought for Christianity what the United Nations gave to the political world.

The founding assembly in Amsterdam was the first time in history that representatives of major Protestant and Orthodox bodies throughout the world had gathered. As one magazine editorial later stated:

> The great achievement of Amsterdam was not what it said but what it did. For the first time since the Reformation, there is now a continuing body which can speak to the world on behalf of non-Roman Christianity.[4]

The Reverend Willem Adolf Visser't Hooft, an ordained minister of the Netherlands Reformed church, was a pivotal figure in the World Council's development. He became WCC's first secretary general in 1948 and guided it through its first, second, and third assemblies at Amsterdam, Evanston, Illinois (1954) and New Delhi, India (1966), until his retirement that year. Under his leadership, the World Council grew from 147 denominations in forty countries to nearly 300 denominations in ninety countries.

Despite criticism, Visser't Hooft insisted that churches in Communist countries be included. He enlarged the role of African and Asian churches, as well as that of Orthodox churches, and sought to include Roman Catholics as members. This latter goal was, unfortunately, one that was never fulfilled. Dr. Visser't Hooft died in 1985 at the age of eighty four.

In 1984, the Reverend Emilio Castro, a Methodist pastor from Uruguay, was named to succeed Dr. Philip Potter who retired after twelve years of service as general secretary of the council. Castro, who was fluent in six languages and author of six books, was also regarded as a "fiery evangelical" by some. The personable South American brought a more moderate bent to the WCC, which was often viewed with suspicion by political and religious conservatives.

Since its 1948 assembly, the World Council has held assemblies every seven years: in Evanston, Illinois (1954); New Delhi (1961); Uppsala, Sweden (1968); Nairobi, Kenya (1975); and Vancouver, British Columbia (1975). As of 1985, 305 member churches representing some 400 million Christians are members of the fellowship. Nearly every tradition is represented, including the churches in Communist nations, developing nations, Western nations, and a growing number of independent churches in Asia, Africa, and Latin America.

The National Council of the Churches of Christ

The National Council of the Churches of Christ (NCCC) was organized in 1950 at a meeting held in Cleveland, Ohio. The Episcopal Church voted to join the proposed organization at its 1946 General Convention. The National Council developed from a merger between twelve ecumenical program agencies.[5] While it resembled its predecessor, the Federal Council of Churches (formed in 1908), its purpose was to combine the program functions of the uniting organizations under one roof. Home and foreign missions, religious education, higher education, stewardship, hunger relief, theological education and communications were among the concerns of these uniting groups.

The Constituting Convention of the NCCC was held in Cleveland, Ohio, from November 28 to December 1, 1950. President Harry S Truman sent a message to the convention which said:

> I extend heartiest congratulations to the National Council of the Churches of Christ in the U.S.A. as it begins its task of drawing together twenty-nine great communions into united action on a still greater scale than in the past. I have followed with a warm appreciation the work which has been done in recent years by the interdenominational agencies which now combine their forces into a new council . . .

The Right Reverend Henry Knox Sherrill, Presiding Bishop of the Episcopal Church, was elected the first president of NCCC. Bishop Sherrill served as president of the National Council from 1950 to 1952, and was elected one of the presidents of the World Council of Churches in 1954. Another

Episcopalian, Dr. Cynthia Wedel, served as NCCC president from 1969 to 1972, as well as one of the six presidents of the World Council of Churches from 1975 to 1983.

In later years, both the National Council of Churches and World Council of Churches came under criticism at various levels of church life. Some popular media critics sought to link the ecumenical bodies to Communist political groups, charges which were never verified. Controversy around a 1978 grant to the Patriotic Front of Zimbabwe by the World Council of Churches taken from special funds in its Program to Combat Racism spotlighted unusual and perhaps unbalanced attention on the WCC.

In 1979, the Executive Council responded affirmatively to the Lambeth Conference request that all churches, "reaffirm their support and strengthen their understanding of (WCC), which is not only the most comprehensive expression of the ecumenical movement, but also the chief vehicle of world-wide ecumenical cooperation and service."

Consultation on Church Union

"I first heard of the consultation aboard a 707 jet flying over the Rocky Mountains to San Francisco. The date was December 2, 1960 and the consultation was still in the womb of time, to be cast screaming into life two days later. Seated next to me was a Presbyterian minister who told me of the proposal which Eugene Carson Blake was planning to make in a sermon at Grace Cathedral that Sunday . . ."[6]

These were the words of George A. Beazley, Jr., chief executive for the Council on Christian Unity of the Christian Church (Disciples of Christ). Eugene Carson Blake's sermon at Grace (Episcopal) Cathedral in San Francisco indeed made history. Blake was the stated clerk (chief executive officer) of the United Presbyterian church. His "Proposal Toward the Reunion of Christ's Church" proved to be an epochal event: It came just after Pope John XXIII's call of the Second Vatican Council in 1959, but before its actual opening in 1962. Blake also timed the sermon for the same day the National Council of Churches convened a San Francisco meeting. The congregation he preached to included a number of distinguished religious leaders.

Blake's sermon read, in part:

Led, I pray by the Holy Spirit, I propose to the Protestant Episcopal church that it together with the United Presbyterian church invite the Methodist church and the United Church of Christ to form with us a plan of church union both catholic and reformed on the basis of the principles I shall later in this sermon suggest.[7]

Eugene Carson Blake was a towering ecumenical figure of the era. He was the stated clerk of the Presbyterian Church in the U.S.A. from 1951 to 1966; president of the National Council of Churches from 1954 to 1957, and general secretary of the World Council of Churches from 1966 to 1972.

Following his sermon, churches responded positively and the first exploratory plenary of the Consultation on Church Union (COCU) was held in Washington, D.C. in April, 1962. COCU's charter called for "a united church, truly catholic, truly reformed, and truly evangelical." A dozen plenaries and twice as many years later, the road for COCU has been a rocky one.

One of COCU's problems is that it has never captured the imagination of the average layperson, a continuing problem of all ecumenical structures. Bishop Francis Bloy of the Diocese of Los Angeles said in his 1961 convention address that the ecumenical movement, "is a top level movement; it has not caught the imagination or interest of the vast majority of Christian people living at the grass roots."

"A Plan of Union for the Church of Christ Uniting," issued after the ninth plenary held in St. Louis, failed to gain acceptance by the member churches. At the 1970 General Convention in Houston, the deputies passed a resolution authorizing the Joint Commission on Ecumenical Relations to continue studying the COCU plan, but added the phrase that such study "does not imply approval of the plan in its present form." While the resolution authorized the commission to commend the plan to Episcopalians for study at all levels of church life, it forbid the Standing Commission to "negotiate the entry of this church into such a plan of union."

A summary statement of the Episcopal Church's position on COCU made by the 1979 Detroit Consultation stated:

> After the publication of the 1970 plan of the consultation, the member churches in their study process made it clear that they did not accept the structure proposed in that plan. It appeared to envisage the loss of treasures and traditions, and to allow absorption into a monolithic structure, neither of which would be acceptable to the Episcopal Church.[8]

In a 1973 interview, the church's ecumenical officer, Dr. Peter Day, said that COCU's Plan of Union was a "casualty of the concept of church government as being the arena in which answers to unity questions are found . . . We have found that the idea of governmental union is not for these times in this country. Here and now it is not the likely way of increasing unity among American Christians."[9]

On the other hand, the Reverend William B. Lawson, a member of the Standing Commission on Ecumenical Relations describes the Episcopal Church's involvement in COCU as important:

> . . . it is the only place in which we maintain an ongoing dialogue with black churches. Also given the grouping of churches involved, our input and participation brings the essential catholic view and tradition to bear on whatever the final results might be.[10]

By 1984, another phase of COCU began, although history is yet to reveal its significance. Delegates from the nine member denominations approved a 28,000 word theology statement and referred it to the member denominations for study and consideration. The theology statement, under development for twenty years, was intended to represent a basis for "covenanting" between the member churches.[11]

The Changing Mood

Charles Austin wrote in the *New York Times* in 1981, "During the 1960s and 1970s, Christians had their Camelot—a vision of a united church, its theological differences reconciled and proclaiming the one gospel of Jesus Christ . . ." The initial hope of ecumenical leaders was for organic unity among all Christian churches, but the focus began to change during the 1970s. The emphasis shifted from "superstructures" to cooperation and sharing at the grassroots level.

At the grassroots level, joint activities developed among numerous congregations, dioceses, and other judicatories. This activity expressed the "Lund Principle," which also shaped the Episcopal Church's ecumenical policy. At the 1976 General Convention, the Lund Principle, first stated by the World Conference on Faith and Order at Lund, Sweden, in 1952, was reaffirmed.

In essence, the Lund Principle calls on Christian churches "to do together everything which conscience does not compel us to do separately." The reaffirmation of the Lund Principle resolved that "The Episcopal Church at every level of its life be urged to act together and in concert with other churches of Jesus Christ in all matters, except those in which deep differences of conviction or church order compel us to act separately."[12]

This shifting emphasis in the ecumenical mood encouraged the recognition—rather than compromise—of differences. William Lawson, a leading ecumenist in the Episcopal Church, writes:

> In the past we too often have tried to equate unity and uniformity. Today we are affirming that the church is not an association of like-minded people . . . We are affirming that unity is best discovered and is more meaningful when it builds on the strength and richness of who we are rather than on compromises . . .[13]

Few today expect the Episcopal Church to reach organic union with any of the churches with whom it holds conversations. The changing mood, however, has made the ecumenical dialogues even more important. A more realistic goal for Christian churches today is intercommunion and the sharing of the eucharistic table. Presiding Bishop John Allin stated the point well in a 1978 interview:

> . . . ecumenism is not now considered to be a matter of trying to create one great uniform church, but rather is a way of trying to bring the richness of our various traditions into unity so that we may come to recognize one ministry and share the sacraments together . . . I think we are just beginning to discover that . . ."[14]

12

The Ecumenical Dialogues

SINCE 1960, THE MOST VISIBLE ecumenical activity of the Episcopal Church has been its officially-sponsored dialogues with Roman Catholics, the Orthodox churches, and Lutherans. Conversations with other Protestant churches have occurred through the Consultation on Church Union (COCU). Furthermore, the concordat agreements brought the church into conversations with churches throughout the world.

To facilitate these dialogues, the 1967 General Convention established an ecumenical policy for the Episcopal Church:

> Our ecumenical policy is to press toward the visible unity of the whole Christian fellowship in the faith and truth of Jesus Christ, developing and sharing in its various dialogues and consultations in such a way that the goal be neither obscured nor compromised and that each separate activity be a step toward the fullness of unity for which our Savior prayed.[1]

This policy expressed the consensus and momentum that had been building in ecumenical relations since 1950 and the establishment of the World Council and National Council of Churches.

Prior to the modern era, the Episcopal Church engaged itself for nine years in merger talks with the Presbyterian church. The 1937 General Convention passed a resolution inviting the Presbyterian Church, U.S.A., to join the Episcopal Church in unity talks:

> The two churches, one in the faith of the Lord Jesus Christ, the Incarnate Word of God, recognized the Holy Scriptures as the supreme rule of faith, accepting the two sacraments ordained by Christ, and believing that the visible unity of Christian Churches is the will of God, hereby formally declare their purpose to achieve organic union between the respective churches.

The goal was nothing less than one church, one government, one ministry, and one communicant list. In May, 1938, the Presbyterian General Assembly accepted the invitation extended by the Episcopal General Convention and appointed a commission to meet with Episcopal representatives.

The short of a long story is that the 1946 General Convention defeated "The Proposed Basis of Union" with the Presbyterians. The proposal was debated for three General Conventions, and the heated Philadelphia debate in 1946 resulted in its defeat by both orders in the House of Deputies. The defeat, spearheaded by Anglo-Catholic leaders, was an affront to the Presbyterians, who had responded to the church's 1937 invitation with hearty enthusiasm and cooperation. George E. DeMille wrote, "The whole episode of the attempted union with the Presbyterian Church is not one on which an Episcopalian can look back with much pride."[2]

The story is told about the Calvinist who slips on a banana peel, tumbles down a flight of stairs, then gets up and says to himself, "Whew, I'm glad that's over." That could have expressed the feeling of Presbyterians after those nine years of talks. Since that time, the Presbyterians have turned to more fertile ecumenical soil and reunited some of their sister bodies.

Since World War II, new organizations and commissions within the life of the Episcopal Church have allowed it to adapt to changing ecumenical needs. A year after the formation of the World Council of Churches, the 1949 General Convention established the Joint Commission on Ecumenical Relations. Replacing the old Commission on Faith and Order, the commission's instructions were:

> To see that the church is kept informed as to progress in this field, especially at the grass roots level, and that it be held responsible for maintaining and furthering our close fellowship and cooperation with the World Council of Churches and National Council of Churches.

Until 1964, there were two other church commissions also dealing with ecumenical relations: the Joint Commission on Approaches to Unity and the Joint Commission on Relations with Eastern and Old Catholic Churches. The 1964 General Convention approved the merger of these three commissions under the title "Joint Commission on Ecumenical Relations" (JCER). Since that year, this enlarged commission has coordinated all aspects of the church's ecumenical relations.

The merger resolution spelled out its tasks:

> . . . to develop a comprehensive and coordinated policy and strategy on relations with other churches, confirming, interpreting, or making fresh definitions in harmony with the faith and canons . . . thus involving a) statements on Faith and Order, b) theological discussions with other churches . . . and c) questions of Church law, tradition, and worship . . .[3]

The Right Reverend Robert F. Gibson, Jr. was the first chairman of the new commission, and served in that post until his retirement in 1974. Prior to that, Gibson, the Bishop of Virginia, was chairman of the Joint Commission on Approaches to Unity from 1955 to 1964. Gibson was a visionary ecumenical leader during the time the Episcopal Church initiated most of its ecumenical dialogues. The Right Reverend Edward Jones, Bishop of Indianapolis, has served as chairman of JCER since 1982.

In 1964, a full-time ecumenical officer was added to the staff of the Episcopal Church Center in New York. Approved by the General Convention in 1961, the office became part of the National and World Mission Unit at the church center. Dr. Peter Day, a layman, was named the first ecumenical officer, and served in that post until his retirement in 1981. The Reverend William Norgren became the assistant ecumenical officer in 1975, and was named the ecumenical officer in 1981. Norgren had previously served as executive director of the Faith and Order Commission for the National Council of Churches of Christ.

Roman Catholic Dialogues

The Archbishop of Canterbury, Robert A. K. Runcie, tells the story of a visit to Uganda where he was honored by Roman Catholic leaders. After an ecumenical service at a cathedral, he was presented with a portrait of himself with Roman Catholic Cardinal Emanual Nsubuga. "The painter was there," the archbishop said, "and I exclaimed, 'My, that's magnificent, but how did you get it done so quickly? I just arrived.' He said, 'Oh, it was like this. When the pope came, I painted a picture of the cardinal greeting the pope. Actually, I painted two pictures, because one wasn't quite as good as the other. On the second one this morning, I painted out the pope's face, and put in yours. So it is still the pope's body, but it is your head.' "

The archbishop laughed as he told the story in 1984 at the sixth meeting of the Anglican Consultative Council in Lagos, Nigeria. "So I was able to say to the crowd, 'If you can have the Archbishop of Canterbury's head on a pope's body, then all things are possible.' "

The archbishop's story illustrates the generally congenial relations between Roman Catholics and Anglicans that developed in the twentieth century, particular after the Second Vatican Council. The Common Declaration by Archbishop of Canterbury Michael Ramsey and Pope Paul VI in 1966 was the first such common declaration since the two churches split in the sixteenth century. They stated that despite many obstacles they were determined, "to inaugurate between the Roman Catholic church and the Anglican Communion a serious dialogue which, founded on the Gospels and on the ancient common traditions, may lead to that unity in truth for which Christ prayed." On an international level, that dialogue began in 1970.

Four years earlier, the historic Second Vatican Council paved the way. Not only did the council commit the Roman Catholic church to full participation in the ecumenical movement, it brought substantial reform to that church and laid a foundation upon which dialogues with other churches could begin.

In the United States, the Anglican Roman-Catholic (ARC) dialogues began in 1965 and were only one of several national Anglican-Roman Catholic dialogues that eventually developed in seventeen countries. The Episcopal Church's co-chairman was the Right Reverend Arthur Vogel, Bishop of West Missouri. The Right Reverend Theodore Eastman, Bishop of Maryland, succeeded him in 1984. The ARC/USA met once or twice a year with eighteen members, an equal number from each church. The ARC statements spoke "to the churches and not for the churches," and bore the authority only of the commission, and not the churches themselves.

ARC's goals "have tended to fluctuate from time to time depending upon the ever-changing composition of the group's membership" as well as the concurrent agenda of the international consultation. However, the fullest expression of its goal came from a 1969 statement in which its members declared, "We see the goal as to realize full communion of the Roman Catholic church with the Episcopal Church and the other churches of the Anglican Communion." ARC then proposed three stages: "Re-Counter through personal exchange and dialogue;" "Growing together: interim steps;" and "Toward full communion and organic unity."

The most significant development of the American dialogues was a twelve-year report issued in 1977 titled "Where We Are: A Challenge for the Future." Summarizing the first nineteen meetings, the report stated:

> After twelve years of study ARC contends that the Episcopal Church and the Roman Catholic church agree at the level of faith on such topics as the Holy Eucharist, Priesthood and Ordination, and the nature and mission of the church . . . Yet agreement even at the level of faith is not always evident in visible expression. The Episcopal and the Roman Catholic churches differ in their forms of worship, their traditions of spirituality, their styles of theological reflection, and in some of their organizational structures of church life.

> Despite these historically conditioned differences, however, ARC finds after nineteen joint consultations that the Episcopal and Roman Catholic churches share so profound an agreement on the level of faith that these churches are in fact 'sister churches' in the one communion, which is the Church of Christ.[4]

However, the report recognized differences in such areas as abortion, human sexuality and marriage and family. ARC found that the answers being given in each church "are not in agreement with one another," and even labelled this a "new area of growing disagreement."

One of the major problems has been the Roman Catholic church's refusal to recognize the validity of Anglican orders of ministry. This refusal of recognition was first declared in 1896 when Pope Leo XIII issued an encyclical declaring that Anglican orders of ministry were invalid. Prior to that time, the Roman Catholic church recognized Anglican orders. However, in modern times, the lack of official recognition has not had a practical effect in relationships between Anglican and Roman Catholic clergy.

In a 1973 interview, the church's ecumenical officer, Dr. Peter Day, said, "One hurdle is whether Roman Catholics can recognize the validity of Anglican orders in a way which doesn't seem to be saying that a bad judgment was made in the past. And, of course, we have the problem of defining a relationship with the Bishop of Rome which, to Roman Catholics, does not damage papal authority. This requires immense good will on both sides."[5]

The major problem between the Episcopal Church and the Roman Catholic church is that of authority. The dialogues have pointed out that Episcopalians have difficulty accepting the infallibility of the pope, as well as the lack of inclusion of laity in decision-making processes of the church. *A Communion of Communions* reports that "these deficiencies give rise to a suspicion and mistrust of the decision-making process and agencies for the implementation of decisions within the Roman Catholic church."[6]

At the international level, the Anglican Roman Catholic International Consultation (ARCIC) began meeting in 1970. There have been nine delegates from each communion. The Right Reverend Arthur Vogel, Bishop of West Missouri, was the only American Episcopalian represented in the international dialogues. ARCIC has produced three historic statements. These were statements on various aspects of Christian doctrines about which the two churches agreed. While at a practical level they represented no formal moves toward unity, they provided a basis for further conversations and efforts. These statements were:

1971—Windsor Statement on Eucharistic Doctrine
1973—Canterbury Statement on Ministry and Ordination
1976—Venice Statement on Authority in the Church

When the Windsor Statement was issued in 1971, it represented the first such public statement since the split between the two communions in the sixteenth century.

The 1979 General Convention approved the Windsor and Canterbury statements by saying they "provide a statement of the faith of this church in the matters concerned and form a basis upon which to proceed in further growth towards unity . . ." The 1985 General Convention considered the Venice Statement on authority. While it referred some questions on the statement to ARCIC II for further discussion, it affirmed that the statement represented "a theological model of convergence towards which both of our churches may grow."

The three statements, as well as a historical summary of the dialogues, were issued in the booklet titled *The Final Report,* published in the United States by Forward Movement Publications in 1982. The book, *Called of Full Unity: Documents on Anglican-Catholic Relations, 1966-1984,* tells the full story of both American and international dialogues.[7]

Reaction to the Ordination of Women

"The judgment of Rome is that Anglican ordination [of women] would not disrupt our negotiations for ecumenical unity, but that ordination [of women] would be regarded seriously as a setback," said Archbishop of Canterbury Donald Coggan at a 1976 press conference following the historic decision to ordain women.[8]

Archbishop Coggan and Pope Paul VI exchanged letters on the subject of the ordination of women in 1975. Archbishop Coggan informed the Pope of a "slow but steady growth of a consensus of opinion within the Anglican communion that there are no fundamental objections in principle to the ordination of women to the priesthood." The Holy Father replied to Coggan, in part, "We must regretfully recognize that a new course taken by the Anglican Communion in admitting women to the ordained priesthood cannot fail to introduce into his dialogue an element of grave difficulty . . ."[9]

Underneath the official reactions to the Episcopal Church's decision to ordain women, various Roman Catholic leaders offered mixed assessments. "We were quite jubilant when the vote came," said Judy Klepperich, who represented the Roman Catholic Women's Ordination Conference at the 1976 General Convention. Sister Marquita Finley, social concerns chairwoman for the National Assembly of Women Religious said, "It's going to have an impact in the Catholic church. We can't ignore it."[10]

A year earlier, the Anglican-Roman Catholic dialogue in the United States had already agreed that the ordination of women would not become a divisive issue in the dialogues. In a joint statement issued in October 1975, ARC members affirmed that if one of the two churches proceeded to ordain women, "This difference would not lead to ARC's termination or to the abandonment of its declared goal." Speaking to the women's ordination question, the members observed, "Though disagreement exists on the answer, the question is based on a common understanding of the issues involved and the meaning of terms common to both churches. We are talking about the same Eucharist and the same three-fold ministry . . ."[11]

Later, however, the religious world was mildly shocked when in August, 1980, the Roman Catholic church announced it would accept married Episcopal priests into its ministry. The move was a gesture of accommodation towards those Episcopal priests who, although married, could not accept their church's decision to ordain women. Catholic officials said the Episcopal priests would be required to accept the doctrine of the Catholic Church— and be ordained again.

Bishop Bernard Law of Missouri, later to become Archbishop of Boston, was appointed liaison between the Episcopal priests and the American Catholic bishops. Bishop Law said that this question had been discussed in closed executive meetings of Catholic bishops for a few years. While some observers called the move a response to the Episcopal Church's decision to ordain women, Law called that "an unfortunate and overly simplistic" explanation. While the move did not produce a mass exodus of Episcopal priests into the Roman Catholic church, some twenty-two Episcopalians had been ordained in the Catholic church by 1985. It should be noted, however, that a far greater number of Roman Catholic priests entered the Episcopal priesthood in the preceding five years.

The second round of talks between Anglicans and Roman Catholics at the international level, ARCIC II, began in 1983. Its responsibilities were set out as follows:

. . . to examine, especially in the light of our respective judgments on the *Final Report,* the outstanding doctrinal differences which still separate us, with a view towards their eventual resolution; to study all that hinders the mutual recognition of the ministries of our communions; and to recommend what practical steps will be necessary when, on the basis of our unity in faith, we are able to proceed to the restoration of full communion.[12]

The first two meetings of ARCIC II focused on fundamental doctrinal principles about salvation, justification by faith, and the role of the church in human redemption.

Dialogues with Orthodox Churches

The Anglican Orthodox Theological Consultation (AOTC) in the United States began in 1962. It was initiated by Presiding Bishop Arthur Lichtenberger and Archbishop Iakovos, president of the Standing Conference of Canonical Orthodox Bishops. The objective was "to identify things held in common, to analyze the nature of differences, and to seek recommendations for presentation to the respective church authorities, with a view to mutual recognition of common faith and . . . the goal of some form of expressed unity between the Anglican and Orthodox communions."[13] Like the Roman Catholic dialogues, consultations were held at both the United States and the international level.

The first twelve American meetings between 1962 and 1979 had both a theological and a pastoral purpose, so theologians and pastors participated in equal numbers. *A Communion of Communions* reports "The mixed purpose was indicated because only in North America do Anglicans and Orthodox live in the same society in which neither is the majority church, and where they are exposed to similar challenges and needs."[14]

In 1974, AOTC agreed in its "Common Statement of Purpose" that "the ultimate purpose of the consultation is the full union of the two communions" and the "proximate purpose is the encouragement of this end through the consideration of the many serious differences still existing between the two bodies, and the many internal problems with which both must contend." A dozen years later, the United States dialogue has helped to promote understanding and friendship, but the Episcopal Church's decision to ordain women has produced some problems.

The decision of the Episcopal Church to admit women to Holy Orders disrupted the dialogue with Orthodox churches much more seriously than it did the Roman Catholic dialogue. After the 1976 Minneapolis vote for the ordination of women, the AOTC meeting scheduled for October was cancelled at the request of the Orthodox delegates and they met separately to assess the new situation. Regularly scheduled meetings of the dialogue were not to resume for two years.

The secretary of the Orthodox delegation, the Reverend Paul Schneirla, wrote a letter to its members stating, "This unilateral action . . . contravening the testimony of Scripture and the unbroken tradition of the Catholic church, has radically changed the Anglican image which Orthodox could cherish . . ."

The Right Reverend John of Thermon, bishop of the eighth district of the Greek Orthodox Archdiocese, said in an interview that the Greek Orthodox church could never unite with a church that has female priests, saying his church "will never change its stand." Alexander Schnemann, dean of St. Vladimir's Seminary, told participants at an ecumenical conference, "The way the questions have been formulated, raised, debated and . . . resolved are certainly not the way the Orthodox church would consider the normal way for an issue of such tremendous importance and decisiveness."[15]

An editorial in *The Orthodox Church* stated that "the era which saw an apparent rapprochement between the Anglican Communion as a whole and the Orthodox church seems to have ended. Many of us will see this as a tragedy and a real setback for ecumenism."

The Episcopal delegates to AOTC adopted a "Message to the Orthodox Members of the Anglican-Orthodox Theological Consultation," stating that "this action of the Episcopal Church does not create a new ground of division. Rather, it is an expression of more fundamental differences which lie at the root of our long-sustained and unhappy separation." Their statement urged the dialogues to continue.

In 1977, Presiding Bishop John Allin paid a visit to the Patriarch of Moscow. The dialogue itself did not hold another meeting until February, 1978 when it heard a paper by the Reverend James Griffiss, professor of systematic theology at Nashotah House Seminary, on "History, Tradition, and Experience." Members of the dialogue also heard a paper by Father Paul Schneirla presenting some Orthodox reactions to our proposed *Book of Common Prayer*. There was also an informal exchange of information on the ordination of women.

The consultation officially resumed its meetings in 1980 with reconstituted membership, and Greek Orthodox Bishop Maximos of Pittsburgh and Suffragan Bishop Robert Terwilliger of Dallas as co-chairmen. Delegates began discussing omitting the *filioque* from the Nicene Creed, a topic which was to be one of AOTC's major concerns for the next few years.

In the Nicene Creed used in the Service of Holy Communion (page 327 and page 359, BCP), Episcopal worshippers proclaim that "We believe in the Holy Spirit . . . who proceeds from the Father and the Son." The words "and the Son" are what is called the *filioque* clause. The use of these words in the creed has been a major source of difference between the Eastern and Western churches since before their division in 1054. They were not in the original Nicene Creed (which originated at the Council of Nicea in 325), but were later added at the Third Council of Toledo in 589 to strengthen church teaching against the prevalent Arian heresy.

"*Filioque* has an ecumenical importance far beyond its small size," said the Standing Commission on Ecumenical Relations in its report to the 1985 General Convention. The Orthodox believe that the original creed, without the *filioque,* more clearly represents the Father as the source of divine life. To assert "and from the Son" at least appears to introduce two principles of origin into the Trinity. It is at best, confusing, and at worst, heretical, according to the Orthodox.

In the revision of the Prayer Book, the Standing Liturgical Commission proposed to the 1976 General Convention that *filioque* be removed from the Nicene Creed in the eucharistic liturgy. The House of Bishops concurred, but the House of Deputies voted to retain *filioque.* The 1979 General Convention received the request of the 1978 Lambeth Conference that restoration of the original wording be considered. The House of Bishops Theology Committee in 1981 accepted the Orthodox criticism that, because the *filioque* had been added without proper ecumenical authority, the original wording should be restored. The 1982 General Convention asked for a study of the question by dioceses through the association of Episcopal Diocesan Ecumenical officers.

The result was a resolution for the 1985 General Convention—which passed—expressing the Episcopal Church's "intention to restore in liturgical usage the original form of the Nicene Creed . . . provided that such restoration is endorsed and commended by the Lambeth Conference" [of 1988]. Other churches in the Anglican communion, notably Burma, Canada, the West Indies and South Africa, had already voted to restore the original wording to the Nicene Creed.

At the international level, talks in 1962 between Archbishop of Canterbury Michael Ramsey and the Ecumenical Patriarch, Athenagoras I of Constantinople, resulted in the appointment of an Anglican Theological Commission to confer with Orthodox church representatives. Two years later, the Orthodox approved the talks at the Third Pan-Orthodox Conference at Rhodes.

The Anglican-Orthodox Joint Doctrinal Commission held its first discussions between 1973 and 1976, and in 1976 produced the *Moscow Agreed Statement,* which included sections on the Knowledge of God, the Inspiration and Authority of Holy Scripture and Tradition, and other doctrinal matters as well. In 1984, it completed the *Dublin Agreed Statement,* which included sections on the Mystery of the Church, Faith in the Trinity, Prayer and Holiness, and Worship and Tradition.[16] The 1985 General Convention of the Episcopal Church commended the Dublin Statement, and asked for study and response from the dioceses and seminaries of the church.

Lutheran-Episcopal Dialogue (LED)

Dialogues with Lutherans began in 1970 at the international level, and in 1969 in the United States. Six meetings of the Lutheran-Episcopal Dialogue (United States) were held between October, 1969 and June, 1972. The co-chairmen were the Reverend O. V. Anderson of the Lutheran Church in America (LCA) and the Right Reverend Richard S. M. Emrich, Episcopal Bishop of Michigan. Along with the Episcopal Church, the Lutheran Church in America, American Lutheran church, and the Lutheran church (Missouri Synod), joined in the dialogue.

Although the objective of the first series was "to define the possibilities and problems for a more extended dialogue, having more specific fellowship or unity or union goals," the dialogue went beyond that objective. "As we discussed the faith and the mission to which Christ calls us," they said, "we discovered both an existing unity and, in the face of massive cultural upheaval, an unavoidable imperative to manifest oneness."[17]

Specifically, the dialogue recognized agreement between Lutherans and Episcopalians on the following fundamentals of church life and doctrine:

1) The primacy and authority of the Holy Scriptures
2) The doctrine of the Apostles' and Nicene Creed
3) Justification by grace through faith as affirmed by both the Lutheran Confessions and the *Book of Common Prayer*
4) The doctrine and practice of baptism
5) Fundamental agreement of the Holy Eucharist, although with some differences in emphasis

The dialogue identified two problem areas which needed further discussion. On the Lutheran side, questions remained about the Episcopal Church's understanding of the nature of the Gospel. On the Episcopal side, there were concerns about the place of the historic episcopate in Lutheran practice and theology. The complete report of the first dialogue was issued in *Lutheran-Episcopal Dialogue: A Progress Report,* published by Forward Movement Publications in 1973.

The second series (LED II) was held between 1976 and 1980. The same Lutheran bodies participated in this series, and were joined in 1978 by the Association of Evangelical Lutheran Churches, a smaller body which had broken off from the Missouri Synod Lutherans. Co-chairmen were the Right Reverend William Weinhauer, Episcopal Bishop of Western North Carolina, and Dr. Robert L. Wietelmann, an Ohio pastor from the American Lutheran church.

These conversations resulted in "joint statements" on Justification, Apostolicity, the Authority of Scripture, the Gospel, and Eucharistic Presence. The most significant result of LED II, however, was the preparation of recommendations to the General Convention and conventions of the three Lutheran bodies, which all met in September, 1982. The three Lutheran bodies added another dimension to the ecumenical progress by voting to merge at their 1982 conventions and form a "new Lutheran church" by 1988.

The resolution passed by the 1982 Episcopal and Lutheran conventions stated that the respective church bodies recognized one another "as churches in which the Gospel is preached and taught" and looked forward to the day "when full communion is established between Anglican and Lutheran churches." Most importantly, the resolution approved "interim eucharistic sharing" so that Episcopalians could be welcomed at Lutheran altars, and Lutherans could be welcomed at Episcopal altars. Under its provisions, Lutheran and Episcopal Church leaders "may by mutual agreement extend the regulations of church discipline to permit common, joint celebration of the eucharist within their jurisdictions." The term "interim eucharistic sharing" was used because the resolution did not intend to signify that "final recognition of each other's eucharists or ministries has yet been achieved."

Third, the historic resolution encouraged mutual prayer and support for the churches, joint programs in Christian education, evangelism and ministry, as well as joint use of facilities. Finally, it authorized a third series of dialogues to study the orders of ministry, and the role and office of the bishop.

The action brought dozens of joint Lutheran-Episcopal worship services around the country in 1983. In the first of these, nearly 2,500 Episcopalians and Lutherans worshipped at an historic service on January 16, 1983, at the Washington Cathedral. Presiding Bishop John Allin joined Bishop David Preus of the American Lutheran church, Bishop James R. Crumley of the Lutheran Church in America, and Bishop William Kohn of the Association of Evangelical Lutheran Churches for a joint celebration of the eucharist.

The third series of the Lutheran-Episcopal Dialogue began in 1983. During the first two years of the meeting, the group addressed four major topics: The Historic Episcopate, the Gospel and its Implications, the Teaching Authority of the Church under the Gospel, and Ways to Full Communion and Mutual Recognition of Ministries. While the Lutheran Church-Missouri Synod did not approve the 1982 agreement, representatives continued to participate in the dialogue.

Southern Baptist Dialogue

In 1979, Southern Baptists and Episcopalians in the state of North Carolina began an unusual set of dialogues. The annual dialogue brought together twelve clergy from each tradition. All three Episcopal dioceses in the state participated. Topics discussed in each of its first seven years are: 1979—the Gospel Imperative for Mission; 1980—Spiritual Formation for Discipleship; 1981—The Problem of Authority in Church and State; 1982—Christian Initiation Rites; 1983—Signs, Symbols, and Sacraments; 1984—The Doctrine of the Church; 1985—Baptist and Episcopal Evaluations of the Lima Report on the Topic of Ordained Ministry.

The goals of this dialogue were to build on earlier dialogues and stimulate ever-deepening doctrinal discussions, stimulate meetings in other states, and eventually involve other Baptist groups, including the American Baptist

Convention and the three major black conventions. The 1976 General Convention passed a resolution instructing the Joint Commission on Ecumenical Relations to establish "ongoing conversations with several Baptist associations" in order to improve understanding, communications, and cooperation in ministry.[18]

The Concordat Relationships

A "concordat relationship" refers to an agreement in which the churches recognize each other as sufficiently similar in faith and practice to allow full communion. William Norgren, the Episcopal Church's ecumenical officer, wrote in 1979 that a concordat "expresses the fact of agreeing or being in harmony between churches; it attests to an existing unity without any constitutional provision or other special act of union."[19]

The General Convention of 1976 entered into a concordat for full communion with the Mar Thoma Syrian church of Malabar. Fifteen years earlier, the 1961 convention established concordat relationships with the Philippine Independent church (Iglesia Filipina Independiente), as well as the Spanish Reformed Episcopal church and the Lusitanian Church of Portugal. In 1931, the Episcopal Church reached a concordat relationship with the Old Catholic Churches of the Union of Ultrecht in the Bonn Agreement.

The terms of the concordat relationships, although reached at different times with somewhat different provisions, contain these essentials:

1. Each communion recognizes the catholicity and independence of the other and maintains its own.

2. Each communion agrees to admit members to the other communion to participate in the sacraments.

3. Intercommunion does not require from either communion the acceptance of all doctrinal opinion, sacramental devotion or liturgical practice characteristic of the other, but implies that each believes the other to hold all the essentials of the Christian faith.

While the 1976 agreement with the Mar Thoma Syrian church did not contain these explicit provisions, it did allow full communion and recognized the Mar Thoma Syrian church "as a true part of the Church Universal, holding the catholic faith and possessing the apostolic ministry of bishops, priests, and deacons."

Episcopal Diocesean Ecumenical Officers

A new organization—the Episcopal Diocesan Ecumenical Officers (EDEO) was started in 1974. Late in the 1950s, the Joint Commission on Ecumenical Relations asked each diocese to appoint an ecumenical officer. The first meeting for these officers was held in 1966 in Chicago. In 1969, the diocesan officers were invited by the Roman Catholics to participate in a National Workshop on Christian Unity in Philadelphia. After a series of meetings, and with the assistance of Dr. Peter Day, the church's ecumenical officer, EDEO was officially organized in Charleston, South Carolina, in March, 1974. Over fifty diocesan ecumenical officers attended the meeting. Officers were elected and bylaws were approved. The Reverend John Bonner of the Diocese of Tennessee was named the first chairman.

EDEO's stated purpose was to initiate, support and communicate ecumenical activity at both the diocesan and local level. The group reports activities to the Executive Council and the Standing Commission on Ecumenical Relations, and seeks to implement the actions of General Convention at the local level.[20]

The 1976 General Convention commended the new network and encouraged its participation in the expansion of local and diocesan ecumenical activity. Presiding Bishop Allin commented in 1980, "The Episcopal Church's diocesan ecumenical officers have been leaders in bringing home to the church at large the fact that there is more to the ecumenical agenda than national and international efforts . . ."

In 1975, the Fifth Assembly of the World Council of Churches, meeting in Nairobi, Kenya, urged its member churches "to review the pattern and degree of their present commitment to the ecumenical structures at local, national, regional, and global levels," with the purpose of determining whether their function provided a "means towards unity" or a "substitute for unity."

The Detroit Consultation

The 1976 General Convention responded to the challenge set forth by the World Council of Churches by calling for a major review of the church's ecumenical activity. The resolution asked the Standing Commission on Ecumenical Relations to undertake:

> through the convening of regional meetings, culminating in a special national conference . . . to assess this church's present ecumenical posture and involvement, to suggest restatement, where necessary, of those essentials to which the Episcopal Church is committed, and to formulate those priorities and goals which can guide our ecumenical activities in the future . . .

As a result, a three-year study was undertaken to assess ecumenical progress. Three questions were being asked at all levels of the church: "Where have we been? Where are we now? Where do we need to go?" This unprecedented study culminated in the National Ecumenical Consultation, which was held November 5-9, 1978, in Detroit, Michigan. The gathering brought a new clarity and consistency to the ecumenical policies of the Episcopal Church, as affirmed by the consensus reached by the Detroit Consultation. The 1979 General Convention approved that consensus in its "Declaration on Unity":

The visible unity we seek will be one eucharistic fellowship. As an expression of and a means toward this goal, the uniting church will recognize itself as a communion of communions, based upon acknowledgement of catholicity and apostolicity. In this organic relationship all will recognize each other's members and ministries. All will share the bread and the cup of the Lord. All will acknowledge each other as belonging to the body of Christ at all places and at all times. . . .

We do not yet see the shape of that collegiality, conciliarity, authority and primacy which need to be present and active in the diocese with its parishes as well as nationally, regionally, universally; but we recognize that some ecclesial structure will be necessary to bring about the expressions of our unity in the body of Christ described above. . . .

All Christians are challenged to express more fully among themselves the biblical call to mutual responsibility and interdependence. We believe ways can now be found to express this call to a communion of the churches in the body of Christ. As the churches become partners in mission, they will move from . . . interrelatedness to interdependence.[21]

13

Some Leave, Some Stay

IN THE EARLY 1970s, THERE WERE several troubling issues developing among conservatives in the Episcopal Church, but the proposal to ordain women was the most alarming. Following the 1973 General Convention, several organizations within the church united under an umbrella group called The Fellowship of Concerned Churchman. The fellowship provided some structural unity for opposing women's ordination—a perceived threat they all shared.

Groups represented in the fellowship included: the American Church News, the American Church Union, the Anglican Digest, the Canterbury Guild, the Certain Trumpet, the Christian Challenge, Comment (Canadian), the Congregation of St. Augustine, the Council for the Faith (Canadian), Episcopal Guild for the Blind, Episcopal Renaissance of Pennsylvania, Episcopalians United, Foundation for Christian Theology, Society of the Holy Cross, Society for the Preservation of the *Book of Common Prayer,* and Speak.

Representatives of the fellowship wrote "An Open Letter to Bishops of the Episcopal Church" in March of 1976. The letter cited their objectives to proposed changes in the Prayer Book, a "relaxed moral code" in the church, and further stated, "We perceive the most immediate threat to the church's life to lie in the proposal to ordain women." It went on to declare "We must proclaim in all conscience, with deep pain, that the proposed changes in the nature of the ordained ministry are unacceptable to us . . . If General Convention were to exceed its authority and purport to authorize the ordination of women . . . we would refuse to accept this action."[1]

For the most part, these organizations were from Anglo-Catholic or "high church" persuasions within the Episcopal Church. While they are conservative, it is a different kind of conservatism than that generally found among evangelicals. Anglo-Catholic conservatism is in relation to church tradition, while evangelical conservatism is in relation to interpretation of

154

Scripture. While some of the evangelicals in the church opposed the ordination of women, it never came with the same degree of force as that found among organizations belonging to the Fellowship of Concerned Churchmen.

After their efforts were defeated at the Minneapolis convention in 1976 (and women were ordained), the fellowship was forced to deal with the inevitable. Following the vote, the fellowship issued a declaration which stated, in part:

> The General Convention of the Episcopal Church . . . has now taken the fateful step of departing from the Apostolic order to which the Episcopal Church has hitherto adhered . . . This action is null and void. The Episcopal Church has no right or authority to change the nature of the Apostolic priesthood and episcopate . . . The Episcopal organizations and publications comprising the Fellowship of Concerned Churchmen rejects this action . . . and all acts and consequences following from it . . .[2]

Why did these groups oppose women in the priesthood? There were a number of arguments, but the following reflect the most commonly held beliefs:

1.) The priest represents Christ at the altar, and since Jesus was a male, then the priesthood must be all-male.

2.) If Jesus had intended for women to be included in the apostolic ministry, then he would have chosen a female apostle.

3.) Ordaining women would deter ecumenical conversations with the Roman Catholic and Orthodox churches.

4.) The church relies partly on tradition for an expression of God's revelation. Since the church has never had women priests, there is no compelling reason to begin at this point in history.

Sometimes these opponents of women's ordination stated that the Episcopal Church had no "right" to make the decision, meaning that the ordained priests of the Episcopal Church were part of the apostolic order of ministry that one also found within the Roman Catholic and Eastern Orthodox churches. If there were going to be any change in the nature of this ministry, then it would have to be one agreed upon by all of these churches. According to the fellowship, any decision by the Episcopal Church to ordain women would be unilateral and invalid.

Representatives of organizations in the fellowship met in Nashville, Tennessee, in November of 1976 for the specific purpose of responding to the actions of the Minneapolis General Convention. The representatives discussed possible courses of action and agreed that it was impossible for Episcopalians who were determined to "keep the faith whole and entire" to remain in communion with the Episcopal Church. The group resolved to hold a church congress the following September for the purpose of "presenting the spiritual principles and ecclesial structure of the continuing Episcopal Church." It also appointed a steering committee to develop detailed plans for the organization and financing of the meeting.[3]

The "St. Louis Congress" was held September 14 through September 1977, and attracted a great deal of attention in both the church and secular press. While the decision to ordain women to the priesthood promoted the most discussion, one observer stated in a later report that a number of grievances had surfaced:

> . . . women's ordination, Prayer Book revision, creeping humanism, homosexuals in the church, homosexuals in the priesthood, the high divorce rate, church funding of minority programs, abortion, the World Council of Churches . . . and all of the seminaries of the Episcopal Church. It is true that they were all united in their anger towards the Episcopal Church. However, that anger came from a hundred different directions.[4]

In three days of meetings, *The Christian Century* reported that these particular grievances were raised:

* The late Bishop James Pike's 'heresies' and the House of Bishops' refusal in 1967 to discipline him. Pike, the Bishop of California, had nettled conservatives and moderates alike with his unorthodox and controversial theological beliefs.
* Bishop Paul Moore's ordination of a lesbian.
* The General Convention Special Program.
* Presiding Bishop John Allin's 'waffling' on crucial issues in an effort to 'hold together two basically incompatible issues.'
* The church's easing of its position on abortion, divorce and remarriage, adultery and homosexuality.[5]

The "Affirmation at St. Louis," the main result of the St. Louis Congress, contained a plan for a new church structure. Tentatively choosing the name Anglican Church of North America (ACNA), they agreed that the church would be governed by a three branch Holy Synod (bishops, priests and deacons, and laity). It would not join the World or National Council of Churches since these organizations were believed to be "non-apostolic, humanist and secular in purpose and practice." Neither would it participate in the Consultation on Church Union—the ecumenical proposal to unite the Episcopal Church with other Protestant denominations. The three orders of ministry—bishops, priests, and deacons—would be all-male. However, the lay order of "deaconess" would be open to women. Later, the church's name was changed to the Anglican Catholic church.

St. Mary's Episcopal Church in Denver, Colorado, was the first parish to withdraw from the Episcopal Church, following the action at the Minneapolis convention. After a four hour meeting on November 28, 1976, they voted 197-79 to dissolve the parish's relationship with the Episcopal Church. Its rector, the Reverend James Mote, became a leader in the Anglican Catholic church and one of its first four bishops. Other parishes soon followed and by the end of 1977, four dioceses had been formed. The Diocese of Christ the King was formed in December, 1977, in Glendale, California, and elected Robert S. Morse as its bishop. Morse was rector of St. Peter's Church in Oakland. The Diocese of the Southeast was also organized that month, and elected Peter Watterson as its bishop. Watterson was rector at Church of the Holy Spirit in Palm Beach, Florida.

Duing a formation meeting for the Diocese of the Holy Trinity in Hollywood, California, nine priests publicly renounced their ordination vows and offered their "fealty and obedience" to the Right Reverend Albert A. Chambers, retired bishop of the Diocese of Springfield (Illinois). The bishop had agreed to furnish episcopal oversight by serving as the interim ecclesiastical authority pending a "restructuring of the Episcopal Church." The Diocese of the Midwest was the fourth diocese to be organized prior to the consecration of the initial four bishops.

The dissident leaders faced the major problem of locating three bishops who would consecrate their new bishops. Both Anglican and Catholic tradition call for at least three bishops to participate in the consecration service of every new bishop. This ensures the "validity of orders" for the new bishop, and guards the apostolic succession. The dissidents only found two who would agree to participate in the service, although a third allegedly gave written "consent" for the ordination.

By January, 1978, four new bishops had been chosen and the consecration service was scheduled for January 28 at Augustana Lutheran Church in Denver. The Lutheran parish, which was affiliated with the Lutheran Church in America, was the only church facility the group could obtain for the service. Denver's Roman Catholic bishops denied them the use of the Cathedral of the Immaculate Conception because of their strong ecumenical relations with the Episcopal Diocese of Colorado and Bishop William Frey.[6]

The four new bishops were: James O. Mote, rector of Denver's St. Mary's Church, and bishop of the Diocese of the Holy Trinity; Charles Dale David Doren, Diocese of the Midwest; Robert S. Morse of Oakland, California, and the Diocese of Christ the King; and Peter F. Watterson of Palm Beach, Florida, and the Diocese of the Southeast.

Bishop Chambers was one of the two consecrating bishops, along with Francisco J. Pagtakhan, a bishop of the Philippine Independent church. On February 9, 1978, the Supreme Council of Bishops of the Philippine Independent church met and passed a resolution stating that Pagtakhan was never given permission or authorization to participate in the consecrations. The Most Reverend Macario Ga, Supreme Bishop of the Philippine church, said in a cable to Presiding Bishop John Allin that he was "shocked and distressed" to hear of Pagtakhan's participation, and that he had not authorized it.[7]

Another dispute arose over a third bishop who was reported to have given "consent" for the consecrations. Bishop Mark Pae of South Korea was scheduled to participate in the service, but withdrew after being threatened with disciplinary action by Donald F. Coggan, the Archbishop of Canterbury. Bishop Pae allegedly wrote Bishop Chambers a letter stating his consent to the ordination.[8]

The new bishops and emerging church never received the recognition from the wider Anglican Communion that they so earnestly coveted. In a February 6, 1978 letter to the bishops of the Episcopal Church, Presiding Bishop John Allin said that he and Donald Coggan, the Archbishop of Canterbury, "agree that the new ecclesiastical body is not in communion with the See of Canterbury, nor in communion with this Province of the Anglican Communion." Allin said that Bishop Chambers "acted without the consent or authorization of this church to ordain to the episcopacy four persons who had been selected to be the leaders of a new ecclesiastical body."[9]

In June, 1978, fifteen bishops of the Episcopal Church filed charges against Bishop Chambers for participating in the consecration service, citing the retired Springfield bishop on three counts:

* For participating in the service without the presiding bishop, and without the consent of the diocesan standing committees and other bishops of the church;
* For failing to secure the consent of the bishop in the diocese where the consecrations took place (the Diocese of Colorado);
* For having "flagrantly breached" his own consecration vows to "conform to the doctrine, discipline, and worship of the Episcopal Church."[10]

The House of Bishops later chose to settle the matter by issuing a strongly-worded censure of Bishop Chambers, thus avoiding the thorny possibility of an ecclesiastical trial. The bishops passed the censure after a four-hour debate at their October, 1978 meeting in Kansas City, Missouri.

Later Results

"The main characteristic of the movement seems to be almost unlimited fragmentation. In five short years, what began at St. Louis . . . has managed to break into as many as eight different jurisdictions with a total of perhaps (at most) 20,000 souls."[11] This was the assessment of Louis Traycik, editor of the conservative, dissident publication, *The Christian Challenge* in an April, 1983 article. *The Challenge* had been edited for years by Dorothy Faber, a colorful personality sometimes called "the dragon lady" because of her fiery commentary. Louis Traycik, her son-in-law, became editor in 1982 following her death.

The Anglican Catholic church had a schism of its own shortly after the consecration of its four bishops in January, 1978. The first group to leav﹖ formed the Pro Diocese of St. Augustine of Canterbury to seek organic union with the Roman Catholic church.

A press release issued by Bishops Robert F. Morse and Peter F. Watterson announced that they found the ACC's constitution and canons unacceptable "on legal and theological grounds." Bishop Watterson's main complaints about the ACC constitution were that "it allows for abortion on demand, doesn't stress the centrality of the mass . . . and sets up an elaborate ecclesiastical polity that is a fantasy."[12] This group eventually dissolved as many of its clergy leaders sought ordination in the Roman Catholic church after that church made the decision in 1980 to allow married Episcopal priests to enter its ordained ministry.

Two of the founding dioceses of the Anglican Catholic church failed to ratify its constitution and remained independent bodies. One of the bishops, Charles Dale David Doren, left to form the United Episcopal church. Only one of the original four bishops who was consecrated in 1978—James O. Mote—remained in the Anglican Catholic church. By 1985, the Anglican Catholic church was comprised of roughly 100 parishes and 6,500 members.

Next to the Anglican Catholic church, the largest schismatic group to develop since 1977 was the American Episcopal church. In 1985, it was made up of approximately seventy-four parishes with 5,000 members. The American Episcopal church was first organized in May 1982, but organizing groups date back to the 1963 Anglican Orthodox church formed in North Carolina. Two dissident bodies which left this church in 1968 and 1972, respectively, later merged to form the American Episcopal church. The Diocese of the Southwest, which left the Anglican Catholic church, affiliated with the American Episcopal church in October 1984.[13]

The chart that follows outlines the several dissident groups that sprang from the St. Louis Congress and subsequent consecrations of the four bishops in the Anglican Catholic church.

However the dissident groups defined "Anglicanism," they each had a different vision of what it meant. In *A Report on the St. Louis Congress,* the Reverend Nathaniel Pierce wrote, "About all they could agree on was this: the Protestant Episcopal Church in the United States (PECUSA) was no longer part of the Catholic and Apostolic church, (and) PECUSA was no longer validly Anglican."[14]

The various factions soon discovered the difficulty of finding unity based on what you *don't* believe in—or in whom you oppose. Critics of the dissident groups asserted that the major reason the groups splintered was because of the power struggles and personality differences of its leaders. Louis Traycik, editor of *The Christian Challenge,* stated "We're going through a period of experimentation and of seeing whose method works best. We have a period of experimentation . . ."[15]

The Reverend Donald Armentrout, a professor of church history at the University of the South's School of Theology, summarizes the initial optimism and later disappointment of these groups:

TABLE II
Groups Which Left the Episcopal Church After 1977*

Table includes organization date, place, primary leader and
available membership statistics as of 1985.

1. **Anglican Catholic church,** organized October, 1978, Dallas. (Originally named Anglican Church of North America, it is the most direct descendent of the 1977 St. Louis Congress.) First bishop and leader is James O. Mote.

   Approximately 10 dioceses, 100 parishes, and 6,500 members.

   Internal Schisms
   a) United Episcopal Church of the U.S.A., formed December 7, 1980. Charles Dale David Doren, organizing bishop.
   b) Diocese of Christ the King, formed December 10, 1977. Robert S. Morse, organizing bishop. When the diocese met in January, 1979, delegates refused to ratify the constitution of the Anglican Catholic church and this diocese continued as a separate body.
   c) Diocese of Southeastern United States, Peter Watterson, organizing bishop. Failed to ratify constitution of the ACC at April, 1979 meeting; voted to dissolve at March, 1984 meeting. Watterson became a Roman Catholic.
   d) Diocese of the Southwest, formed July 1978. Mark Holliday elected bishop, but never consecrated. Merged with the American Episcopal church in October, 1984.

2. **American Episcopal church,** formed May 20, 1982. Primary leader is Anthony F. M. Clavier.

   Approximately 74 parishes with 5,000 members.

   The American Episcopal church was formed as a result of a merger between the American Episcopal church (organized 1968) and the Anglican Episcopal church of North America (organized 1972). Both of these bodies were originally part of the Anglican Orthodox church, formed 1963 in North Carolina by James Parker Dees. The Diocese of the Southwest (formerly with the Anglican Catholic church) affiliated in October, 1984.

3. **Diocese of Christ the King,** formed December, 1977. Primary leader is Bishop Robert S. Morse.

   Approximately 60 parishes, 48 clergy, and 3,000 members

   Originally a part of the Anglican Catholic church, it never ratified the constitution and remained an independent body.

4. **Anglican Rite Jurisdiction of the Americas,** organized October 18-20, 1979, in Indianapolis. Primary leader is Philippine Bishop Francisco J. Pagtakhan.

   Approximately 11 churches and 700 members.

   The Anglican Rite Jurdisdiction was formed by Bishop Francisco J. Pagtakhan of the Philippine Independent church as an "umbrella jurisdiction" for those dissatisfied with the Anglican Catholic church and other groups.

5. **United Episcopal Church of the U.S.A.,** formed December, 1980 in Coshocton, Ohio. Primary leader is Bishop Charles Dale David Doren.

   Approximately 10 churches and 700 members.

*There were two United States Anglican groups prior to the 1976 General Convention. The Reformed Episcopal church was organized December, 1883 and the Anglican Orthodox church was organized November, 1963.

At the time of the St. Louis Congress, there were predictions of an initial membership in the new group of 75,000 to 100,000. This clearly did not materialize and in the post-1976 groups, there are about 15,000 members. Their future impact on American Christianity is dependent upon uniting the different groups. Even then, the story of continuing Anglicanism will be a small chapter of American church history."[16]

Why did the Episcopal Church Lose Members?

"The Episcopal Church has lost a member every five minutes for the past ten years," said one church leader in 1977. The Episcopal Church's baptized membership peaked in 1966 at 3,647,297. It declined steadily until it began levelling off in the 1980s. There was a slight increase to 3,024,105 in 1983, and then it dipped downward again in 1984.

"It's because they decided to ordain women and revise the Prayer Book" said one irate defector. "The Episcopal Church just got too radical in the 1960s with those grants to radical, activist groups," said another loyal communicant. "The church never takes a stand on anything," commented one evangelical. "If we could ever get our act together on evangelism, things would come alive again."

While speculations abound on why the Episcopal Church lost half a million members in fifteen years, the reasons appear to defy a single explanation. Whatever the reasons, they weren't entirely unique to the Episcopal Church. Mainline Protestant church membership losses have generally paralleled those found in the Episcopal Church, both in years of origin and in duration. While Episcopal Church membership peaked in 1966, United Presbyterian church (U.S.A.) membership peaked in 1965; the United Methodist church peaked in 1964; the Lutheran Church in America peaked in 1967; the American Lutheran church peaked in 1966; and the United Church of Canada peaked in 1965. None of these churches have shown any subsequent years of increases.

The statistical evidence doesn't suggest that declines in membership were a result of the 1976 General Convention decisions over the ordination of women and Prayer Book revision. While the church lost approximately 68,000 members between 1976 and 1984, the most serious membership losses occurred prior to 1976. Between 1968 and 1976, the church lost 516,000 members—almost eight times as many. Shifts in population demographics may offer some clue to membership declines among the Protestant denominations. In the fall of 1975, Widick Schroeder published a study of demographic patterns and church membership in the *Chicago Theological Seminary Register*.[17] In this study, Schroeder proposed the concept of the "family life cycle." On the basis of age group patterns in the general population, he explained losses in membership of the mainline denominations, and even predicted a leveling off and subsequent increase in the 1980s. In the 1950s, when membership increased rapidly, "The number of people in age groups from which church members were most likely to be drawn were growing fairly rapidly, and the number of people in the age group from which church members were least likely to be drawn was actually declining," he said. During the 1960s and 1970s, when losses were great, Schroeder said that "The number of people in the age group from which most loyal church members are drawn [35-65] increased moderately, while the number of people in the age group from which defections were most likely increased substantially" [20-34].

Furthermore, he concludes that "The Episcopal Church and the United Presbyterian church, the denominations with the largest proportion of upper and upper middle status members and (those) most susceptible to the impact of the family life cycle on church membership, lost the largest proportion of members between 1960 and 1973."[18]

One study of Episcopal Church membership has documented a high statistical correlation between the U.S. birthrate and Episcopal Church membership.[19] The U.S. birthrate peaked in 1958 and Episcopal Church membership peaked in 1966. The birthrate then declined and reached its low point in 1973. Episcopal Church membership reached its lowest ebb in 1981. This suggests that after children are born, parents and families join churches several years later—particularly the mainline churches. When adults are single, or married without children, they are less likely to be church members. When children reach schoolage, then they tend to join the church. This phenomenon, well-known to pastors and parish priests, has been demonstrated in a number of studies.

These suggestions are not meant to absolve the church, its leaders, or its members of responsibility for the membership losses. Whatever the reasons, disappointment over the losses may mask the changing constituency of the Episcopal Church. According to an 1984 *State of the Church* report by The Reverend John Schultz, between 1966 and 1984, the Episcopal Church has baptized 120,000 adults, confirmed an estimated 93,000 adults baptized elsewhere, and received 82,000 new members from other branches of the catholic church. Schultz reports, "This infusion of new blood has changed the make up of our constituency, so that now nearly 60 percent of our membership was not raised in the Episcopal Church, but came to us by choice as adults."[20]

14

A Mission Church:
At Home and Abroad

ON OCTOBER 16, 1984, A NORWEGIAN DIPLOMAT arrived on the campus of New York's General Theological Seminary to tell a visiting professor he had won an award. After he had informed Bishop Desmond Tutu that he had been selected to receive the Nobel Peace Prize, he escorted the bishop through an overflow crowd to the seminary chapel for a service of prayer and thanksgiving. The Right Reverend Desmond Tutu focused the attention of the world on the racial injustice of South Africa and became Anglicanism's most celebrated leader. In one sense, he had already become an Anglican missionary to the United States. In the fall of 1984, he was a visiting professor of Anglican Studies at General Theological Seminary. But beginning with visits in the 1980s, he had spoken to numerous Episcopal church groups, and had addressed the 1982 General Convention.

If Bishop Tutu had become, in one sense, a "missionary" to the United States, his activity merely reflected the changing missionary strategy throughout the Anglican Communion. The years after World War II witnessed the indigenization and growth to maturity of what had been the footholds of white western missionary activity—the churches of Africa, Asia, and South America. Mission work in the Anglican Communion traditionally took the form of "sending-receiving." Typically this meant that white westerners were the "senders" while blacks or hispanics elsewhere were the "receivers." The pattern was broken once the church realized that *all* are engaged together in one worldwide mission. The Mutual Responsibility and Interdependence in the Body of Christ (MRI) concept, originated at the 1963 Anglican Congress, and the notion later expressed by Partners in Mission reflected this changing strategy of worldwide missions.

The declining number of missionaries sent overseas also reflected the changing strategy. In 1965—the peak year—the Episcopal Church supported 459 missionaries and spouses working overseas. By 1977, however, this number had dropped to 124.[1]

163

Mutual Responsibility and Interdependence

Through "Partners in Mission," more than sixty dioceses in the United States are linked to companion dioceses overseas. The Partners in Mission idea had its origins at the 1973 meeting of the Anglican Consultative Council. However, its predecessor, *Mutual Responsibility and Interdependence in the Body of Christ,* emerged at the Anglican Congress held in 1963 at Toronto. The basic idea behind MRI was to link isolated provinces and countries of the Anglican Communion into a common sense of mission and ministry. The MRI document, issued August 17, 1963, paired off "companion dioceses" in widely scattered parts of the Anglican communion. The MRI document also marked the beginning of the shift away from "sending-receiving" churches to an equal partnership in the Gospel. It declared: "Mission is not the kindness of the lucky to the unlucky; it is mutual, united obedience to the one God whose mission it is . . ."

In their message to Anglicans throughout the world, the primates and archbishops of the Anglican Communion stated at the Toronto meeting:

Our professed nature as a world-wide fellowship of national and regional churches has suddenly become a reality—all but ten of the 350 Anglican dioceses are now included in self-governing churches . . . It is now irrelevant to talk of "giving" and "receiving" churches. The keynotes of our time are equality, interdependence, and mutual responsibility.[2]

Credit as the "chief architect" of MRI goes to an American bishop: the Right Reverend Stephen Bayne, who served as the first executive officer for the Anglican Communion from 1960 to 1964. The 1958 Lambeth Conference called for the creation of the post, "Anglican Executive Officer." Archbishop of Canterbury Geoffrey Fischer appointed Bayne to the post in 1959. Bishop Bayne had been Bishop of Olympia (Washington) since 1947. As the first executive officer of the Anglican Communion, Bayne served on behalf of the Lambeth Conference "over all matters affecting the welfare of the worldwide Anglican Communion." He also served as executive officer of the Anglican Advisory Council on Mission Strategy.

During his four years serving in that position, Bayne travelled half a million miles "without well thumbed maps and with few letters of instruction." One observer writes, "It has been Stephen Bayne's task to discover a vocation and a purpose for the loosely joined company of Christians that constitutes the Anglican Communion throughout the world . . ."[3] Commenting on the MRI document in a newspaper interview shortly after the Anglican Congress, Bayne said, "Some church members will have to cease thinking of the church as a kind of memorial association for a deceased clergyman named Christ."[4]

By the mid-sixties, the hippies had become a new counter culture force in American society. Race riots took place in Watts, the 24th amendment abolished the poll tax, and Martin Luther King, Jr. led a march from Selma to Montgomery. Following the Tonkin Gulf incident, the war in Vietnam escalated and so did American casualties. As this tumultous decade came to an end, a rock festival celebrating music and free love drew half a million youths to Woodstock. In the midst of the domestic turmoil, how did the Episcopal Church respond to its mission challenge?

The 1964 General Convention took the initial steps to organize the church around its mission. "MRI is a call to a greater maturity and a more appropriate form of obedience to mission. It is a summons to a greater and clearer understanding of the divine mission, and our obedience to it," said Bishop Bayne. By this time, Bayne had resigned his position as executive officer of the Anglican Communion in order to become director of the overseas department at the Episcopal Church Center. He challenged his fellow Episcopalians to:

> . . . respond to immediate needs by initiating over and above the budget, the acceptance of projects equaling $6 million during the next three years . . . What we do with our money is significant as a symbol of what we are doing with our lives.[5]

The 1964 General Convention appointed a commission to study the Mutual Responsibility and Interdependence proposal—and the commission's subsequent recommendations were to have some far-reaching results. One could see in Bayne's remarks threads of the future General Convention Special Program.

Another result of this changing strategy was the Anglican Consultative Council (ACC). Established by the 1968 Lambeth Conference of bishops, the ACC was officially organized after all the Anglican provinces had approved the worldwide body. The 1970 General Convention approved Episcopal Church participation and elected its first three delegates. One of the first delegates was Dr. Marion Kelleran, a professor at Virginia Theological Seminary, who later served as chairperson of the ACC between 1974 and 1979.

Resolution 69 of the 1968 Lambeth Conference assigned functions to the Anglican Consultative Council. Its basic tasks were to encourage the sharing of information among the Anglican provinces; to assist in the development of new provinces and dioceses; to develop a common mission policy; and to enable Anglican participation in the worldwide ecumenical movement, including the international dialogues and the World Council of Churches.

The first meeting of ACC was held in Limura, Kenya, in 1971. Later meetings were held in Dublin, Ireland (1973), Trinidad (1976), London, Ontario (1979), Newcastle Upon Tyne, England (1981), and Lagos, Nigeria (1984). The Reverend John Howe of Ireland was named the ACC's first executive secretary and served in that London post until 1982.

The Reverend Samuel Van Culin, Executive for World Mission at the Episcopal Church Center, was named ACC's executive secretary that same year. In his opening address to ACC-6 on July 17, 1984, Van Culin noted that the Council's sixty-three delegates spoke twenty-one different languages as a first language, while all spoke English as a second or third language. "We have members whose first languages include Japanese, Arabic, Melanesian, Greek, Igorot, Chinese, Malayalam, Xhosa, Burmese, Zulu, Kiswahili Ibo/Ijaw and Spanish," Van Culin remarked. The Archbishop of Canterbury also stressed the diversity of the Anglican Communion in his opening sermon at the Cathedral Church of Lagos. The Most Reverend Robert A. K. Runcie stated, "Now the truth that the Anglican church is numerically stronger in Africa than in any other part of the world begins to be seen. No longer can it be said that the Anglican church is the Church of England. Rather the Church of England is a member of the Anglican Communion . . ."[6]

He pointed out that at his Lambeth Palace home, there is a photo of bishops who participated in the 1887 Lambeth Conference. "There is only one African face—just one," he said, but by 1978, the number of African bishops at Lambeth had increased to 102, or 25 percent of all participants.[7]

Partners in Mission

The Reverend Tunde Abiala, a Nigerian priest, wrote the following in a letter to an American friend:

My assignment with the church has been growing steadily. Apart from my main job as the diocesan evangelist and youth chaplain, I have been given a new congregation to oversee . . . God has been on our side, and we are now the fastest growing church in the area. We expect 5,000 people before the close of the year . . ."[8]

The friendship between the Nigerian priest and his new-found American friend was made possible through the Partners in Mission process. An outgrowth of "MRI," the "Partners in Mission" idea originated at the second meeting of the Anglican Consultative Council, held in Dublin, Ireland, in 1973. The report of *ACC-2*, which was entitled *Partners in Mission*, stated:

The emergence everywhere of autonomous churches in independent nations has challenged our inherited idea of mission as a movement from 'Christendom' in the West to the 'non-Christian world.' In its place has come the conviction that there is but one mission in all the world, and that this one mission is shared by the worldwide Christian community.[9]

In 1977, a major Partners in Mission consultation was held in Louisville, Kentucky, with representatives from all nine provinces of the Episcopal Church. Each province had already held its own consultation to discuss its mission concerns, and representatives brought to Louisville an agenda for the other provinces of the church to consider. James W. Kennedy, former director of Forward Movement Publications, reported a number of common concerns that emerged at this meeting:

In the area of mission, the partners chided the Episcopal Church for using the term "mission diocese" and "mission parish," suggesting that these terms imposed a limited understanding of mission and reinforced the attitude that "missions" were burdens instead of opportunities.[10]

"Partners in Mission is a process and the way mission is done today in the Anglican Communion," said Patrick Mauney, director of overseas ministry for the Episcopal Church. "The companion diocese program is only one expression of the Partners in Mission idea," he explained. Through the companion diocese program, which was established in 1962, a United States diocese is "linked" to a partner diocese of an overseas nation. The dioceses exchange visits, hold conferences, share resources, or develop whatever activities that can enhance their understanding of mission. By 1982, sixty-eight U.S. Episcopal dioceses were linked to an overseas diocese through the companion diocese program.

It's hard to determine at what point the barriers break . . . but I am sure something has happened. No longer do we sort out our sentences so carefully and rehearse the dialogue before we approach our Nigerian brethren. And tonight, after evening prayer, the Nigerian women began a spontaneous song and dance to the accompaniment of a tune tapped out on a soda bottle. We joined in, feeling slightly foolish, slightly exhilarated. We were sharing—not thinking, planning, or even politely discussing.[11]

These thoughts were shared by Harriet Heithaus of Troy, Ohio, during a ten-day companion diocese consultation held between her Episcopal diocese in the United States and its companion Anglican diocese in Nigeria. Organized by Bishop William Black of Southern Ohio, this 1983 international get-together in Geneva, Switzerland, between American Episcopalians and Nigerian Anglicans was but one result of the companion diocese program and the emergence of *sharing* as a missionary concept. Some dioceses sent teachers overseas, others developed student and clergy exchanges or educational exchange programs. At the least, almost all exchanged visits of lay and clergy leaders.

Venture in Mission

The twentieth century in the Episcopal Church brought the sense of "mission" and all that it entailed from overseas to the back doorsteps of most Episcopalians. Mission's emphasis was no longer something we do for "them" who live "over there;" it became a central part of each Christian's responsibility. Indeed, it always was "in theory." The structures and programs of the church began to accommodate the shift. Nowhere was this more evident than in the Venture in Mission (VIM) program.

"Venture in Mission is not *a* program, it is *the* program of the church and provides the primary criterion for all of our programs," said Presiding Bishop

John Allin at a 1977 meeting of the Executive Council. Venture in Mission, initiated by the 1970 General Convention, set out to raise $100 million for special mission and ministry projects. By 1985, more than eighty-five dioceses had participated, and raised more than $170 million. However, it was more than a fundraising campaign because it sought to *educate* its participants about the nature of mission. The 1970 General Convention called for "a program which would enable the church to fulfill its responsibilities for mission and ministry at home and abroad." The 1973 General Convention in Louisville called for the Executive Council "to design a strategy to release the human and financial resources of the church." The Executive Council responded to this mandate and presented an imaginative proposal to the 1976 General Convention for Venture in Mission.

Through Venture in Mission, the national church asked each diocese to set a goal for funding projects. Often the diocese chose half of its projects within the diocese, and half in some other part of the United States or world. While the convention designated a number of project criteria, one was particularly significant:

Each project must be communicable to the whole church and should educate the church to larger dimensions of the total mission and ministry, the individual responsibility and interdependence of the whole church.[12]

From all over the church, at home and overseas, there came appeals for projects "we've always wanted to do but never dared think we could," as one diocesan official put it. The diocese, not the national church, decided which projects to fund and what its financial goals would be. The Diocese of Atlanta's "Toward Tomorrow" VIM program set a goal of $2.5 million. Before the program was over, $3.1 million in cash and pledges had been received. "We've got a whole new spirit here," said Atlanta's VIM chairman Paul Kennedy. South Carolina's "Mission and Renewal" campaigners sought $1.5 million and surpassed it. Almost 1,400 people came to South Carolina's kickoff meetings in Charleston and Florence. "That's the first time so many Episcopalians had been together here in 300 years" said Mission and Renewal co-chairman John W. Wilson.[13]

Presiding Bishop John Allin described Venture in Mission this way:

The three words "Venture in Mission" have been examined as gingerly as one looks for counterfeits among new issue of common currency. Some see the words as the designation of a formula, the sole purpose of which is to produce money. Some declare these to be code-words of a code without a key. Some treat the words as a lost phrase looking for a convention resolution. They have been read as the title of some new version of an old ecclesiastical game . . .

Venture in Mission is more than a fundraising effort. It is a sacramental adventure—a challenging opportunity for every Episcopalian to gain new insights and to make a new commitment to the mission of this church . . . [14]

The Episcopal Church Foundation

In 1955, St. Matthew's Mission was founded in Albuquerque, New Mexico. The congregation rented a dance studio—the Barling Academy of Fine Arts—because it was the only available space where they could hold Sunday worship services. On Sunday mornings, the men of the church had to rise early in order to set up the altar and chairs in time for the eight o'clock service, then stayed into the early afternoon to dismantle the furnishings.

Two years later, a loan from the Episcopal Church Foundation made it possible for the church to buy land and construct a new building for the growing congregation. Today, with three priests on its staff, it is one of the largest parishes in the diocese.

The Episcopal Church Foundation was established at the 1949 General Convention under the leadership of Presiding Bishop Henry Knox Sherrill. He saw the need for a church-related organization which could support the "advance work" of parishes and dioceses with funds not available through normal channels. Sherrill and a group of over twenty lay business leaders raised several million dollars to permanently endow the work of the foundation.

The foundation's first efforts focused on providing funds for the construction of church buildings during the prosperous 1950s. Later, it started funding other innovative projects of parishes and dioceses, as well as fellowships for doctoral students who planned to teach at Episcopal seminaries. In 1984, the Episcopal Church Foundation donated $365,000 for various grants and fellowships, and had provided $656,000 for building construction through its revolving loan fund.

Jubilee Ministry

When the Reverend Nelson Foxx came to Philadelphia's St. Matthias Church in 1983, he counted ten worshipers scattered in the pews. The story was a familiar one. The parish was a victim of a decaying neighborhood with a dwindling economic base. The struggling northwest Philadelphia parish was nearly forced to close its doors.

Just three years later, the congregation had tripled in size while its outreach ministries included an after-school tutoring program, a teen-age pregnancy prevention project, and workshops on child abuse prevention. In its second year the pilot tutoring program offered individualized instruction in basic skills, including reading, mathematics and science. A grant from the Diocese of Pennsylvania paid the salaries of four tutors.

"Jesus didn't tell people to go look up the answers, he struggled with them," the parish's rector wrote. "The Gospel is full of hard questions that we all must face . . . In confronting these questions and those who ask them, we will discover the truth about our commitment and our faith in the one we are called to serve."[15]

Jubilee Ministry is a program of the national church which now recognizes and supports these kinds of neighborhood ministries in local congregations. Established by the 1982 General Convention, Jubilee Ministry called the church to "a major new commitment to a ministry of joint discipleship with poor and oppressed people . . . to meet basic human needs and to build a just and peaceful global society." Jubilee's functions include consciousness raising, establishing Jubilee Centers, training, creating a human resources bank, research and evaluation, publishing a journal, evangelism and congregational development, coordinating a public policy network, and awarding Jubilee grants.[16]

The recognition and support of "Jubilee Center" parishes became the program's most publicized effort. By 1985, more than forty-five Episcopal parishes had been designated as Jubilee Centers by their dioceses and the national church's Executive Council. Jubilee Centers had to meet certain criteria, including engagement "in mission and ministry among and with the poor," a foundation in worship, and at least one human rights advocacy program and one human service program.

In addition to the Jubilee Centers, the quarterly magazine *Jubilee Journal* was established to report on issues affecting the poor and dispossessed. Among other subjects, the magazine contained stories about the ministry and programs of the Jubilee Centers.

The 1985 General Convention reaffirmed the Jubilee Ministry program with an expanded budget and opportunities for individual involvement. A residency program for Jubilee interns was established to provide opportunities for college and seminary students to work at Jubilee Centers. A program called "Jubilee Volunteers for Mission" was established to give adults the opportunity to commit themselves to two years of service at Jubilee Centers.

The Appalachian People's Service Organization

The Appalachian People's Service Organization (APSO) is another expression of the Episcopal Church's mission at home. Started in 1964, APSO is a coalition of fourteen dioceses in the states of Georgia, Tennessee, North Carolina, Kentucky, Virginia, West Virginia, Ohio, Maryland, and Pennsylvania, and carries out its work in both urban and rural regions of those states.

That same year, President Lyndon Johnson visited Martin County, Kentucky, and stepped onto the porch of Tom Fletcher's house. Fletcher was an unemployed laborer who had earned only $400 in 1963. From that porch, Johnson announced that "the greatest war the United States ever waged" was about to begin.

That "war" was of course the Johnson administration's "War on Poverty." APSO, in effect, was the Episcopal Church's response to it. A declining coal industry had reduced employment from half a million to less than 200,000. In 1963, one in three Appalachian families lived in poverty.

The president's dramatic gesture helped call attention to the abysmal poverty of the Appalachian region, and churches began to pay more attention to the plight of families in the region as well.

A coalition of churches and denominations formed the Commission on Religion in Appalachia (CORA), based in Knoxville, Tennessee, and a group of Episcopal dioceses formed Appalachia South, Inc. in 1964—soon to be called the Appalachian People's Service Organization.[17] Bishop Dan Corrigan, director of the national church's Home Missions Office, called together six Appalachian bishops to discuss a regional coalition. Bishops from the dioceses of Tennessee, West Virginia, Southwest Virginia, Western North Carolina, Lexington (Kentucky), and Virginia signed the articles of incorporation which stated that APSO's purpose was "to attempt to meet the challenge of the Christian church presented by the economic, social, and cultural problems inherent in those portions of the United States known as Appalachia." In addition, its "activities are to consist of bringing together the forces of the church and any other available organizations, groups or individuals having the means and/or skills necessary for relief of such problems."[18]

The Right Reverend William Sanders, Bishop of Tennessee, said that prior to APSO's formation, the major priorities of the Episcopal Church in Appalachia were the maintenance of small congregations in the area, and support of scattered social ministries already being offered by various church agencies there.

The Right Reverend William Marmion, Bishop of Southwest Virginia, stated that "The major priority for APSO's work was to attack Appalachia's number one problem—poverty." The Reverend George Abele of Kingsport, Tennessee, became APSO's first executive director in 1965. In 1968, the Reverend R. Baldwin Lloyd was named APSO's second executive director and continues to serve in that position. Lloyd had been the Episcopal chaplain at Virginia Polytechnic Institute in Blacksburg, Virginia.

During its early years, APSO worked to coordinate church and non church-related projects which provided assistance to the Appalachian people. Sometimes APSO assumed an advocacy role and challenged tax policies which allowed absentee corporate landowners to pay less than their "fair share" of local taxes. The Urban Ministry Program Unit was started in 1973, when the church recognized that Appalachians who left the hills to search for jobs in the cities had not found the lifestyle they sought or one with which they were comfortable. Many lived in "hillbilly" ghettoes.

"This program (The Urban Ministry Program Unit) has worked to train urban churches to respond to the needs of urban Appalachian migrants, and has helped spawn local service projects in Atlanta, Cincinnati, Charleston, and East Baltimore," wrote Stephen B. Smith, former communications director for APSO.[19] In 1984, the APSO Urban Unit initiated a series of "Working Class Ministry" Conferences. With nationwide participation, Louisville hosted the first one, while the next two were both held in Newport, Kentucky in the Greater Cincinnati area.

APSO's Youth Ministry Unit was also started in 1973. The program features week-long "work camp" experiences for youth who do minor repairs, winterization, and painting homes for poor Appalachians. APSO's Social and Specialized Ministries Unit has produced educational materials for Appalachians on land use and ownership, lifestyles, and money stewardship. The Intramont Unit provides training for ordained and lay persons for ministry in the small congregations of Appalachia.

In the spring of 1984, the APSO Board of Governors identified issues affecting the Appalachian region and ranked them in priority. The stewardship of land, resources and environment, employment, human services, and public education were targeted as priority issues for APSO to address through its four ministry units in succeeding years.

Other Groups

Six years after the eastern dioceses formed APSO in 1964, a coalition of western dioceses formed Coalition 14 (C-14) in 1971. Most of these dioceses, previously called "missionary districts," required financial assistance from the national church. After its formation, Coalition 14 received one block grant from the national church each year. Individual members then divided it according to their own needs.

The coalition's organizational meeting was held in May, 1971, in Sedalia, Colorado. Original diocesan members were the dioceses of Eau Claire, Montana, Wyoming, Eastern Oregon, South Dakota, North Dakota, Nevada, Idaho, Western Kansas, Hawaii, Arizona, Utah, Rio Grande, and Nebraska.[20]

The Right Reverend Richard Trelease, Bishop of the Rio Grande, told a later meeting of C-14 that prior to its formation, dioceses went individually to the national church office in New York City to seek funds. He explained that as a matter of course the "most charismatic of the bishops" got most of the money. Trelease said he had heard stories of some bishops who purposely wore shirts with frayed sleeves so that their appearance would make a visual statement about their need for money.

Recognizing the need for a better way to distribute funds, several national church staff members met with the missionary bishops at the 1970 General Convention in Houston. This resulted in the May, 1971 organizational meeting. One of the cornerstones of the coalition was "honesty, complete and full honesty," said Trelease. The coalition also developed formal guidelines to provide for identical budget processes in each diocese. The guidelines provide, in part, that "each jurisdiction will review its total budget with full disclosure in the presence of the fourteen member dioceses in consultation with representatives of the Executive Council, staff and members responsible for jurisdictional relations." C-14 dioceses also agreed to coordinate requests for United Thank Offering (UTO) grants from the Episcopal Church Women.

Since its formation, Hawaii has left Coalition-14, while the dioceses of Alaska, Northern Michigan, and San Joaquin have joined. Of the sixteen members in 1985, six receive no grant from the national church, but share in the "mission and ministry" of the coalition.

Like Coalition 14, the aim of "Coalition O" is cooperation in missionary work rather than competition. "O" stands for "overseas." Coalition O, which was established at the 1973 General Convention, is comprised of the nineteen overseas missionary dioceses of the Episcopal Church. While Coalition 14 includes priests and laity in its organizational structure, Coalition O membership is limited to bishops. Travel distances and costs have prohibited wider participation. While the eventual goal of each of these dioceses is autonomy and independence, Coalition O provides a fully open, joint decision-making structure for allotting the national church's funds.

Two additional overseas missionary organizations developed within the Episcopal Church in the 1970s as well. The South American Missionary Society (SAMS) established an American base of operations in 1976 to support missionary work in Latin and South American countries. An affiliate of the 138-year-old British parent organization of the same name, the United States office established its home in Union Mills, North Carolina. Although independent of the national church, SAMS worked cooperatively with the world mission office at the Episcopal Church Center in New York. The home office recruited and trained Episcopal missionaries from throughout the United States, while each missionary was asked to raise financial backing from supporting parishes. In addition to the United States and England, SAMS also maintains training centers in Australia, Canada, Ireland, and New Zealand.

The Episcopal Church Missionary Community (ECMC) was founded in 1974 by the Reverend and Mrs. Walter W. Hannum in Pasadena, California. ECMC is another independent missionary organization which works cooperatively with the national church. "We started it to enable Episcopalians to be more informed, active, and effective in world missions in obedience to the Great Commission," said Hannum, who spent twenty years working as a parish priest in Alaska. ECMC serves primarily as a training center for new missionaries, and works with candidates supplied by the South American Missionary Society, as well as the national church. By the mid-1980s, it had presented "Mission Awareness Seminars" in more than thirty-five dioceses and helped to sponsor a number of world mission training conferences.

The Ministry of the Laity

"I use music to teach multiple handicapped children skills that enable them to cope with the demands of living . . . When we sing, dance or listen together, we are creating a harmony that helps keep ourselves in balance. With ourselves in balance, our handicaps (and we all have them) become manageable. Surely this is a form of ministry, a most joyful one."

These words, written by a midwestern teacher in her diocesan newspaper, reflected the church's changing concept of ministry. As the Episcopal Church moved into the 1980s, the ministry of all Christians, or "total ministry" became more of a concern for all Episcopalians. Scores of articles and books told Episcopalians that all Christians were called to ministry, not just their parish priests.

The term "lay ministry" decreased in use because of its connotation of being carried out by a "novice" or that it was in some way a "second-class" ministry. The term was replaced by the concept of a "total ministry." That term came into the official language of the Episcopal Church at the 1976 General Convention through its use in various reports and resolutions. "Total ministry," sometimes used synonomously with "ministry of the laity," was officially defined as "the ministry of all God's people in all areas of life. It is carried out by the people of God in a style called mutual ministry: laity and clergy in roles which are mutually affirming."

The change was also reflected in the church's Prayer Book, music, and liturgy. "With the Spirit's gifts empower us for the work of ministry," asserts the refrain of one of the new hymns from the *Hymnal 1982* (Hymn No. 528). The Prayer Book attests:

Q. Who are the ministers of the church?

A. The ministers of the church are lay persons, bishops, priests, and deacons. (BCP, page 855)

These are words from the Catechism of the 1979 *Book of Common Prayer.*

The emerging lay movement was not without its gurus and spokespersons. Verna Dozier, a retired English teacher from Washington, D.C., became one of the most widely-known speakers and writers on the subject. Another well-known lay leader was Jean Haldane, who founded the Lay Academy of the Diocese of California in San Francisco, and served as its dean until 1984. This continuing education center for the laity served as a model for efforts in several other dioceses.

An important event in the total ministry movement was a meeting of forty-five clergy and laity in September, 1978 in Cincinnati. Together they drafted an outline of a report to the church on what total ministry is and how to support it at the diocesan level:

Total ministry is a claim upon all the baptized by the Gospel. We of the church are called to develop education and training resources which will challenge and support our members of all ages in the following ways:
a) By developing a common theological understanding of the ministry of all Christians;
b) By identification and development of gifts and skills for ministry;
c) By affirming and testing of ministries within and outside the structures of the church;
d) By identifying and developing various practical models of mutual ministry . . .[21]

The Task Force on Total Ministry developed from the 1978 meeting, and became the primary national effort of the Episcopal Church to promote the ministry of the laity. Funded and supported through the Episcopal Church Center, this group consisted of clergy and laity from around the country. They sponsored national conferences, organized a network of seminarians planning lay vocations, and developed lay leadership models for parishes and dioceses. In 1980, the task force began a study of the church's canons on ministry. It subsequently developed changes—approved by the 1985 General Convention—which clarified and strengthened the role of the laity in the church's ministry. For example, the canons had previously used the word "minister" to refer only to an ordained priest or deacon. The word, if used, was expanded to include both clergy and laity.

Overseas Mission Work Continues

"It is a monumental drought, and people are dying by the thousands. It affects an area larger than the United States," said Dr. David Crean, hunger officer for the Episcopal Church, describing the African famine of 1984-85. While the ministry of the laity was emerging at home, the Episcopal Church's overseas ministry was beginning to develop a new vitality. In response to the African famine crisis, the Presiding Bishop's Fund for World Relief received record numbers of contributions. In 1984, the fund received more than $4 million dollars, more than twice the average of previous years.

While the Episcopal Church continued to support permanent missionaries, Volunteers for Mission developed as a result of a vote by the 1976 General Convention. The program provided short-term opportunities for teachers, veterinarians, journalists, nurses, farmers, and other laity to work in projects directed by Anglican bishops overseas. By 1985, 286 Episcopalians had served as Volunteers for Mission, mostly in Central and South America and Africa.

Stewardship

As the Episcopal Church moved towards the twenty-first century, a number of encouraging signs of church health emerged. The most surprising trend was in stewardship. By 1985, the Episcopal Church ranked first among mainline denominations in per capita giving, a dramatic increase from seventh a few years earlier. Among all denominations the Episcopal Church ranked fourth in recorded per capita giving. Presiding Bishop John Allin stated, "From 1974 to 1983, the combined giving to congregations and dioceses went up from $375 million to more than $816 million."

Most observers attributed the dramatic improvements in financial stewardship to two factors: Venture in Mission and the 1982 General Convention resolution on tithing. Venture in Mission had initiated the trend of giving more freely. It seemed that after pledges were fulfilled, giving became a habit, and parishioners continued with their pledge payments, directing them to their individual churches. The 1982 General Convention affirmed the "biblical tithe as the standard for giving," and for the first time in the church's history, Episcopalians began talking about tithing. No other Episcopal church convention had ever before affirmed that 10 percent of one's income was the biblical standard of giving.

Indeed, during the 1970s and 1980s, a new focus for the Episcopal Church was emerging. After internal debates on Prayer Book revision and the ordination of women, the Episcopal Church turned its attention outward. Whether through *Venture in Mission, Partners in Mission,* or one of the many other expressions of mission, Episcopalians discovered anew some of the Bible's most familiar words: "I have not come to be ministered unto, but to minister . . ."

Archbishop of Canterbury Robert Runcie stated the point eloquently in a 1985 sermon at Westminster Abbey: "Every generation has its own problems to solve and fresh forms of evil to resist. There is no retirement from the service of God, or from the struggle to establish his reign of love and justice upon earth."[22]

15

Edmond Browning:
"There shall be no outcasts"

"I WANT TO BE VERY CLEAR: this church of ours is open to all—there shall be no outcasts—the convictions and the hopes of all will be honored. . . ."

These words of Edmond Lee Browning in his acceptance speech as presiding bishop on September 12, 1985, reflected a recurring theme throughout the previous forty years. "There shall be no outcasts" included the struggle to include women, blacks and other minorities at all levels of church life, and the recognition of the wider Christian fellowship in ecumenical relations. Fifteen years after the first women were seated as deputies, one-fourth of the deputies at the 1985 General Convention were female, including twenty-four female clergy. "This is our first successful convention for blacks," said the Venerable Lorentho Wooden, the archdeacon from the Diocese of Southern Ohio. In his remarks, the archdeacon pointed to the election of two blacks to the Executive Council and one to the board of General Theological Seminary.

When Edmond Lee Browning was elected presiding bishop, a new era in the Episcopal Church's leadership had begun. The Most Reverend John Allin ended his twelve years as presiding bishop with courage and grace as he addressed his final convention: "I thank you all for this hour and for your companionship through the years . . . I expect a change of pace, time for reflection and further inquiry and new adventures in 'the way.' "

As history passes, John Allin's contributions as presiding bishop will be increasingly valued. It is difficult to measure his leadership through such recent historical perspective. When he was elected in 1973, however, the Episcopal Church was torn, divided, and rapidly losing membership. The 1985 convention was characterized as one of the most harmonious and unified in history. By that time, membership losses had levelled off and increases in membership were evident. In 1973, the national church budget was $13.6 million. Twelve years later under Allin's leadership, it had doubled to $27.5 million.

In 1985, John Allin addressed the last Executive Council meeting he would preside over, stating that reconciliation was the primary goal of his administration. "Our Lord's mission was to reconcile us with God and each other," he stressed at the meeting held in Memphis, Tennessee. Allin fought hard to avoid threatened schism after the 1976 General Convention which voted to admit women to the priesthood. The fact that the Anglican schismatic movement has had such limited success, a "small chapter in American church history" as one historian stated it, could be largely credited to Allin.

Next to reconciliation, he may be credited for the highly successful Venture in Mission campaign. With an original aim of $100 million, the campaign for domestic and overseas missions raised over $170 million. VIM helped increase the Episcopal Church's per capita giving from seventh to first among mainline denominations, and eleventh to fourth among all denominations.

Probably Allin's greatest trial and source of criticism was the dispute over ordaining women to the priesthood. However, one of his last public statements on the issue was in 1977, when he said he was "unable to accept women in the role of priests." In a 1985 interview, he pointed out that personally, "I had to get out of that argument. My role [as presiding bishop] was to keep the two sides in conversation and to have the church do what she said she would do—ordain women priests."

As Allin moved toward the end of his term in 1985, the Episcopal Church prepared to elect its next leader. The 1982 General Convention had elected a Joint Nominating Committee consisting of bishops, priests, and laity, and chaired by Bishop John Coburn of Massachusetts. In February 1985, the Committee announced its four nominees for presiding bishop: Edmond Browning, Bishop of Hawaii; William Frey, Bishop of Colorado; Furman Stough, Bishop of Alabama; and John T. Walker, Bishop of Washington (D.C.). As momentum built towards the September convention, speculation over the eventual winner became the biggest issue.

On September 10, two days after the convention opened in Anaheim, California, 200 active and retired bishops travelled to St. Michael's Church to meet behind locked doors. They went through four ballots. Two hours later, the result was announced publicly to a crowded House of Deputies. After jubilant applause, the deputies confirmed the bishop's choice of Browning with only a sole dissenting vote.

"I don't know what this means," said Bishop Browning in a dry and cracking voice. "I was interviewed by the Nominating Committee on Ash Wednesday, informed of my nomination on my birthday" [March 11], and elected "today on the thirty-second anniversary of our marriage."

The Right Reverend Edmond Lee Browning had spent only seven of his thirty-one years in ordained ministry within the continental United States. A graduate of the college and seminary of the University of the South, Browning is widely known for his missionary experience and global involvement. After his ordination in 1954, he spent his first five years in parish positions in his native Texas. He then went to Okinawa where he was a rector, archdeacon, and later bishop of the Pacific diocese. Between 1971 and 1974, he was bishop of the Convocation of American Churches in Europe. Between 1974 and 1976, he was Executive for National and World Mission at the Episcopal Church Center in New York. The Diocese of Hawaii elected him as its bishop in 1976. He and his wife, Patricia, have five children: Mark, John, Peter, Philip, and Paige.

At this same convention, the Very Reverend David Collins, former dean of St. Philip's Cathedral in Atlanta, was elected president of the House of Deputies, and Pamela Chinnis of Washington, D.C. was elected vice-president. Collins was known as a leader in the charismatic renewal movement, while Chinnis became the first female vice-president in the convention's history.

The diversity and inclusiveness which Browning and the convention illuminated has served as a unifying theme for the past forty years of the church's history. While critics have pointed out that the Episcopal Church has been a church of the wealthiest, best-educated, and most socially-conscious Americans, that image is changing. In the late twentieth century the church has clearly demonstrated a trend toward pluralism and diversity. As American society changed, so, too, has the Episcopal Church in terms of its increasing diversity of membership.

"There shall be no outcasts" as a church dictum began in the 1940s when the church had to face the issue of prejudice within its ranks. ". . . There are no racial distinctions in the mind of the Father, and 'all are one in Christ Jesus,' " stated the church's National Council in 1943. While one can't say the church was always ready to welcome minorities as members of the body, the years since World War II have clearly moved the doors further open. By 1954, all dioceses had eliminated the color bar for representation at conventions, and all the seminaries were integrated. And while seminaries opened their doors to blacks and women, other church agencies and parishes sought them for leadership positions as well.

The enormous strides in ecumenical relations can also be seen as an extension of this theme. Officially-sponsored dialogues with Lutherans, Roman Catholics, and Orthodox churches began in the 1960s. The church has increasingly recognized that there is truly "one body" of Christ as it sought intercommunion and common recognition of ministries with these other bodies. Larger agencies, such as the World Council of Churches, brought together Christians from around the world to share in the common cup and fellowship of Christ.

When all is said and done, the threatened schism of the Episcopal Church in the late 1970s barely created a ripple in its statistical sea. On the other hand, the explosive growth of Anglicanism in Africa made American Episcopalians realize that, by 1985, there were more black than white Anglicans throughout the world. The constituency of the Episcopal Church was also changing. By 1985, an estimated 60 percent of all Episcopalians came to the church "by choice," confirmed as adults. So when Edmond

Browning said, "There shall be no outcasts," he was not predicting the future as much as he was summarizing the past. The period from 1945 to 1985 was one of reaching out to "all sorts and conditions" of humanity. "Diversity in unity, and unity in diversity" is one way Episcopalians like to describe their church. While diversity is one of its strengths, its hope is not within itself, but indeed rooted in Jesus, the Lord of history, the creator and the sustainer of life.

> He gives strength to the weary
> and increases the power of the weak.
> Even youths grow tired and weary,
> and young men stumble and fall;
> but those who hope in the Lord
> will renew their strength.
> They will soar on wings like eagles;
> they will run and not grow weary,
> they will walk and not be faint.
>   Isaiah 40:29-31 (NAS)

Notes

Chapter 1

[1]Diocesan Press Service of the Episcopal Church, January 1, 1968.
[2]Roger Rosenblatt, "The Atomic Age," *Time* magazine, July 29, 1985, p. 54.
[3]George E. DeMille, *The Episcopal Church Since 1900* (New York: Morehouse-Gorham Company, 1955), p. 154.
[4]"Site Purchased," *The Living Church* 141, September 14, 1960, p. 141.
[5]George E. DeMille, op. cit. p. 184.
[6]*Bishop Henry Knox Sherrill Oral History Project: Reminiscenses of Bishop Arthur E. Walmsley* (New York: Columbia University Oral History Research Office, 1981), p. 11. Transcripts held at the Yale Divinity School Library and the Archives of the Episcopal Church.
[7]*Bishop Henry Knox Sherrill Oral History Project: Reminiscenses of Bishop Roger Blanchard* (New York: Columbia University Oral History Research Office, 1981), p. 52-53. Transcripts held at the Yale Divinity School Library and the Archives of the Episcopal Church.
[8]Norman Pittenger, "Continuing Anglicanism and the Challenge of Our Times," *Anglican Theological Review,* Vol. XXX (1948) p. 12.

Chapter 2

[1]Ruth Jenkins, "I Still Feel Indignant," *The Witness,* November 1983, p. 13.
[2]"A Woman Deputy," *The Living Church* 124, June 29, 1952, p. 19.
[3]"No Voice, No Vote, No Women," *The Living Church* 119, October 9, 1949, p. 9. See also David E. Sumner, "Women Deputies' Struggle Overshadowed by Ordination," *The Witness,* November 1983, p. 10.
[4]Ruth Jenkins, op. cit. p. 13.
[5]"Episcopalians Debate Status of Women," *The Christian Century* 66, October 12, 1949, p. 1188.
[6]"Report of the Commission on Women," *The Living Church* 124, June 22, 1952, p. 10-11. The report is signed by its members: The Right Reverend Malcolm E. Peabody, Chairman; the Right Reverend Richard A. Kirchhoffer, the Right Reverend Girault Jones, the Reverend William P. Barnds, the Reverend Robert H. Dunn, Philip Adams, C. Clement French, Ronald L. Jardine, Miss Leila Anderson, Miss Ruth Jenkins, and Mrs. Edward G. Lasar.
[7]"Still No Women," *The Christian Century* 72, October 2, 1955, p. 25.
[8]"Women and the Franchise," *The Episcopalian,* April 1964, p. 20.
[9]Clifford P. Morehouse, "A Matter of Segregation," *The Episcopalian,* April 1964, p. 22.

[10]Mary Eunice Oliver, "The Last Woman Not to be Seated," *The Witness,* November 1983, p. 10.

Chapter 3

[1]Mary Cochran, "Jean Dementi: A Wilderness Experience," *The Episcopalian,* May 1977, p. 11.

[2]Quoted from Paul Moore, *Take a Bishop Like Me* (San Francisco: Harper and Row, 1979), p. 88.

[3]Thomas L. Ehrich, "Pat Park: Ordination Dynamo," *General Convention Daily* (Minneapolis: September 21, 1976), p. 1.

[4]_____ "Deep Rift in the Soul of the Church," *General Convention Daily* (Minneapolis: September 21, 1976), p. 1.

[5]Janette Pierce, "Women Priests Still Controversial," *The Episcopalian,* December 1976, p. 3.

[6]Heather Huyck, "Indelible Change: Women Priests in the Episcopal Church," *Historical Magazine of the Protestant Episcopal Church* 51, (December 1982), p. 389.

[7]Ted Harrison, "A Priestly Trail-Blazer," *The Church Times,* May 10, 1985, p. 11. See also Harrison, *Much Beloved Daughter: The Story of Florence Li,* (London: Darton, Longman, and Todd, 1985).

[8]Ibid. p. 13.

[9]William Stringfellow and Anthony Towne, *The Death and Life of Bishop Pike* (Garden City, New York: Doubleday and Company, 1976), p. 317.

[10]*Journal of the General Convention, 1967,* Supplements, Part V, p. 7.

[11]"Deaconess Now Functions as Deacon," *The Living Church* 150, March 23, 1965, p. 5.

[12]James B. Simpson and Edward M. Story, *The Long Shadows of Lambeth X* (New York: McGraw-Hill, 1969), p. 184.

[13]"Theological Seminary to Accept Women Next Fall," *The Living Church* 136, March 6, 1958, p. 9.

[14]Heather Huyck, op. cit. p. 386.

[15]Ibid. p. 387.

[16]James B. Simpson and Edward P. Story, op. cit. p. 187.

[17]"Caucus Formed," *The Living Church* 163, December 5, 1971, p. 5.

[18]Barbara Schlachter, "The Beginning: 1971-1975" *Ruach,* Autumn, 1981, p. 1. *Ruach* is the newsletter of the Episcopal Women's Caucus. This tenth anniversary issue contains a large amount of historical information on the women's movement in the Episcopal Church.

[19]Paul Moore, op. cit. p. 1.

[20]Suzanne R. Hiatt, "How We Brought the Good News from Graymoor to Minneapolis: An Episcopal Paradigm," *Journal of Ecumenical Studies* 20 (Fall 1983), p. 580.

[21]"An Open Letter to the House of Bishops," *Journal of the General Convention, 1976,* p. B-182.

[22]Robert L. DeWitt, "Why the Other Bishops Balked," *The Witness, Special Anniversary Issue, 1984,* p. 14. This undated anniversary issue contains several articles about the July 1974 Philadelphia ordinations.

[23]Diocesan Press Service of the Episcopal Church, July 25, 1974.

[24]"Do You Remember?" *Ruach* 3, Autumn 1981, p. 6.

[25]*Journal of the General Convention, 1976,* p. B-198.

[26]Erwin M. Soukup, "Advocates of Women's Ordination Muster Momentum," Diocesan Press Service of the Episcopal Church, January 27, 1975.

[27]Diocesan Press Service of the Episcopal Church, April 11, 1975.

[28]*Journal of the General Convention, 1976,* p. B-326.
[29]"Bishop Allin Reaffirms Ordination Position," Diocesan Press Service of the Episcopal Church, April 12, 1976.
[30]Polly Bond, "Sixty-Seven Bishops Sponsor Women's Ordination," *Interchange* (Diocese of Southern Ohio) September 4, 1976, p. 8.
[31]Paul Moore, op. cit. p. 83.
[32]Heather Huyck, op. cit. p. 397.
[33]*Journal of the General Convention, 1979,* p. B-202.
[34]Ibid. p. B-193.
[35]Michael M. Marrett, *The Lambeth Conferences and Women Priests* (Smithtown, New York: Exposition Press, 1981), Appendix, p. 153.
[36]Heather Huyck, op. cit. p. 398.

Chapter 4

[1]J. Carleton Hayden, *Struggle, Strife and Salvation: The Role of Blacks in the Episcopal Church* (Cincinnati: Forward Movement, 1976), p. 19.
[2]Ibid. p. 20.
[3]*The Living Church* 119, August 14, 1949, p. 8.
[4]*The Living Church* 171, November 7, 1975, p. 11.
[5]Henry Knox Sherrill, *Among Friends: An Autobiography* (Boston: Little, Brown, and Company, 1962), p. 226.
[6]Odell Greenlead Harris, *A History of the Seminary to Prepare Black Men for the Ministry of the Protestant Episcopal Church.* (Alexandria, Virginia: Virginia Theological Seminary, 1980), p. 3.
[7]Donald S. Armentrout, *The Quest for the Informed Priest: A History of the School of Theology* (Sewanee, Tennessee. University of the South Press, 1979), p. 281.
[8]Ibid. p. 307.
[9]Henry Knox Sherrill, op. cit. p. 247.
[10]Russell Porter, "Episcopal Convention Cancelled Over Racial Segregation," New York Times, September 9, 1954, p. 1.
[11]Ibid. p. 1.
[12]Henry Knox Sherrill, op. cit. p. 257.
[13]*The Church Speaks: Christian Social Relations at General Convention 1955* (New York: The National Council, 1955), p. 15.
[14]David Wallechinsky and Irving Wallace, "Headline 1955: Rosa Parks," *The People's Almanac* (Garden City, New York: Doubleday and Company, 1975): pp. 728-729. This book contains a full account of the story.
[15]*The Living Church* 135, October 6, 1957, p. 10.
[16]John L. Kater, Jr. "The Episcopal Society for Cultural and Racial Unity and its Role in the Episcopal Church, 1959-1970" (Ph.D. diss. McGill University, Toronto, 1973), p. 28.
[17]*The Christian Century* 80, September 20, 1963, p. 63. See also "Episcopal Group Held in Jackson," *New York Times,* September 14, 1963, p. 32.
[18]John L. Kater, Jr., "The Episcopal Society for Cultural and Racial Unity," p. 50.
[19]General Convention News Release No. 11 (Detroit, 1961), September 16, 1961.
[20]*Journal of the General Convention, 1961,* p. 418.
[21]Zebulan Vance Wilson, *They Took Their Stand: The Integration of Southern Private Schools,* (Atlanta: Mid-South Association of Independent Schools, 1980), p. 5.
[22]Ibid. p. 5.
[23]"Church School Turns Down Negro Child," *The Living Church* 146, March 24, 1963, p. 6. See also "Clergy Sign Protest," Ibid., November 3, 1963, p. 9.
[24]John L. Kater, Jr., "Dwelling Together in Unity: Church, Theology and Race 1950-1965, *Anglican Theological Review* 58, (October 1976), p. 451.

²⁵David E. Sumner, "The Episcopal Church's Involvement in Civil Rights: 1943-1973" (Sewanee, Tennessee: S.T.M. thesis, University of the South, 1983), p. 39.

²⁶"Disability Forces Resignation," *The Living Church* 148, April 12, 1964, p. 5.

²⁷*The Living Church* 149, July 12, 1964, p. 5.

²⁸Margaret Frakes, "Episcopal Dichotomy," *The Christian Century* 81, November 11, 1964, p. 1390.

²⁹John L. Kater, Jr. "Dwelling Together in Unity," p. 452.

³⁰*The Living Church* 150, March 21, 1965, p. 8.

³¹John L. Kater, Jr., "Experiment in Freedom: The Episcopal Church and the Black Power Movement," *Historical Magazine of the Protestant Episcopal Church,* 48 (March 1979), p. 71.

³²*Church and Society in Crisis: Social Policy of the Episcopal Church 1964-67* (New York: The Executive Council, 1968), p. 23.

³³John L. Kater, Jr., "Experiment in Freedom," p. 72.

³⁴John B. Morris, "Power: Black and White—Some Reflections," September 27, 1966. Atlanta, Georgia: Martin Luther King, Jr. Liberary, ESCRU Archives. Cited in Kater dissertation, p. 121.

³⁵J. Carleton Hayden, "Different Names But the Same Agenda: Precursors to the Union of Black Episcopalians," in *The Union of Black Episcopalians* (UBE Pamphlet, 1985).

³⁶*The Episcopalian,* October 1969, p. 21. See also the April 1967 issue for the advertisement.

Chapter 5

¹*Journal of the General Convention, 1967,* p. 2.

²"House of Deputies Minority Report of the Program and Budget Committee," *Journal of the General Convention, 1967,* p. 241.

³Vine Deloria, Jr. "GCSP: The Demons at Work," *Historical Magazine of the Protestant Episcopal Church* XLVII (Winter 1979), p. 84.

⁴*What is GCSP?* (New York: The Executive Council of the Episcopal Church, 1972), p. 2.

⁵Ibid. p. 2.

⁶David E. Sumner, "The Episcopal Church's Involvement in Civil Rights: 1943-1973" (Sewanee, Tennessee: S.T.M. thesis, University of the South, 1983), p. 109.

⁷Diocesan Press Service of the Episcopal Church, December 16, 1968.

⁸*The Living Church* 153, September 25, 1965, p. 5.

⁹David E. Sumner, op. cit. p. 75.

¹⁰Clifford P. Morehouse, "The General Convention Special Program: Past and Future," General Convention News Release No. 38 (Houston, 1970), October 14, 1970.

¹¹Leon E. Modeste, *Mission: Empowerment* (Unpublished, undated), cited in John L. Kater, Jr. "Experiment in Freedom . . . ," p. 77.

¹²*The Living Church* 159, October 12, 1969, p. 22.

¹³Philip Deemer, ed. *Episcopal Year 1969* (New York: Jarrow Press, 1970), p. 34.

¹⁴David E. Sumner, op. cit. p. 79.

¹⁵Deemer, op. cit. p. 103.

¹⁶*Journal of Special General Convention II, 1969,* p. 204.

¹⁷"Churches Protest GCSP," *The Christian Century* 86, October 15, 1969, p. 1306.

¹⁸Vine Deloria, Jr., op. cit. p. 87.

¹⁹Ibid. p. 87.

²⁰Clifford P. Morehouse, op. cit.

²¹Vine Deloria, Jr., op. cit. p. 89.

²²*What We Learned from What You Said* (New York, The Executive Council, 1973), p. 2.

[23]Executive Council Minutes, December 12-13, 1973 (New York: Episcopal Church Center, Henry Knox Sherrill Resource Center).
[24]Diocesan Press Service of the Episcopal Church, February 22, 1973.
[25]Diocesan Press Service of the Episcopal Church, May 2, 1973.
[26]Vine Deloria, Jr. op. cit. p. 90.
[27]David E. Sumner, "Exhausted Church Needs Central Focus," *North Carolina Churchman* (Diocese of North Carolina), June 1978, p. 8.
[28]David E. Sumner, "The Episcopal Church's Involvement in Civil Rights," op. cit. p. 110.

Chapter 6

[1]Philip Deemer, *Episcopal Year 1970* (New York: Jarrow Press, 1971), p. 309.
[2]Richard N. Current, et al. *A Survey of American History Since 1865, Vol. II.* (New York: Alfred A. Knopf, 6th edition, 1983), p. 903.
[3]*Journal of the General Convention, 1973,* p. 513.
[4]"Deputies Don't Back Bishops on Viet Nam," *General Convention Daily* (Houston: October 23, 1970), p. 1.
[5]*Journal of Special General Convention II, 1969,* p. 513.
[6]"A Dangerous Precedent," *The Living Church* 133, December 16, 1956, pp. 8-9.
[7]Trevor Moore, "Plowshares into Swords," *The Christian Century* 88, March 3, 1971, p. 295.
[8]Sandra Anderson, "Bishop Consecrated," *The Living Church* 176, March 26, 1978, p. 6.
[9]"Episcopal Bishop Bars Homosexual Wedding," *The Christian Century* 88, March 3, 1971, p. 279.
[10]Paul Moore, *Take a Bishop Like Me* (San Francisco: Harper and Row, 1979), p. 110.
[11]Ibid. p. 172. See also "Statement to the House of Bishops," *Journal of the General Convention, 1979,* p. B-177 and "Lesbian Ordained," *The Living Church* 174, February 6, 1977, p. 5.
[12]Nancy Axell, Curtis Axell, *Report: Human Sexuality: Diocesan Survey* (New York: Seabury Professional Services, 1981), p. 22.
[13]*General Convention Daily* (Denver, September 18, 1979), p. 1. For a text of the resolution which passed, see *Church and Society: Social Policy of the Episcopal Church, 1967-1979* (New York: The Executive Council, p. A-53.)
[14]From the official liturgy for ordination of a priest, *Book of Common Prayer,* p. 527.
[15]Dorothy Mills Parker, "Ordination Sparks Protest," *The Living Church* 187, July 7, 1985, p. 6.
[16]*Lambeth Conference Report, 1958,* p. 148.
[17]John Goodbody, The Episcopal Church Looks at Issues: Social Ministry" *The Episcopalian,* June 1985, pp. 13-16.

Chapter 7

[1]Quoted in Peter Day's, "Revolution in the Sunday School," *The Living Church* 131, August 7, 1955, p. 10.
[2]Ibid. p. 10.
[3]"House of Bishops: New Plans for Christian Education," *The Living Church* 110, February 11, 1945, p. 7.
[4]Dorothy L. Braun, "A Historical Study of the Origin and Development of the Seabury Series of the Protestant Episcopal Church" (Ph.D. diss., New York University, 1960), p. 16.

[5] *Journal of the General Convention, 1946,* p. 256.
[6] *Journal of the General Convention, 1949,* pp. 479-480.
[7] Dorothy L. Braun, op. cit. p. 76-77.
[8] George E. DeMille, *The Episcopal Church Since 1900* (New York: Morehouse-Gorham Company, 1955), p. 128.
[9] Dorothy L. Braun, op. cit. p. 321.
[10] National Council Minutes, February 12-14, 1952 (New York: Episcopal Church Center: Henry Knox Sherrill Resource Center), p. 34. Cited in Dorothy L. Braun, op. cit. p. 178.
[11] Dorothy L. Braun, op. cit. p. 326.
[12] Peter Day, "Revolution in the Sunday School," *The Living Church* 131, August 7, 1955, p. 20.
[13] Peter Day, " 'Go' Signal for the Seabury Series," *The Living Church* 137, November 9, 1958, p. 14.
[14] Don Frank Fenn, "What Parishes Think of Church School Materials," *The Living Church* 136, June 1, 1958, p. 12.
[15] Ann Proctor McElligott, "The History of the Department of Christian Education of the Executive Council of the Episcopal Church," (Master of Divinity thesis, The General Theological Seminary, 1984), p. 27.
[16] Ann Procter McElligott, op. cit. p. 111.
[17] Ibid. p. 116.
[18] "Education for Ministry Plays in More than Peoria," *Interchange* (Diocese of Southern Ohio), January 1984, p. 9.
[19] Dorothy L. Braun, op. cit. p. 141.
[20] "Twelve Years of the Forward Movement," *The Living Church* 113, August 18, 1946, pp. 16-19.
[20] *Forward Year by Year, 1934-1982.* (Cincinnati: Forward Movement Publications, 1982), p. 10.

Chapter 8

[1] Thomas L. Ehrich, ed., *New Perspectives on Episcopal Seminaries,* (Cambridge, MA: Episcopal Divinity School, 1986), p. 69.
[2] "Too Many Clergy," *The Christian Century* 95, May 10, 1978, p. 495.
[3] Lynn Bauman, "Is the Clergy Surplus a Myth or a Matter of History?" *Crossroads* (Diocese of Dallas), April 1986, p. 3.
[4] *Fact Book on Theological Education for the Academic Year 1985-86* (Vandalia, Ohio: Association of Theological Schools, 1986), p. 13.
[5] "Report of the Board for Theological Education," *Journal of the General Convention, 1979,* pp. AA-316.
[6] William E. Swing, "Where Have All the Young Men Gone," *The Living Church* 185, December 2, 1984, p. 9.
[7] "Report of the Board for Theological Education," *Journal of Special General Convention II, 1969,* p. 381.
[8] Ibid. p. 381. See also "James L. Lowery, Jr., "The Clergy Deployment Office," *The Living Church* 178, June 17, 1979, p. 10.
[9] Christopher Walters-Bugbee, "Going Public: Seminaries in Search of Support," *The Christian Century* 98, May 13, 1981, p. 538.
[10] Ibid. p. 540.
[11] "Report of the Board for Theological Education," *Journal of the General Convention, 1976,* p. AA-164.
[12] "Report of the Board for Theological Education," *Journal of the General Convention, 1970,* p. 734.

[13]*Fact Book on Theological Education for the Academic Year 1985-86,* op. cit. p. 141.

[14]*Theological Education in Accredited Episcopal Seminaries* (New York: A Report by Peat, Marwick, Mitchell and Company prepared for the Board for Theological Education, January, 1982), p. 16.

[15]David E. Sumner, "One Percent Plan: It's Working" *The Living Church* 184, March 11, 1984, p. 7.

[16]Douglass Lewis, "Should Every Minister Have a Doctorate?" *The Christian Century* 81, February 4, 1981, p. 137.

[17]Charles L. Taylor, ed. *Ministry for Tomorrow: Report of the Special Committee on Theological Education* (New York: Seabury Press, 1967).

[18]*Journal of the 94th Annual Convention, 1968, Diocese of Southern Ohio* (Cincinnati: Diocese of Southern Ohio, 1968), p. 93.

[19]*Journal of the 103rd Council, 1952, Diocese of Texas* (Houston: Diocese of Texas, 1952), p. 77.

[20]"Report of the Board for Theological Education," *Journal of the General Convention, 1979,* p. AA-317.

[21]O. C. Edwards, Jr., "The Strange Case of Diocesan Training Schools," *The Christian Century* 97, February 6, 1980. p. 131.

Chapter 9

[1]Jean Caffey Lyles, "Common Prayer and an Uncommon Convention," *The Christian Century* 93, October 6, 1976, p. 829.

[2]Ibid. p. 829.

[3]Bayard Jones, editor. *Prayer Book Studies 4: The Eucharistic Liturgy* (New York: The Church Pension Fund, 1953), p. 4.

[4]Charles P. Price, *Prayer Book Studies 29: Introducing the Book* (New York: The Church Hymnal Corporation, 1976), p. 12.

[5]"Toward Prayer Book Revision: Report of the Standing Liturgical Commission," *The Living Church* 118, June 12, 1949, p. 5.

[6]*Prayer Book Studies 4: The Eucharistic Liturgy,* (New York: The Church Hymnal Corporation, 1953), pp. 135-136.

[7]"Report of the Standing Liturgical Commission," *Journal of the General Convention, 1967,* Appendix 23.10.

[8]*Prayer Book Studies 15: The Problem and Method of Prayer Book Revision* (New York: The Church Pension Fund, 1961), p. 8.

[9]"Deputies Approve Draft Book," *General Convention Daily,* September 20, 1976, p. 1.

[10]"Prayer Book Society Stunned," *General Convention Daily,* September 20, 1976, p. 1.

[11]Betty Gray, "Episcopalians Shape a New Liturgical Life," *The Christian Century* 93, September 1, 1976, p. 731.

[12]Earl H. Brill, "The Episcopal Church: Conflict and Cohesion," *The Christian Century* 95, January 18, 1978, p. 41.

[13]Marion J. Hatchett, *Commentary on the American Prayer Book* (New York: The Seabury Press, 1980), p. 345.

[14]_____, "Twenty-five years of Eucharistic Development," *National Bulletin on Liturgy,* 15 (Jan.-Feb. 1982), p. 39.

[15]Diocesan Press Service of the Episcopal Church, December 6, 1976.

[16]Sherodd Albritton, "What's Going On with the Hymnal?" *Historical Magazine of the Protestant Episcopal Church,* vol. XLVIII (Summer 1979), p. 140.

[17]David E. Sumner, "The New Hymnal: An Interview with Charles Price," *Interchange* (Diocese of Southern Ohio), October 1981), p. 4.

[18]*The Hymnal 1982* (New York: The Church Hymnal Corporation, 1985), contained in the Preface.
[19]"Report of the Standing Committee on Church Music," *The Blue Book for General Convention, 1982,* p. 205.
[20]Diocesan Press Service of the Episcopal Church, January 16, 1986.

Chapter 10

[1]Michael J. McManus, "At St. Paul's, Darien, the Holy Spirit is Alive, Well and Active" *The Episcopalian,* September 1978, p. 13.
[2]Richard Quebedeaux, *The New Charismatics II* (San Francisco: Harper and Row, 1983), p. 1.
[3]Ibid. p. 61.
[4]"Rector and a Rumpus," *Newsweek,* July 4, 1960, p. 77.
[5]"Speaking in Tongues," *Time,* August 15, 1960, p. 55.
[6]Richard Quebedeaux, op. cit. p. 10.
[7]W. Graham Pulkingham, *They Left Their Nets: A Vision for Community Ministry,* (New York: Morehouse-Barlow, 1973), p. 13.
[8]Ibid. p. 96. See also, "Positive Pentecostalism: A Visit to the Church of the Redeemer, Houston, Texas," *The Living Church* 171, September 14, 1975, p. 16.
[9]"Pentecostal Voices," *The Living Church* 141, July 17, 1960, p. 9.
[10]"New Movements in the Church," *Journal of the General Convention, 1964,* p. 978.
[11]"First National Episcopal Charismatic Conference," *The Living Church* 166, March 18, 1973, p. 13.
[12]*Your Fourth Day* (Dallas: Ultreya Publications, 1985), p. 1.
[13]John E. Borrego, "What is Cursillo?" *The Living Church* 187, October 20, 1985, p. 8.
[14]Allen W. Brown, "PEWSACTION," *The Living Church* 167, September 9, 1973, p. 10.
[15]"National Conference on Renewal First for Episcopal Church," *The Living Church* 169, November 24, 1974, p. 9.
[16]Philip Deemer, *Renewal Movements in the Episcopal Church* (Cincinnati: Forward Movement, 1975), p. 4. For a series of articles on renewal organizations, see *New Life,* October 1975 and May 1974.
[17]Peter R. Rodgers, "Fellowship of Witness," *New Life,* May 1974, p. 21.
[18]Clark W. Trafton, OHC, "Order of the Holy Cross," *New Life,* January 1976, p. 9-10.
[19]*Anglican Religious Communities in the United States and Canada,* (Sandy, Oregon: Conference on the Religious Life, 1975), p. 34. For a series of articles on the religious communities, see *New Life,* January 1976.
[20]Andrew Rank, SSP, *A Directory of the Conference on the Religious Life in the Anglican Communion* (Published by the Conference on the Religious Life, 1985), p. 5.

Chapter 11

[1]Henry Knox Sherrill, *Among Friends: An Autobiography,* (Boston: Little, Brown, and Company, 1962), p. 314.
[2]"The Church and the Churches," *Time,* March 26, 1951, p. 68.
[3]Paul A. Crow, Jr., and William Jerry Boney, eds. *Church Union at Midpoint,* (New York: Association Press, 1972), p. 21. Chapter 2 contains a summary of these early unity attempts.
[4]"Amsterdam in Retrospect," *The Living Church* 117, October 17, 1948, p. 19.

⁵These were the Foreign Mission Conference of North America, Home Missions Council of North America, International Council of Religious Education, Missionary Education Movement of the U.S. and Canada, National Protestant Council on Higher Education, United Council of Church Women, United Stewardship Council, Church World Service, Interseminary Committee, Protestant Film Commission, and the Protestant Radio Commission.

⁶Paul A. Crow, Jr. and William Jerry Boney, op. cit. p. 13.

⁷Eugene Carson Blake, "A Proposal Towards the Reunion of Christ's Church," *The Ecumenical Review* 38, April 1986, p. 140.

⁸J. Robert Wright, ed., *A Communion of Communions: One Eucharistic Fellowship, The Detroit Report and Papers of the Triennial Ecumenical Study of the Episcopal Church, 1976-79* (New York: Seabury Press, 1979), p. 18.

⁹Diocesan Press Service of the Episcopal Church, June 15, 1973.

¹⁰William B. Lawson, *Moving Toward Unity: A Summary of Current Relationships Between the Episcopal Church and Other Churches* (Cincinnati: Forward Movement, 1984), p. 8.

¹¹Gerald F. Moede, ed., *The COCU Consensus: In Quest of a Church Uniting* (Princeton: Consultation on Church Union, 1985), p. 1.

¹²J. Robert Wright, op. cit. p. 289.

¹³William B. Lawson, op. cit. p. 11.

¹⁴Robert Mercer, "Lambeth 1978: An Interview with Bishop John Maury Allin," *Ecumenical Trends* 7, (Graymoor Ecumenical Institute), October 1978, p. 1.

Chapter 12

¹*Journal of the General Convention, 1967,* p. 362.

²George A. DeMille, *The Episcopal Church Since 1900* (New York: Morehouse-Gorham Company, 1955), p. 159. This work includes a complete discussion of the merger proposal in Chapter 7.

³J. Robert Wright, ed., *A Communion of Communions: One Eucharistic Fellowship. The Detroit Report and Papers of the Triennial Ecumenical Study of the Episcopal Church, 1976-1979.* (New York: Seabury Press, 1979), p. 25.

⁴"Where We Are: A Challenge For the Future, A 12-Year Report," *Ecumenical Bulletin* 27, January-February, 1978, p. 1.

⁵Diocesan Press Service of the Episcopal Church, June 15, 1973, pp. 1-6.

⁶J. Robert Wright, op. cit. p. 25.

⁷*Called To Full Unity: Documents on Anglican-Catholic Relations, 1966-1984* (Washington, D.C.: National Conference of Catholic Bishops, 1985). Available from Forward Movement Publications, Cincinnati, Ohio.

⁸"Relationships Between Churches Which Do and Do Not Ordain Women," *Ecumenical Bulletin* 20, November-December, 1976, p. 6.

⁹"Letters Exchanged by Pope and Anglican Leader," *Origins* 6 (National Catholic Documentary Service), August 12, 1976, p. 33.

¹⁰"Relationships Between Churches Which Do and Do Not Ordain Women, op. cit. p. 6.

¹¹"ARC Agreed Statement: Christian Unity and Women's Ordination," *Ecumenical Bulletin* 15, January-February 1976, p. 25.

¹²"Report of the Standing Commission on Ecumenical Relations," *Blue Book of the General Convention Journal, 1985,* p. 33.

¹³*Journal of the General Convention, 1964,* p. 454.

¹⁴J. Robert Wright, op. cit. p. 71.

¹⁵"More Response to Women in Priesthood from Roman Catholics and Orthodox," *Ecumenical Bulletin* 21, January-February 1977, p. 21.

[16]The Dublin Statement has been published with the 1976 Moscow Agreed Statement in *Anglican-Orthodox Dialogue: Dublin Agreed Statement, 1984* (Crestwood, NY: St. Vladimir's Seminary Press, 1985), p. 8.

[17]*Lutheran-Episcopal Dialogue: A Progress Report* (Forward Movement, 1973), p. 13. For additional information, see *Lutheran-Episcopal Dialogue: Report and Recommendations.* (Cincinnati: Forward Movement Publications, 1981) and William H. Peterson and Robert J. Goeser, *Traditions Transplanted, The Story of Anglican and Lutheran Churches in America* (Forward Movement, 1981).

[18]"Report of the Standing Commission on Ecumenical Relations," *Journal of the General Convention,* p. AA-33.

[19]William Norgren, "The Concordat Relationships," published in J. Robert Wright, op. cit. p. 184.

[20]*Handbook for Diocesan Ecumenism, 1980-82 Edition* (New York: The Executive Council, 1980), p. 13.

[21]*Journal of the General Convention, 1979,* p. B-40. See also J. Robert Wright, op. cit. p. 3.

Chapter 13

[1]"An Open Letter to the Bishops of the Episcopal Church," *The Christian Challenge* (May 1976), p. 1.

[2]*Episcopalians United,* September 22, 1976, p. 4.

[3]Donald S. Armentrout, *Episcopal Splinter Groups: A Study of Groups Which Have Left the Episcopal Church, 1873-1985* (Sewanee, Tennessee: School of Theology of the University of the South, 1985), p. 41.

[4]Nathaniel W. Pierce, A Report on the St. Louis Congress, September 1977 (Nampa, Idaho: privately published, 1977), p. 8.

[5]Jean Caffey Lyles, "The Old Schism Trail," *The Christian Century* 94, October 5, 1977, p. 867.

[6]Anglican Secessionists Consecrate Four Bishops," *The Christian Century* 95, February 15, 1978, p. 149.

[7]"Breakaway Body Shunned," *The Christian Century* 95, February 22, 1978, p. 183.

[8]Donald S. Armentrout, op. cit. p. 46.

[9]"Another Group Formed," *The Living Church* 176, March 12, 1978, p. 6.

[10]"Bishop Chambers Charged," *The Episcopalian,* August 1978, p. 2.

[11]Louis E. Traycik, "The Continuing Church Today, Part III: The Future of the Movement," *The Christian Challenge,* April 1983, p. 9.

[12]"Splinter Group Splits," *The Christian Century* 94, September 12, 1977", p. 842.

[13]Louis E. Traycik, "The Continuing Church Today, Part II: The Other Churches," *The Christian Challenge,* March 1983, p. 9.

[14]Nathaniel W. Pierce, op. cit. p. 2.

[15]Personal interview with Louis E. Traycik, Austin, Texas, February 18, 1985.

[16]Donald S. Armentrout, op. cit. p. 20.

[17]Widick Schroeder, "Age Cohorts, the Family Life Cycle, and Participation in the Voluntary Church in America: Implications for Membership Patterns, 1950-2000," *Chicago Theological Seminary Register* LXV (Fall 1975), pp. 13-28.

[18]Ibid. p. 23.

[19]David E. Sumner, "The Children Shall Lead Us: The Relationship Between U.S. Birthrate and Episcopal Church Membership," *Historical Magazine of the Protestant Episcopal Church* LIV (September 1985), p. 253.

[20]John Schultz, "State of the Church, 9/9/84" (New York: Episcopal Church Center, 1984, unpublished report).

Chapter 14

[1]Neil Lebhar and Martyn Minns, "Why Did the Yankees Go Home? A Study of Episcopal Missions: 1953-1977," *Historical Magazine of the Protestant Episcopal Church,* XLVIII (March 1979), pp. 27-43.

[2]*Proceedings of the Anglican Congress, Toronto, 1963.* (New York: distributed in the U.S. by Seabury Press, 1963), p. 118.

[3]Cecil Northcott, "New Anglican Horizon," *The Christian Century* 81, January 29, 1964, p. 134. See also "Headquarters Chief," *The Living Church* 138, April 26, 1959, p. 7.

[4]James B. Simpson and Edward M. Story, *The Long Shadows of Lambeth X* [1978] (New York: McGraw-Hill, 1979), p. 250.

[5]General Convention News Release No. 30 (St. Louis: October 15, 1964).

[6]*Bonds of Affection: Proceedings of ACC-6* (London: Anglican Consultative Council, 1985), p. 19.

[7]Ibid. p. 19.

[8]David E. Sumner, "U.S. Dioceses Evaluate Companion Diocese Programs," *Interchange* (Diocese of Southern Ohio), March 1986, p. 6.

[9]*Partners in Mission: Anglican Consultative Council, Second Meeting, Dublin 1973.* (London: SPCK, 1973), p. 53.

[10]James W. Kennedy, editor, *Partners in Mission. The Louisville Consultation, 1977* (Cincinnati: Forward Movement, 1977), p. 102.

[11]Harriet Heithaus, "Excerpts from a Geneva Diary," *Interchange,* (Diocese of Southern Ohio) July-August 1983, p. 7.

[12]*Journal of the General Convention, 1976,* p. C-130.

[13]Henry L. McCorkle, "Early Venture Campaigns Pass Goals," *The Episcopalian,* September 1978, p. 6.

[14]James W. Kennedy, op. cit. p. 10.

[15]Nelson Foxx, "St. Matthias Takes to the Streets," *Jubilee,* Winter 1986, p. 22.

[16]Jane Oglesby, "The Roots of Jubilee," *Jubilee,* Winter 1986, p. 18.

[17]For a complete account of APSO history, see Stephen B. Smith, "Development of the Appalachian People's Service Organization" *Historical Magazine of the Protestant Episcopal Church* LII (December 1983), pp. 405-426.

[18]Ibid. p. 411.

[19]Ibid. p. 424.

[20]"Coalition-14," *Episcopal Year 1971,* Philip Deemer, ed. (Lenox, Massachusetts: Jarrow Press, 1972), p. 64.

[21]*Journal of the General Convention, 1979,* p. AA-185.

[22]Robert A. K. Runcie, "Great Afflictions Call Forth Great Virtues," *The Church Times,* May 10, 1985, p. 5.

Appendices

A. A Chronology of Episcopal Church History

1946   General Convention, Philadelphia (September 10-20):
—Merger proposal with Presbyterian church is defeated.

—Mrs. Randolph Dyer from Diocese of Missouri is seated as a deputy; only woman to be seated as a deputy until 1970.

—Henry Knox Sherrill, Bishop of Massachusetts, is elected presiding bishop.

—Supreme Court Justice Owen Roberts is elected first lay president of House of Deputies.

—Presiding Bishop's Fund for World Relief is established.

1948   World Council of Churches is organized at First Assembly in Amsterdam, Holland (August 22-September 4).

Lambeth Conference in London, England, denies Synod of Hong Kong's request for permission to ordain women as priests on the grounds "the time has not yet come."

1949   General Convention, San Francisco (September 26-October 7):
—Department of Christian Education is established; national church begins revitalization program for Christian education.

—Four elected women deputies refused seating; measure to allow women to be seated as deputies is defeated; same measure defeated at each successive General Convention until 1967.

—Joint Commission on Ecumenical Relations is established to succeed Joint Commission on Faith and Order.

—Theological Education Offering Sunday is established.

Episcopal Church Foundation is established by Presiding Bishop Henry Knox Sherrill.

Bishop Payne Divinity School (Petersburg, VA) closes; assets merged with Virginia Theological Seminary in 1953.

Representatives of nineteen religious communities establish the Conference on the Religious Life.

1950   Prayer Book Studies I published—first of a series of twenty-nine Prayer Book Studies booklets leading to the revision of the *Book of Common Prayer* in 1976.

1951   National Council of Churches established at Cleveland meeting by twenty-nine American Protestant churches and four Eastern Orthodox churches (November 28-December 3). Presiding Bishop Henry Knox Sherrill is elected first president.

Seabury Press established as an agency of the Department of Christian Education.

1952   General Convention, Boston (September 8-19):
—Dean Claude W. Sprouse collapses and dies on platform shortly after being re-elected president of House of Deputies; succeeded by Canon Theodore O. Wedel.
—Resolution declares Christ's teaching to be "incompatible with every form of discrimination based on color or race."

Dean and seven faculty members at University of the South's School of Theology submit resignations because of board's refusal to admit black students (October 6).

Episcopal Theological Seminary of the Southwest (Austin, Texas) is established by the Diocese of Texas.

Episcopal Church hosts second Anglican Congress, Minneapolis (August 4-13):
—First representative gathering of worldwide Anglicans to be held outside British Isles.

Second Assembly of World Council of Churches, Evanston, Illinois (August 15-31).

1954   Diocese of South Carolina is last diocese to eliminate color bar for delegates at a diocesan convention.

1955   General Convention, Honolulu (September 4-15):
—Moved from Houston because of failure to receive assurances of racial integration of facilities.

1958   General Convention, Miami Beach (October 5-17):
—Arthur Lichtenberger is elected presiding bishop; replaces Henry Knox Sherrill.
—Clifford P. Morehouse is elected president of House of Deputies.

Episcopal Theological School, Cambridge, Massachusetts, becomes first seminary to adopt policy for admitting women to Bachelor of Divinity program.

1959   Episcopal Society for Cultural and Racial Unity organizes in December meeting at Raleigh, North Carolina.

1960   *The Episcopalian* is established to replace *Forth* as the monthly magazine of the Episcopal Church. Henry McCorkle is named editor.

The Right Reverend Stephen Bayne, Bishop of Olympia, is named first Anglican executive officer.

The Reverend Dennis Bennett resigns as rector of St. Mark's Church in Van Nuys, California; begins leadership in national charismatic movement.

Eugene Carson Blake preaches at Grace Cathedral, San Francisco; proposes Consultation on Church Union to bring merger between the Episcopal Church, Presbyterian Church in the U.S.A., United Methodist church, and United Church of Christ.

1961   General Convention, Detroit (September 17-29):
—Votes to join Consultation on Church Union.

—Principle of "trial use" for Prayer Book services is approved.

—Full communion with Philippine Independent church is approved.

1962   Construction of Episcopal Church Center at 815 Second Avenue, New York, is completed.

Second Vatican Council paves way for Anglican-Roman Catholic dialogues.

Anglican-Orthodox consultations begin.

John Burgess becomes Bishop of Massachusetts on November 8; first black to become bishop of a predominantly white diocese.

House of Bishops issues Pastoral Letter on War and Peace; In 1979, it becomes the mandate for the Joint Commission on Peace.

1963   Third Anglican Congress, Toronto, Ontario (August 13-23):

—Produces "Mutual Responsibility and Interdependence" document calling upon every Anglican to measure every activity by the test of service and mission to others.

1964   General Convention, St. Louis (October 11-23):

—John E. Hines, Bishop of Texas, is elected presiding bishop.

—Martin Luther King, Jr. addresses House of Deputies.

—Name of National Council changed to Executive Council, and membership enlarged to forty.

—Canon on deaconesses is changed to read "ordered" rather than "appointed;" also permits deaconesses to marry.

Appalachia South, Inc. is established in December. Name later changed to Appalachian People's Service Organization.

House of Bishops elects Arnold Lewis, bishop of the missionary district of Western Kansas, as first Suffragan Bishop for the Armed Forces.

Dr. Peter Day named as church's first ecumenical officer.

1965   Anglican-Roman Catholic Consultation in the U.S.A (ARC) is established.

Jonathan Daniels, seminarian from Episcopal Theological School in Cambridge, Massachusetts, is killed in Alabama August 25 while doing civil rights work.

1966   James A. Pike resigns as Bishop of California.

1967   First of successive annual declines in membership in the Episcopal Church until 1981. Number of baptized members peaked at 3,647,297, in 1966.

General Convention, Seattle (September 17-27):

—General Convention Special Program is established.

—Plan for Prayer Book revision is approved.

—Laymen are authorized to administer the chalice.

—Women are granted approval to serve as deputies.

—Board for Theological Education is established.

—Resolution on abortion issue is passed for the first time.

—The Very Reverend John Coburn is elected president of House of Deputies.

1968   Lambeth Conference, held in London, England, establishes Anglican Consultative Council.

The Reverend R. Baldwin Lloyd is named first executive director of Appalachian People's Service Organization.

Bexley Hall Seminary, Gambier, Ohio, moves to Rochester, New York.

1969   Special General Convention, South Bend, Indiana (August 31-September 5):
—Voted to participate in the Anglican Consultative Council.

—Women are permitted to become lay readers.

—A resolution rejects "much of the ideology of the Black Manifesto" but a grant of $200,000 is given to the Black Economic Development Conference.

—A thorough review and updating of the overseas missionary strategy is mandated.

Lutheran-Episcopal Dialogue I begins in Detroit, Michigan (October 14-15).

Anglican-Roman Catholic International Consultation (ARCIC) is established.

1970   General Convention, Houston (October 11-22):
—First women deputies are seated (approved by 1967 convention).

—Ordination of women to the diaconate is approved.

—General Convention Special Program is re-affirmed, but with tighter restrictions on grants.

Services for Trial Use ("Green Book") is published.

First Episcopal Cursillo weekend in the Episcopal Church held in Diocese of Iowa.

1971   Clarence Hobgood elected and consecrated Suffragan Bishop for the Armed Forces, Washington Cathedral (February 2); Episcopal Peace Fellowship stages peaceful protest.

Bishop Gilbert Baker of Hong Kong, acting with the approval of his synod, ordains two women to the priesthood: Jane Hwang Hsien-Yung and Joyce Bennett.

Absalom Jones Theological Institute in Atlanta, Georgia, established as part of Interdenominational Theological Center.

First meeting of Anglican Consultative Council in Limura, Kenya; resolution states it is "acceptable to this Council" for any province of the Anglican Communion to ordain women to the priesthood.

Episcopal Women's Caucus is organized in October.

Church Deployment Office begins operation.

Berkeley Divinity School in New Haven, Connecticut, merges with Yale Divinity School.

Coalition-14, network of Western dioceses, is organized at May meeting.

1972   PEWSACTION coalition is organized.

1973   General Convention, Louisville (September 26-October 22):
—John M. Allin, Bishop of Mississippi, is elected presiding bishop.

—General Convention Special Program is merged with other minority programs—no longer a "special program."

—Marriage canons are changed to allow re-marriage of divorced persons within the church.

—Resolution to allow ordination of women as priests is defeated.

Authorized Services, 1973 ("Zebra Book") is published.

Anglican Consultative Council meets in Dublin, Ireland (July 17-27):
—"Partners in Mission" process is established.

1974 Irregular ordination of eleven women to the priesthood at Church of the Advocate in Philadelphia, Pennsylvania (July 29).

Philadelphia Divinity School merges with Episcopal Theological School in Cambridge, Massachusetts. Name is changed to Episcopal Divinity School.

Episcopal Diocesan Ecumenical Officers (EDEO) established as formal organization.

First national renewal conference held at St. Philip's Cathedral, Atlanta, Georgia.

1975 First national meeting of *Integrity,* organization for gay Episcopalians, held in Chicago, Illinois (August 8-10). James Wickliff and Ellen Barrett are elected co-presidents.

Five women irregularly ordained to the priesthood by Bishop George Barrett in Washington, D.C. (September 25).

House of Bishops meeting in Portland, Maine (September 19-26) votes 118-18 to censure bishops participating in Philadelphia ordination of eleven women.

Education for Ministry extension program developed by the University of the South.

1976 General Convention, Minneapolis (September 11-22):
—Ordination of women to the priesthood is approved.

—Revised Prayer Book is approved.

—Venture in Mission launched; by mid-1978, 86 of 93 U.S. dioceses agreed to participate.

—Dr. Charles Lawrence elected president of House of Deputies; first black to hold the office.

Lutheran-Episcopal Dialogue II begins with January meeting in Alexandria, Virginia.

Publication of Draft Proposed *Book of Common Prayer* (February 2).

Anglican Consultative Council meets at Trinidad (March 23-April 2).

John Walker, Suffragan Bishop of Washington, elected Bishop of Washington. Becomes second black diocesan bishop of predominantly white diocese.

Trinity Episcopal School for Ministry established by Fellowship of Witness in Ambridge, Pennsylvania. Receives full accreditation in 1985.

1977 House of Bishops meeting, Port St. Lucie, Florida (September 30-October 7):
—"Conscience clause" is established which affirms that "no bishop, priest, or lay person should be coerced or penalized in any manner" for opposing the 1976 General Convention decision to ordain women.

—Presiding Bishop John Allin states he is "unable to accept women in the role of priests."

Jacqueline Means ordained priest in All Saints' Church, Indianapolis, Indiana (January 1). First woman ordained after official approval by General Convention.

St. Louis Congress sponsored by Fellowship of Concerned Churchman (September 14-16). Leads to formation of "Anglican Catholic church."

"Living the Good News" curriculum is developed by the Diocese of Colorado.

1978 First national ecumenical consultation held in Detroit, Michigan to evaluate church's ecumenical relations (November 5-9).

Anglican Church in North America (later named Anglican Catholic church) consecrates its first four bishops at Augustana Lutheran Church, Denver, Colorado.

Charles L. Burgreen is consecrated Suffragan Bishop for the Armed Forces (February 27).

1979   General Convention, Denver (September 8-20):

—Final approval of Prayer Book.

—Process begun for new hymnal by directing Standing Committee on Church Music to present a collection of proposed hymn texts to the 1982 convention.

—"Protestant" dropped from official name of church. Becomes "The Episcopal Church in the United States of America" or "The Episcopal Church."

—Resolution states "we believe it isn't appropriate for this church to ordain a practicing homosexual."

—Joint Commission on Peace created "to present a comprehensive program for implementing the 1962 House of Bishops letter as it pertains to peace and war."

Seabury Press published revision of *The Church's Teaching Series.*

National Episcopal Peace Conference in Denver, Colorado (September 6-8) celebrates fortieth anniversary of Episcopal Peace Fellowship.

Southern Baptist-Episcopal dialogue begins in North Carolina.

1980   Final session of Lutheran-Episcopal Dialogue II, in Nashotah, Wisconsin (November).

1982   General Convention, New Orleans (September 5-15):

—Authorized and approved texts for the *Hymnal 1982* and directed the Music Commission to "perfect the details of its work and complete the pew and accompaniment editions."

—Asked each parish to give annually one percent of its budgeted income to one of the accredited seminaries.

—Affirmed the biblical tithe as the "minimum standard of Christian giving."

—Approved "The Next Step" by asking all congregations to evaluate their mission and ministry through Service, Worship, Evangelism, Education, and Pastoral Care (SWEEP).

—Established a relationship of "interim eucharistic sharing" with the American Lutheran church, Lutheran Church in America, and Association of Evangelical Lutheran Churches.

Seabury Press sold to Winston Press of Minneapolis, Minnesota.

Third series of Lutheran-Episcopal dialogues begins.

1984   The Right Reverend Desmond Tutu notified of winning Nobel Peace Prize while teaching at General Theological Seminary.

Fiftieth anniversary of Forward Movement Publications.

1985   General Convention, Anaheim, California (September 8-15):

—The Right Reverend Edmond L. Browning, Bishop of Hawaii, is elected presiding bishop.

—The Very Reverend David Collins of Atlanta is elected president of House of Deputies.

—Mrs. Pamela Chinnis of Washington, D.C. is elected first woman vice president of House of Deputies.

—House of Bishops votes 112-31 that it did not intend to withhold consent to the election of a bishop "on the grounds of gender."

—The Exeuctive Council is asked to withdraw any of its $7.5 million in investments from companies doing business in South Africa; asks Church Pension Fund, parishes, and dioceses to consider similar action.

—Expresses opposition to Present Reagan's "Star Wars" program as well as economic and military aid to Nicaragua.

—Calls for parishes and dioceses to undertake three-year study of abortion issue.

B. Baptized Membership, Parishes, and Clergy

	Baptized Membership	Parishes and missions	Ordained Priests
1945	2,269,962	7,818	6,449
1946	2,300,575	7,648	6,450
1947	2,349,631	7,740	6,443
1948	2,436,589	7,864	6,506
1949	2,512,265	7,909	6,547
1950	2,540,548	7,784	6,654
1951	2,643,488	7,851	6,805
1952	2,715,825	7,954	6,958
1953	2,790,935	7,999	7,233
1954	2,907,321	7,912	7,367
1955	3,013,570	8,053	7,573
1956	3,111,440	7,200	7,889
1957	3,163,126	7,290	8,070
1958	3,274,867	7,347	8,234
1959	3,359,048	7,485	8,785
1960	3,444,265	7,657	9,079
1961	3,519,685	7,721	9,343
1962	3,565,470	7,735	9,811
1963	3,587,104	7,705	9,994
1964	3,591,164	7,992	9,978
1965	3,615,643	7,539	10,309
1966	3,647,297	7,593	10,615
1967	3,584,613	7,595	11,115
1968	3,588,435	7,546	11,362
1969	3,536,099	7,511	11,505
1970	3,475,164	7,464	11,772
1971	3,445,317	7,417	11,961
1972	3,385,436	7,506	12,082
1973	3,207,702	7,506	12,407
1974	3,081,936	7,395	12,469
1975	3,039,136	7,382	12,035
1976	3,072,760	7,507	12,641
1977	3,070,436	7,465	12,720
1978	3,057,612	7,587	12,945
1979	3,095,080	7,417	12,978
1980	3,037,420	7,591	13,089
1981	3,020,920	7,578	13,184
1982	3,014,982	7,590	13,605
1983	3,024,105	7,775	13,733
1984	3,004,758	7,796	13,924
1985	2,972,607	7,858	14,482

Source: *Episcopal Church Annuals*

C. General Conventions and Presiding Bishops

Date	Location	Presiding Bishop
1946 Sept. 10-20	Philadelphia	Henry St. George Tucker
		(Henry Knox Sherrill elected)
1949 Sept. 26-Oct. 7	San Francisco	Henry Knox Sherrill
1952 Sept. 8-19	Boston	Henry Knox Sherrill
1955 Sept. 4-15	Honolulu	Henry Knox Sherrill
1958 October 5-17	Miami Beach	Henry Knox Sherrill
		(Arthur Lichtenberger elected)
1961 Sept. 17-29	Detroit	Arthur Lichtenberger
1964 October 11-23	St. Louis	Arthur Lichtenberger
		(John E. Hines elected)
1967 Sept. 17-27	Seattle	John E. Hines
1969 Aug. 31-Sept. 5	South Bend, IN	John E. Hines
1970 October 11-22	Houston	John E. Hines
1973 Sept. 26-Oct. 22	Louisville	John E. Hines
		(John M. Allin elected)
1976 Sept. 11-22	Minneapolis	John Allin
1979 Sept. 6-20	Denver	John Allin
1982 Sept. 5-15	New Orleans	John Allin
1985 Sept. 7-14	Anaheim, CA	John Allin
		(Edmond Lee Browning elected)

D. New U.S. Dioceses Since 1945

For former missionary districts, date of organization as a missionary district is in parentheses. For dioceses formed from existing diocese, name of parent diocese is in parentheses.

1946	Missionary district of Western Nebraska reunited with Diocese of Nebraska
1958	Northwest Texas (1910)
1961	San Joaquin (1910)
1961	Hawaii (1902)
1968	Idaho (1896)
1968	Wyoming (1884)
1969	Central Florida, Southeast Florida, Southwest Florida (organized from Diocese of South Florida)
1970	Central Gulf Coast (Florida and Alabama)
1971	Eastern Oregon (1908)
1971	Nevada (1906)
1971	North Dakota (1884)
1971	Western Kansas (1903)
1972	Utah (1899)
1972	Alaska (1892)
1973	San Diego (Los Angeles)
1980	Western Louisiana (Louisiana)
1983	Ft. Worth (Dallas)
1983	West Tennessee (Tennessee)
1985	East Tennessee (Tennessee)

For a complete historical listing of dioceses added to the Episcopal Church, see *The General Convention of the Episcopal Church* by Bob N. Wallace (New York: Seabury Press, 1976) pp. 5-10.

E. Accredited Seminaries and their Deans

All deans are ordained priests titled "The Very Reverend"

Berkeley Divinity School at Yale
363 St. Ronan Street
New Haven, Connecticut 06511

Lawrence Rose, 1942-47
Percy L. Urban, 1947-57
Richard H. Wilmer, Jr., 1957-69
J. C. Michael Allen, 1969-70 (Acting Dean) 1970-76 (Dean)
Rowan Allen, III, 1976-77 (Acting Dean)
Charles H. Clark, 1977-82
James E. Annand, 1982-83 (Acting Dean) 1983-   (Dean)

Bexley Hall
1100 S. Goodman Street
Rochester, New York 14620

Corwin C. Roach, 1942-58
Robert J. Page, 1958-59 (Acting Dean)
Almus M. Thorp, Sr. 1959-69
Daniel Corrigan, 1969-70 (Acting Dean) 1970-71 (Dean)
Hays H. Rockwell, 1970-76
Richard H. Mansfield, 1977-83
William H. Petersen, 1983-

Bishop Payne Divinity School
Petersburg, Virginia
(Closed in 1949)

Robert A. Goodwin, 1940-49

Church Divinity School of the Pacific
2451 Ridge Road
Berkeley, California 94709

Henry H. Shires, 1935-50
Sherman E. Johnson, 1951-72
Frederick H. Borsch, 1972-81
William S. Pregnall, 1981-

Episcopal Divinity School
99 Brattle Street
Cambridge, Massachusetts 02138

Charles Lincoln Taylor, Jr., 1944-57
John B. Coburn, 1957-69
Edward G. Harris, 1974-76 (Co-Dean)
Harvey H. Guthrie, Jr., 1969-74, 1974-76 (Co-Dean) 1976-85 (Dean)
Bishop E. Otis Charles, 1985-

Episcopal Theological Seminary of the Southwest
P.O. Box 2247
Austin, Texas 78768

Gray M. Blandy, 1952-67
R. Francis Johnson, 1967-68 (Acting Dean)
T. Hudnall Harvey, 1968-72
Lawrence L. Brown, 1972-73

Gordon T. Charlton, 1973-82
George L. McGonigle, 1982-84 (Provost)*
Durstan R. McDonald, 1984-

The General Theological Seminary
175 Ninth Avenue
New York, New York 10011

Hughell E. W. Fosbroke, 1917-47
Lawrence Rose, 1947-66
Samuel J. Wylie, 1966-72
Bishop Stephen F. Bayne, Jr., 1972-73 (Acting Dean)
Roland Foster, 1973-78
James C. Fenhagan, II, 1979-

Nashotah House
Nashotah, Wisconsin 53058

Edmund J. M. Nutter, 1925-47
William H. Hess, 1947-52
Edward S. White, 1952-59
Walter C. Klein, 1960-63
Donald J. Parsons, 1963-64 (Acting Dean) 1964-73 (Dean)
Otis C. Edwards, 1973-74 (Acting Dean)
John S. Ruef, 1974-84
Bishop Stanley Atkins, 1984-85 (Acting Dean)
Jack C. Knight, 1985-

Philadelphia Divinity School
Philadelphia, Pennsylvania
(Merged with Episcopal Theological School,
Cambridge, Massachusetts, in 1974)

Allen Evans, 1937-47
Frank D. Gifford, 1947-59
Albert H. Lucas, 1959-61
Edward G. Harris, 1961-74

School of Theology
of the University of the South
Sewanee, Tennessee 37375

Bayard H. Jones, 1938-40 (Acting Dean)
Fleming James, 1940-47
Robert F. Gibson, Jr., 1947-49
Francis Craighill Brown, 1949-53
Edmund P. Dandridge, 1953-56 (Acting Dean)
George M. Alexander, 1956-72
Stiles B. Lines, 1972-73 (Acting Dean)
Urban T. Holmes, III, 1973-81
Girault M. Jones, 1981-83
John E. Booty, 1983-85
Donald S. Armentrout, 1985-86 (Acting Dean)
Robert E. Giannini, 1986-

*Layman; all others are ordained priests

Seabury-Western Theological Seminary
2122 Sheridan Road
Evanston, Illinois 60201

Frank A. McElwain, 1938-44
Alden D. Kelley, 1944-57
Charles U. Harris, Jr., 1957-72
Armen D. Jorjorian, 1972-74
Otis C. Edwards, 1974-83
Bishop James W. Montgomery, 1983-84 (Acting Dean)
Mark S. Sisk, 1984-

Trinity Episcopal School for Ministry
311 Eleventh Street
Ambridge, Pennsylvania 15003

Bishop Alfred Stanway, 1976-78
John H. Rodgers, Jr., 1978-

Virginia Theological Seminary
Alexandria, Virginia 22304

Alexander C. Zabriskie, 1940-1950
Stanley Brown-Serman, 1950-52
E. Felix Kloman, 1952-56
Jesse McLane Trotter, 1956-69
G. Cecil Woods, Jr., 1969-82
Richard Reid, 1982-83 (Acting Dean) 1983-   (Dean)

Source: *Episcopal Church Annuals* and *Clerical Directories*

F. Religious Orders in the Episcopal Church
(Dates of founding, if available, are in parentheses)

For Men

Congregation of Companions
of the Holy Savior (1891)
305 N. Broadway
Pennsville, New Jersey 08070

Oratory of the Good Shepherd
1550 Waverly Way
Baltimore, Maryland 21239

Order of the Holy Cross (1884)
West Park, New York 10031

Order of the Holy Family (1969)
Abbot Galisteo Priory
1204 Galisteo Parkway
Sante Fe, New Mexico 87501

Company of the Paraclete (1971)
P.O. Box 55
Jersey City, New Jersey 07302

Order of St. Benedict
St. Gregory's Abbey
Three Rivers, Michigan 49093

Society of St. Francis
Little Portion Friary
P.O. Box 399
Mt. Sinai, New York 11766

Brotherhood of St. Gregory
St. Bartholomew's Church
82 Prospect
White Plains, New York 10606

Society of St. John-Evan
Monastery of St. Mary and St. John
980 Memorial Drive
Cambridge, Massachusetts 02138

Society of St. Paul (1959)
St. Paul the Apostle Monastery
44-660 San Pablo Avenue
Palm Desert, California 92260

Servants of Christ
6533 N. 39th Avenue
Phoenix, Arizona 85019

Society of St. Barnabas
St. Barnabas House
North East, Pennsylvania 16428

Community of Servants of Jesus (1981)
Bethlehem Monastery
430 North Limestone
Lexington, Kentucky 40589

For Women

All Saints' Sisters of the Poor
All Saints' Convent
P.O. Box 3127
Catonsville, Maryland 21228

Sisterhood of Holy Nativity (1882)
101 East Division
Fond du Lac, Wisconsin 54935

Community of the Holy Spirit
St. Hilda's Convent
621 West 113th Street
New York, New York 10025

Poor Clares of Reparation
P.O. Box 342
Mt. Sinai, New York 11766

Order of St. Anne (1910)
St. Anne's House
15 Craigie Street
Cambridge, Massachusetts 02138

St. Benedict's House
RR 1, Box 4383
Camden, Maine 04043

Community of St. Francis
St. Francis House
3743 Army Street
San Francisco, California 94110

Order of St. Helena (1945)
Convent of St. Helena
P.O. Box 426
Vails Gate, New York 12584

Community of St. John Baptist (1874)
P.O. Box 240
Mendham, New Jersey 07945

Society of St. Margaret (1873)
St. Margaret's Convent
17 Louisburg Square
Boston, Massachusetts 02108

Community of St. Mary (1865)
St. Mary's Convent
Peekskill, New York 10566

Sisters of Charity (1869)
St. Vincent de Paul
P.O. Box 818
Boulder City, Nevada 89005

Teachers of the Children of God
Maycroft
Sag Harbor, New York 11963

Community of the Transfiguration (1898)
495 Albion Avenue
Cincinnati, Ohio 45246

Community of the Way of the Cross (1944)
4588 S. Park Avenue
Buffalo, New York 14219

For Men and Women

Order of Agape and Reconciliation (1971)
St. Michael's Forest Valley Priory
P.O. Box 43
Tajique, New Mexico 87057

Third Order of St. Francis
The Rev. Robert J. Goode
P.O. Box 608
Eagle River, Wisconsin 54521

Order of the Servants of Christ the King
Brother Martin SCK
2630 Kingsbridge Terrace 2-UA
The Bronx, New York 10463

Transfiguration Retreat Monastery (1968)
Fr. Christopher
Rt. 1, Box 63A
Pulaski, Wisconsin 54162

Worker Sisters of the Holy Spirit (1972)
Worker Brothers of the Holy Spirit
P.O. Box 276
Cary, Illinois 60013

Glossary of Church Terms

These are terms with which new Episcopalians or non-Episcopalians may not be familiar. They relate mainly to the structure and organization of the Episcopal Church and do not include liturgical and theological terms. For a more complete glossary, *A New Dictionary for Episcopalians* by the Reverend John N. Wall, Jr. (Winston Press, 1985) is recommended.

Anglican Communion. The worldwide body of Anglican churches represented in forty-six countries with a membership of about 65 million. Each national church, or "province," is in communion with the Church of England, and recognizes the leadership of the Archbishop of Canterbury. While the Church of England is "first among equals" in a historic sense, each national church is independent and autonomous.

Anglican Consultative Council (ACC). An international meeting of Anglicans held approximately once every three years. The ACC was established by the Lambeth Conference of Bishops in 1968 to provide a forum for members of the Anglican Communion. Its purpose is to develop a common mission policy, to assist in the development of new provinces, and to enable Anglican participation in the ecumenical movement.

Anglo-Catholic. The tradition within Anglicanism which emphasizes the Roman Catholic origins of the Church of England. Anglo-Catholics stress a "high" style of liturgical worship, along with emphasis on the divine origins of the ordained ministry, the sacraments, and the church's historic continuity with the early church. Anglo-Catholics may practice frequent communion and sacramental confession. Churchmanship differences between "low church" and "high church" Episcopalians are much less pronounced in the 1980s than they were prior to 1950.

Apostolic Succession. The doctrine that bishops are the direct inheritors of the ministry which Jesus first gave the twelve apostles. This "apostolic ministry" has been passed down through the church's bishops. This doctrine is the source for the Episcopal Church's belief in its "historic episcopacy," the belief that the office of bishop had its origins with the twelve apostles. The historic episcopacy is one of the four doctrinal points contained in the Chicago-Lambeth Quadrilateral (see BCP, p. 876). The

Quadrilateral is a statement of four beliefs on which the Episcopal Church refuses to compromise in its ecumenical conversations. As a result, the historic episcopacy has sometimes been a stumbling block in ecumenical dialogues with other churches which do not have bishops.

Archbishop. A bishop who has administrative and disciplinary authority over other bishops in a geographical area called a province (usually, but not necessarily, one country). In most of the provinces of the Anglican Communion, the chief bishop is an archbishop. In the United States, the chief bishop is called "Presiding Bishop, Chief Pastor, and Primate," which is usually shortened to "Presiding Bishop."

Archdeacon. The archdeacon of a diocese is a priest (not a deacon) who normally serves as chief administative assistant to the bishop of his or her diocese. Not all dioceses have an archdeacon and among those which do, the responsibilities vary. The archdeacon is addressed as "The Venerable," which is abbreviated "The Ven."

Bishop. A bishop is elected by each diocese as its chief pastor, spiritual leader, and administrative officer. "Episcopal" comes from the Greek word *Episkopas,* meaning *overseer* or *bishop.* Thus, the Episcopal Church is one "governed by bishops." Only bishops can ordain a person to the priesthood or diaconate. Bishops are also required to visit the parishes of their diocese at regular intervals and perform confirmation services. While there are other kinds of bishops, the bishop in charge of a diocese is called "diocesan bishop" or simply "diocesan." See also *suffragan bishop* and *coadjutor bishop.*

Book of Common Prayer. The *Book of Common Prayer* (BCP) is the primary guide for worship in the Episcopal Church, and contains services for Holy Communion, Morning Prayer, Baptism, Marriage, Burial, and others. In its history, the Episcopal Church adopted its first Prayer Book in 1789 and made three subsequent revisions: 1892, 1928, and 1979. The first Anglican Prayer Book was written by Thomas Cranmer in 1549 for the purpose of compiling into one volume a number of books and manuals required by English priests to conduct a service. Today, the *Book of Common Prayer* gives the Episcopal Church its character by providing a common worship among a wide diversity of liturgical and theological emphases.

Canons. The written "rules" governing church policy, structure, and procedure. There is a set of canons for the national church, determined by the General Convention, as well as a set for each diocese. The national canons deal with the church's organization and administration, clergy and ministry, worship, and other areas. Diocesan canons focus more on the relationship of the diocese to its congregations and must conform to the national church's canons. Each diocesan convention has the authority to adopt and modify the diocesan canons.

Canon (of a cathedral or diocese). A priest on the staff of a cathedral or diocese may be given the title "Canon." On a cathedral staff, the canon is an assistant to the dean. On a diocesan staff, the canon is an assistant to the bishop. Both are addressed as "The Reverend Canon. . . ."

Cathedral. A cathedral is the primary congregation in a city where the diocesan office is located (customarily called "See City") with a historical affilation to the bishop's office. The chief pastor of a cathedral is called a "dean," while clergy assistants may be called "canons." No diocese will have more than one cathedral church, and some have none. The cathedral church may be an elegant, historic edifice, or it may be a church building in a simple style. The Cathedral of St. John the Divine in New York City, the Cathedral of St. Peter and St. Paul in Washington, D.C., and Grace Cathedral in San Francisco are among the best-known Episcopal cathedrals in the United States.

Chicago-Lambeth Quadrilateral. The four articles adopted by the Lambeth Conference of bishops in 1888 which states what Anglicans believe are essential for a reunited church. They are intended as a guide for the ecumenical conversations and statements of doctrine on which Anglicans will not compromise: 1) the sufficiency of Holy Scriptures, 2) the Apostles Creed and Nicene Creed, 3) the Sacraments of Baptism and Holy Communion, and 4) the Historic Episcopate. These are found on page 876 of the *Book of Common Prayer.* The four articles were first agreed upon by the House of Bishops which met in Chicago in 1886 and were later adopted by the Lambeth Conference in 1888. The Chicago-Lambeth Quadrilateral comes closer than any other statement as representing an "official" Anglican theology.

Coadjutor bishop. The Coadjutor bishop is an assistant bishop of a diocese. When planning retirement, the bishop calls for the election of a coadjutor bishop. The coadjutor then assists the bishop until he retires and automatically succeeds him as bishop. Coadjutor bishops are nominated and elected by the clergy and laity of the diocese in which they will serve. Any ordained priest of the Episcopal Church is eligible to become a coadjutor bishop. The suffragan bishop is also elected as an assistant bishop, but does not automatically become bishop.

Communicant. A communicant in an Episcopal parish is a member who has received communion at least three times within the previous year. A member is received by baptism, confirmation, or transfer from another Episcopal parish. Because of similar theology and tradition, new members may be "received" without confirmation from a Roman Catholic or Orthodox church. One can be a member of an Episcopal parish without being a communicant, but not a communicant without being a member.

Confirmation. A Prayer Book rite in which the confirmand expresses faith and commitment to Christ and receives the strengthening of the Holy Spirit through the "laying on of hands" by the bishop. In normal practice, children are confirmed between the ages of ten and twelve. New adult members coming from other churches are also confirmed, except for those coming from Roman Catholic and Orthodox churches who are "received." Confirmation is always preceded by a series of instructional classes. Since 1970, confirmation is no longer required for children to receive Holy Communion. Most parishes, however, provide instruction for children on the meaning of Holy Communion.

Constitution. The Constitution sets forth how the Episcopal Church is to be organized and governed. The majority of the articles regulate such matters as the structure and activity of General Convention, qualifications for bishop and other ordained offices, the bishop's jurisdiction, and clerical discipline. While the canons may be changed by vote of one General Convention, the constitution can only be amended by vote of two successive conventions.

Curate. In current practice, the term is used to refer to one employed to assist the rector in the performance of his or her duties in a parish. Usually the curate is a recently ordained deacon or priest in his or her first parish assignment.

Deacon. A deacon is a member of one of the three orders of the ordained ministry: bishops, priests, and deacons. The diaconate has traditionally been considered a "stepping stone" to the ordained priesthood, although there has been renewed emphasis on the permanent or *perpetual diaconate* as a distinct vocation. Deacons may distribute the chalice and the bread, but cannot celebrate Holy Communion. Deacons have traditionally had a special responsibility to serve the sick, the weak, the poor, and to "interpret the world to the church."

Deaconess. The office of deaconess, a historic role for women, was abolished in 1970 when women were allowed to be ordained to the diaconate. A deaconess used to be a "devoted, unmarried woman" (from the old canon) appointed by the bishop to work in a parish or church institution. They were often given duties to lead Morning and Evening Prayer services, Christian education programs, and home and hospital visitation.

Dean. There are three kinds of deans in the Episcopal Church: The dean of a cathedral (selected by the congregation), the dean of a seminary (selected by the board of trustees), and at times, the dean of a geographic area of a diocese (appointed by the bishop). A cathedral dean is essentially the chief pastor of a cathedral church, often with one or two assistants. A seminary dean is normally the chief administrative and academic officer of a seminary. While some seminaries will call the chief officer a "president," the traditional and historic Anglican term is "dean." A dean may also be a priest in a geographical area of a diocese elected or appointed to preside over local councils and represent the bishop on special occasions.

Deputy (General Convention). Each diocese elects four clerical representatives and four lay representatives to the General Convention, called deputies. Together, they make up the "clerical order" and the "lay order" of the House of Deputies at the General Convention.

Diaconate. The office of deacon. A deacon is one who has been ordained to the diaconate. The term is used in the same way that the "episcopacy" refers to the office of bishop.

Diocese. The diocese is the basic geographical unit within the Episcopal Church and is governed by a bishop, diocesan committees and commissions. Depending on the number of Episcopal church members in a given area, some states will have several dioceses within their borders, while other states will function as a single diocese. As of 1985, there were ninety-eight domestic dioceses and fifteen overseas dioceses of the Episcopal Church.

Episcopal Church Annual. An annual "directory" of the Episcopal Church, now published by the Morehouse-Barlow Company, Inc. It contains the names and addresses of all parishes and diocesan offices, bishops, priests and deacons, seminaries, publications, conference centers, social agencies, and religious orders. It also contains national church statistics, and information on each province in the worldwide Anglican Communion.

Episcopal Church Center. The national church office located at 815 Second Avenue, New York, New York 10017. The building was erected in 1962 and is owned by the Episcopal Church. The presiding bishop's office is located here where he has administrative responsibility for the staff. National offices for Christian education, ecumenical relations, communication, national and world mission, stewardship and others are located here. It is often called simply "815."

Eucharist. In the last thirty years, the eucharist became the primary service of worship in most Episcopal churches. Eucharist comes from the Greek word *eucharisto* meaning "to give thanks." It is also known as Holy Communion.

Executive Council. The national governing council of the Episcopal Church, consisting of a total of forty ordained and lay members. The members are elected by General Convention and meet three times yearly to carry out the programs set forth at the previous General Convention. It could be described as the "vestry" of the national Episcopal Church. Prior to 1970, it was called "National Council."

General Convention. The General Convention is the official legislative body of the Episcopal Church and meets once every three years. It is similar in structure to the United States Congress in that it includes a House of Bishops and a House of Deputies. The House of Bishops consists of approximately 250 active and retired bishops; the House of Deputies consists of approximately 900 deputies, eight from each domestic and overseas diocese of the Episcopal Church.

Historic Episcopate. See apostolic succession.

Holy Orders. The three "orders" of ordained ministry in the Episcopal Church: bishops, priests and deacons. The term should not be confused with "religious orders," which is a term reserved for monastic organizations.

Morning Prayer. Historically called Matins, it is an office of the *Book of Common Prayer* intended for both public worship and private devotional use. The office allows more use of Scripture and canticles (songs of praise) than does the service of Holy Communion. Many Episcopal churches alternate between Morning Prayer and Holy Communion as the primary Sunday worship, although an increasing number use the eucharist only.

Ordinand. A person who is being ordained to the priesthood or diaconate.

Parish. A term referring to a local, self-supporting Episcopal congregation. Parishes are not defined by geographic boundaries in the United States. Any communicant may attend any parish he or she wishes.

Postulancy. The first stage of a process leading to ordination which is usually conferred just prior to or during the first year in seminary. After a person has been examined by the bishop and appropriate committees, he or she is designated a "postulant."

Presiding Bishop. The presiding bishop is the chief administrative officer and spiritual leader of the Episcopal Church in the United States. The office for the presiding bishop is located at the Episcopal Church Center in New York City. Historically, the presiding bishop was elected by the House of Bishops as the bishop who presided over their meetings. With the growing church and scope of office, the job of presiding bishop became a full-time one in 1946 when Henry Knox Sherrill assumed the office. He was the first presiding bishop not to hold diocesan duties along with the office. The full title for the office is "Presiding Bishop, Chief Pastor, and Primate" as voted on at the 1979 General Convention.

Priest. One of the three orders of ordained ministry of the Episcopal Church: bishops, priests, and deacons. Men and women are ordained as priest after ordination to the diaconate. Male priests are addressed as either "Father" or "Mister," while female priests are usually addressed by "Mrs." or "Miss." A priest may work in a parish as rector or assistant rector, in an institutional chaplaincy, a church agency or office, or be employed in secular work. While the bishop may provide guidance and assistance, priests are free to choose their place of employment.

Province. a) The dioceses of the Episcopal Church in the United States are divided into nine geographic areas called provinces. Each province has a governing structure with an elected president, officers and committees. b) Internationally, each national church which is a member of the Anglican Communion is called a province. In this use, the Episcopal Church is one province, while Anglican churches in Nigeria, Australia, England, and so on, make up other provinces.

Rector. The priest who is in charge of a congregation. A parish may have several priests on its staff, but can have only one rector. The term "rector" is unique to Anglicans, with "pastor" or "minister" being the more common term among Protestant denominations.

Religious order. A community of men and/or women who live together under common vows, usually the traditional vows of poverty, chastity, and obedience. Members of orders may be called friars, monks, or nuns, and may be either lay men or women or ordained. In the Episcopal Church (as of 1985), there are thirteen orders for men, seventeen orders for women, and seven orders for men and women.

Suffragan Bishop. The suffragan bishop is elected to assist the bishop of a diocese at the request of that bishop. Unlike the coadjutor bishop, a suffragan bishop does not automatically become bishop when the diocesan bishop retires.

United Thank Offering (UTO). The UTO is collected by the Episcopal Church Women (ECW) in practically every congregation in the Episcopal Church each year. The proceeds are distributed by a national board to mission projects throughout the United States and the world. The offering started in 1889 and has become an annual tradition in the Episcopal Church.

Vestry. The vestry is the primary governing body for each local congregation. Vestry members are normally elected by church members at the parish's annual meeting and serve rotating terms of one to three years.

Vicar. The vicar of a parish is usually appointed by the bishop, and serves at the pleasure of the bishop in a parish which is financially dependent on the diocese for its operating budget. Such parishes may be called "missions" or "aided congregations," according to particular diocesan practices. The vicar of a congregation has the same duties and responsibilities as a rector.

Bibliography
and
Suggested Reading

Anglican-Orthodox Dialogue: Dublin Agreed Statement, 1984 (Crestwood, NY: St. Vladimar's Seminary Press, 1985).

Anglican-Roman Catholic International Consultation: The Final Report (Cincinnati: Forward Movement, 1982).

Armentrout, Donald Smith. *The Quest for the Informed Priest: A History of the School of Theology* (Sewanee, Tennessee: University of the South Press, 1979).

Bayne, Stephen F. *An Anglican Turning Point* (New York: Seabury Press, 1965).

Bonds of Affection: Proceedings of the Anglican Consultative Council, 6th Meeting, Lagos, 1984 (London: Anglican Consultative Council, 1985). See also reports from ACC Meetings at Limura, 1971; Dublin, 1973; Trinidad, 1976; London, Ontario, 1979; and Newcastle-on-Tyne, England, 1981.

Carroll, Jackson W., Johnson, Douglas W., and Marty, Martin E. *Religion in America: 1950 to the Present* (San Francisco: Harper and Row, 1979).

Church and Society: Social Policy of the Episcopal Church, 1967-1979. (New York: The Executive Council, 1979).

Crow, Paul, Jr. and Boney, William J. *Church Union at Midpoint* (New York: Association Press, 1972).

Deemer, Philip, ed. *Episcopal Year 1969* (New York: Jarrow Press, 1970).

_____. *Episcopal Year 1970* (New York: Jarrow Press, 1971).

_____. *Episcopal Year 1971* (New York: Jarrow Press, 1972).

DeMille, George E. *The Episcopal Church Since 1900* (New York: Morehouse-Gorham Company, 1955).

Fact Book on Theological Education for the Academic Year 1985-1986 (Vandalia, Ohio: Association of Theological Schools, 1986).

Gaustad, Edwin S. *A Documentary History of Religion in America* (Grand Rapids, Michigan: Eerdmans, 1983).

Hatchett, Marion J. *Commentary on the American Prayer Book* (New York: Seabury Press, 1980).

Heyward, Carter. *A Priest Forever. The Formation of a Woman and a Priest* (San Francisco: Harper and Row, 1976).

Hodges, George. *A Short History of the Episcopal Church* (Cincinnati: Forward Movement, 1967).

Howe, John. *Highways and Hedges: Anglicanism and the Universal Church* (Toronto: Anglican Book Centre, 1985).

Jones, Bayard H. *Prayer Book Studies IV: The Eucharistic Liturgy* (New York: The Church Pension Fund, 1953).

Kendall, Patricia, ed. *Women and the Priesthood: A Selected and Annotated Bibliography* (Philadelphia: Diocese of Pennsylvania, 1976).

Kennedy, James W. *Partners in Mission: The Louisville Consultation, 1977* (Cincinnati: Forward Movement, 1977).

Konolige, Kit and Frederica. *The Power of their Glory. America's Ruling Class: The Episcopalians* (New York: Wyden Books, 1978).

Krumm, John M. and Kelleran, Marian. *Denver Crossroads: General Convention 1979* (Cincinnati: Forward Movement, 1979).

Long, Charles Henry. *Vancouver Voices: The Sixth Assembly of the World Council of Churches* (Cincinnati: Forward Movement, 1983).

Lutheran-Episcopal Dialogue: A Progress Report (Cincinnati: Forward Movement, 1972).

Lutheran-Episcopal Dialogue: Report and Recommendations (Cincinnati: Forward Movement, 1981).

Manross, W. W. *A History of the American Episcopal Church* (New York: Morehouse-Gorham Company, 1959).

Marrett, Michael M. *The Lambeth Conferences and Women Priests* (Smithtown, New York: Exposition Press, 1981).

Moede, Gerald F. *The COCU Consensus: In Quest of a Church Uniting* (Princeton: Consultation on Church Union, 1985).

Moore, Paul, *Take a Bishop Like Me* (San Francisco: Harper and Row, 1983).

Peterson, William H. and Goeser, Robert J. *Traditions Transplanted: The Story of Anglican and Lutheran Churches in America* (Cincinnati: Forward Movement, 1981).

Prayer Book Studies XV: The Problem and Method of Prayer Book Revision (New York: The Church Pension Fund, 1961).

Price, Charles P. *Prayer Book Studies 29: Introducing the Proposed Book* (New York: Church Hymnal Corporation, 1976).

Proceedings of the Anglican Congress, Toronto, 1963 (New York: Seabury Press, 1963).

Sherrill, Henry Knox. *Among Friends: An Autobiography* (Boston: Little, Brown and Company in association with Atlantic Monthly Press, 1962).

Simpson, James B. and Story, Edward M. *Discerning God's Will: The Complete Eyewitness Account of the Eleventh Lambeth Conference* (Nashville, Tennessee: Thomas Nelson, Inc., 1979).

Simpson, James B. and Story, Edward M. *The Long Shadows of Lambeth X, 1968* (New York: McGraw-Hill, 1969).

Stringfellow, William, and Towne, Anthony. *The Death and Life of Bishop Pike* (Garden City: Doubleday and Company, 1976).

Taylor, Charles, ed. *Ministry for Tomorrow: Report of the Special Committee on Theological Education,* (New York: Seabury Press, 1967).

Wall, John N., Jr. *A New Dictionary for Episcopalians* (Minneapolis, Winston Press, 1985).

Wallace, Bob N. *The General Convention of the Episcopal Church* (New York: Seabury Press, 1979).

Welsby, Paul A. *A History of the Church of England: 1945-1980* (Oxford: Oxford University Press, 1984).

Wright, J. Robert. *A Communion of Communions: One Eucharistic Fellowship.* (New York: Seabury Press, 1979).
Young, Frances M. *Thankfulness Unites: The History of the United Thank Offering, 1889-1979* (Cincinnati: Forward Movement, 1979).

Serials

(The following books and documents are published at least every three years, and some are published annually. An asterisk (*) indicates those which are no longer published. All contain biographical, statistical, or other information used in this book. The latest year of publication and publisher is included with each document).

The Blue Book. Reports of the committees, commissions, boards, and agencies of the General Convention. (The Executive Council, 1985).
The Church Speaks: Christian Social Relations at General Convention. (The Executive Council, 1958-1964)*
Episcopal Church Annual. (Morehouse-Barlow Company, 1986)
Episcopal Clergy Directory. (Church Hymnal Corporation, 1985)
Episcopal Lay Leadership Directory. (Church Hymnal Corporation, 1985)
Journal of the General Convention. (The Executive Council, 1985)
Summary of General Convention Actions. (The Executive Council, 1985)
Yearbook of Canadian and American Churches. (Abingdon Press, 1986)

Index

Abele, George, 171
Abiala, Tunde, 166
abortion, 68-70
Absalom Jones Theological Institute, 104
Acquired Immune Deficiency Syndrome (AIDS), 68
Adelman, Judith, 18
African Methodist Episcopal Church, 14
Alaska, Diocese of, 172
Allin, John M. (presiding bishop), and ordination of women, 23-24, 26, 29, 178; peace issues, 63, 72; ecumenical relations, 139, 150, 152; schismatic groups, 158; Venture in Mission, 167-168; accomplishments, 177-178.
Alianza grant (GCSP), 50-51
All Saints' School, Vicksburg, Mississippi, 38
Altizer, Thomas J. J., 46
American Church Institute for Negroes, 33
American Church Union, 21, 23
American Episcopal church, 159-160
American Lutheran church, 14, 133, 149
Anders, Bill, 1
Anderson, Carol L., 21
Anderson, Leila, 9
Anglican Catholic church, 156-157
Anglican Church of Canada, 14, 29
Anglican Congress, (Toronto, 1963), 164
Anglican Consultative Council, 20, 165-166
Anglican-Orthodox Theological Consultation, 146-148
Anglican Fellowship of Prayer, 125-127
Anglican Rite Jurisdiction of the Americas, 159-160
Anglican-Roman Catholic dialogue (U.S.), 142-144

Anglican-Roman Catholic International Consultation (ARCIC), 144-145
Anglican School of Theology, Dallas, Texas, 105
apartheid, 70-72
Appalachian People's Service Organization, 170-172
Association of Evangelical Lutheran Churches, 150
Association of Theological Schools in the U.S. and Canada, 104
Atkins, Stanley H., 13, 26
Atlanta, Diocese of, 40, 168
Augustana Lutheran Church, Denver, 157
Authorized Services, 1973, 112

Baker, Gilbert, 15, 20
Barrett, Ellen M., 64-66
Barrett, George W., 25
Bayne, Stephen F., Jr., 7, 164-165
Bazley, George A., Jr., 137
Beebe, Peter, 24
Benitez, Maurice M., 128
Bennett, Dennis J., 121-122
Bennett, Joyce, 15
Berkeley Divinity School, New Haven, Conn., 18, 102
Bexley Hall Seminary, 102
Bible Reading Fellowship, 126, 128
Bishop Payne Divinity School, 34, 102
Bishop, Shelton H., 32
Bishop, Hutchens C., 32
Bittner, Merrill, 23
birthrate and church membership, 161-162
Black Economic Development Conference, 51-53